MW00990524

Going In Cold

*How to Turn Strangers into Clients
and Get Rich Doing It*

Going In Cold

*How to Turn Strangers into Clients
and Get Rich Doing It*

By Chuck Piola

The King of Cold Calls
With Jay Finegan

ISBN 0-7414-1913-0

Published by:

PUBLISHING.COM

519 West Lancaster Avenue
Haverford, PA 19041-1413
Info@buybooksontheweb.com
www.buybooksontheweb.com
Toll-free (877) BUY BOOK
Local Phone (610) 520-2500
Fax (610) 519-0261

Printed in the United States of America

Printed on Recycled Paper

Published January 2004

DEDICATION

For my lovely wife, June, who supported me and maintained our home while I went out every day to slay the dragon.

WHY I WROTE THIS BOOK

I stuttered and have Attention Deficit Disorder. By all practical analysis, I shouldn't have "made it." But I did (o' miracle of miracles).

This is a book about something more than sales, more than being in the top ten, more than winning. It's a book about hope, because without hope none of us would get out of bed in the morning. It's also a book about balance, the constant battle to try and achieve it and keep it, and lose it, and try to get it back again. It's a book for the risk takers, and the wanna-be risk takers. It's a book for the entrepreneurs.

I wrote it because I'm still a teacher at heart, and I know how tough it is to keep believing in yourself under the pain of ridicule, rejection, low self-esteem and negative opinions. My wish for you, my desired end result, is that it'll give you a shot in the arm that will last.

Good luck. And never give up.

TESTIMONIALS

"Chuck Piola - A Great Speaker, a Great Man, and a Great Inspiration...Thanks for making me Think! You challenged me!"
        —*Ralph H. Palman, Author of 8 Critical Lifetime Decisions*

"As you can imagine, in more than 20 years running Inc Magazine I've seen just about every major and minor business speaker in the country. Some deliver real value with regard to useful content. Some of those are actually entertaining. A few just grab you by the lapels--challenge you, provoke you, inspire you-- make you want to go out and (in Chuck's case) sell something. I guarantee he'll make you laugh, he'll make you cry--and you won't want your money back."
        —*George Gendron, former Editor-in-Chief Inc. Magazine*

"Chuck Piola is one of the most dynamic speakers we have had in quite some time. Our membership thoroughly enjoyed his no-nonsense approach to sales and marketing. Whether speaking on business or real life issues, Chuck is an engaging and lively speaker. He can certainly motivate your sales force and empower people to act."
        —*Rob Powelson, President Chester County Chamber of Business & Industry*

"A brilliant, experienced-based 'how to' book on not only sales tactics of cold calling but more importantly self management of the emotional underpinnings required to achieve consistent sales success!"Good luck. And never give up.
        —*Dick Falcone, Chairman & CEO Evercom, Inc.*

"Far better it is to dare mighty things to win glorious triumphs, even though checkered by failure, than to take rank with those poor spirits who neither enjoy much nor suffer much because they live in the gray twilight that knows not victory, nor defeat."

—*Theodore Roosevelt*
Speech before the Hamilton Club
Chicago, IL
April 10, 1899

CONTENTS

GOING IN COLD

Foreword by W.R. 'Max' Carey, Jr.

Author of "The Superman Complex: Achieving the Balance that Leads to True Success"

When Chuck Piola first told me that he was going to write a book about turning strangers into clients and that the finished product would be titled *Going in Cold,* I had to smile. I wished I'd had a book like that twenty-seven years ago. That was when I left the cockpit of a jet aircraft as a combat Naval aviator. I went to two weeks of sales training in Chicago, Illinois and I hit the streets as an entry-level salesperson selling insurance-based consulting services to automobile dealers. To this day, it was the toughest job I've ever had. Selling intangibles to car dealers is the worst. And you have to resell them every visit. But it was a good place for me to cut my teeth.

During those 27 years, I've sold in good times and bad, I've sold great product and I've sold average product, I've sold in recession and I've sold in prosperity and with that context in mind I can honestly make the following statement: I have never, in those 27 years, seen a better time or a more opportunistic time to sell value-added products and services for value-added prices at high levels within business America. At the same time, I've never seen a greater propensity for all products and services to be pushed downward to a commodity level. What this statement means for you is that you must become more important to your customers in spite of a marketplace where there is nothing your customers can't buy on the internet.

Selling is the most important function that takes place in America on any given day. In fact, 92% of the GNP is created when someone sells something to someone else. It is the activity without which no other activity takes place. No products are manufactured, no deliveries are made, no paychecks are issued until someone extends their hand and says, "You have a deal". So if your goal is to bring more value to your customer than they can get by shopping from their lap tops, then in many cases that will mean giving personalized service … in other words, going in cold.

If those words send a chill of fear up your spine, congratulations! Fear is a natural and a normal human response to doing that which makes us feel uncomfortable. But fear has such a negative connotation that we often tend to overlook the positive aspects of fear. In reality, it can be an incredibly powerful tool that can be used to your advantage. First of all, fear tells you to run or to fight. If you choose to stay and fight, that decision initiates a sequence of nerve cells firing a chemical release that prepares your body for battle. Your awareness intensifies. Your reflexes quicken. Your perception of pain diminishes. You become prepared—physically and psychologically—for fight or flight.

Secondly, fear tells you what your priorities are. The things that you fear the most are typically the things that are the highest priority in your world. If you are a sales person and you're afraid of not hitting your quota, let the fear be a positive indicator that your quota is one of your biggest priorities. If you are an entrepreneur and the thought of not having enough money for payroll frightens you, that fear simply means, as it certainly should, that taking care of your staff is a priority. Fear has a way of elevating the most important of our priorities while at the same time giving less anxiety to those things which can be looked after at a later time. So if you sit down quietly and asses the things you are most afraid of, you will probably find that what those fears actually reveal are not your weaknesses, not your failures, but rather those things which are most critical to your success.

The third positive aspect of fear is that fear tells you what you don't know. The fear of the unknown plagues all of us, even from early childhood. Why? Because we generally fear what we do not understand. That is why so many sales people sit in their cars unable to move when faced with the task of canvassing a large building. It isn't because of imminent danger or the threat of bodily harm. It is simply because of lack of knowledge. For those of you who know all too well the feeling I am describing, the following pages will be invaluable. By learning from the wisdom of one who has walked in your shoes you will be able to understand the fear and get an edge on your competitors by doing those things which they themselves are afraid to do. Once you can understand the fear, you can fight it.

Lastly, fear allows you to celebrate when you have conquered it. As I turned the pages of *Going in Cold,* awed by the case studies and personal stories, it became increasingly apparent to me that the King of Cold Calls is one person who has not only conquered fear, but actually embraces it. His stories caused me to reflect on some of my own fear-related experiences, and I was reminded of the days when I was training to be a fighter pilot at the academy now known as Top Gun. We had a phrase that was used to describe those pilots that got more out of their aircraft than the other pilots. We'd say, "That pilot flies the aircraft right to the edge of the envelope, right to the edge of its capabilities". If you saw the movie "Top Gun", you may remember that when they were in heavy maneuvering getting maximum performance, it was so rough the cockpits would vibrate! That's called aircraft airframe buffet. The key was to get close to the edge and be able to live in buffet. Many pilots, when they experienced heavy buffet, eased up on the stick to get to a safer more comfortable flight regime. Unfortunately though, in combat with an aggressor at six o'clock and a heat-seeking missile on your tail pipe, if you give in to fear you're probably going to die.

Keep in mind, that as you recalibrate your own sales goals you will experience your own form of buffet. When you do, you are going to have to make the same decision a combat pilot makes: can I live in buffet, can I handle the fear, can I fail and try again, or am I going to give up and go back to where it's comfortable? My challenge for you is this: that you have the courage to take it to the edge and not turn back. That you have the determination to defy your fear ... and even to go in cold.

Try it. And when you do, don't be surprised on your way home from work if you suddenly get the urge to roll down your window and yell at the top of your lungs, "I feel the need, the need for speed"!

A Brief History of My Life in Sales

At age 28, I switched careers and went into sales. Selling promised a higher income and control over my own destiny, with no limit on how much I could earn. The harder and smarter you worked, people told me, the better you could do.

It turned out to be true.

For five years after college, I had been teaching junior high. My annual salary was $10,500. Everyone says teaching is a rewarding profession, and it is. From the standpoint of *financial* rewards, however, it appeared to be a dead end. And I was married, with two kids. I wanted more financial security. Much more.

That move into selling eventually changed everything. Nine years into my sales career, my business partner and I went to work for ourselves – I sold, he handled operations. Together, we revived a tiny collection agency, now a publicly traded company with revenues of more than $700 million. It's the largest collection company in the world, and still growing.

My lifestyle has changed dramatically, with enough financial security for a lifetime or two.

What does it take? Patience, skill and guts. I didn't start out at the top. Read on.

Getting Into the Game

My first sales job wasn't glamorous. In fact, it was about as far down the pecking order as you can get – selling space ads on plastic covers for telephone books.

Each community – this was in Connecticut – had its own cover, with 14 small business ads on each side. The company gave them away free to area residents. Ad sales generated every cent of our income.

For all its lack of prestige, the job was a good boot camp on the basics of salesmanship. We learned to gather intelligence first, targeting a town and assimilating the relevant facts. What did the demographics look like? Which local companies liked to advertise, even if just at a Little League field or on bowling alley score sheets? Which statistics would fortify my pitch to a typical client, who might be a real estate broker, a car dealer, or the owner of a pizza place?

Armed with information like that, I could go into any town with my marketing plan and a memorized set of opening and closing lines we'd been taught.

There was no debate about how to sell these ads. You went right to the street and walked in cold. If you couldn't make a sale on the spot, you pushed for an appointment to come back. You kept moving, playing the percentages. That was the system and nobody questioned it. You wore out a lot of shoe leather, but it made sense to concentrate on working the field. After all, that's where the customers lived.

COLD CALLING ADVANTAGE   #1

When you walk into someone's office looking for business, it's obvious that you're an enterprising individual. Most people respect a guy or gal who shows some grit and hustle. A "can-do" spirit is a major sales asset.

The job was straight commission – no advance, no base salary, no car allowance, no medical benefits, not even an office. I worked out of my condo. It was so tough that after a month, my training class of 40 people had dwindled to two.

But with a family to feed, quitting wasn't an option for me. I drove from town to town, making as many as 60 cold calls a day. Numbers like that generate plenty of rejection, but I convinced myself that rejection was nothing personal; it was simply part of business. As a matter of fact, rejection made me even more determined to succeed. I kept studying my sales manual. I solicited referrals and practiced my presentation skills. I followed every lead, and generally did everything possible to increase my sales volume.

Quick Tip

The Best Sales Strategy I Know

As my sales career began to take off, it became increasingly clear that going in cold – walking in doors and telling my story – was the most powerful and most effective sales strategy I could use. It was direct, dynamic, and it supplied plenty of action and variety. No two days were ever the same.

The Theory of Large Numbers

Before long, my "stop-to-appointment" ratio to was topping 90 percent. If I stopped someplace, locking up an appointment was almost a done deal. The other sales reps joked that a person would have to be "six feet under" to turn me down for an appointment – that's how determined I was.

Having coffee at six-thirty in the morning at the regular stop for contractors, I'd get an appointment on the way out. In a line of traffic, stopped at a red light next to a truck, I'd set up a meeting. If the truck had a name on the side – A1 Appliance Repair – I would lower the window and ask the driver if he owned the company. Sometimes I'd get out of my car to give him a business card, with all the horns blowing because the light had changed.

Quick Tip 🏃

Each Call Is an Adventure

For many people, face-to-face cold calling can be a chilling, intimidating experience. I know the feeling well – I frequently had to face down my own internal demons. I've heard it said that cold calling is the bane of the sales world. I've heard it described as one of the most dreaded of human experiences. Over time, however, you can conquer fears and anxieties, as we'll discuss soon.

This book is full of the stories of people who mastered their fears and discovered that they had "the right stuff" to excel at selling. Once you give it a fair shot, you'll discover that you, too, have the right stuff. And having the right stuff in sales means that you can make good money.

And that's not the only advantage. I discovered that cold calling sharpened my approach. It threw me into many different situations that kept me on edge. And the sheer adventure and action of the undertaking built up my stamina and strength. Meeting new people and trying to turn them into customers kept me attuned to opportunities and openings. It was an invigorating way to cut my teeth in selling, and it got me up to running speed in a hurry.

Cold calling involves converting a "suspect" to a "prospect," and then converting the prospect to a customer. That's the chain I worked on, and it hinged on the theory of large numbers. If you put up big numbers at the front end, in appointments and presentations, you'll close a certain number of deals on the back end. It's almost like a law of nature. And when it came to pushing big numbers into the chute, I was relentless.

That first year I finished fifth out of 135 sales reps and won a trip to the Super Bowl. National Merchandising – that was the plastic-cover company – promoted me to manager of a sales division. I turned the job down – I didn't want the hassle of dealing with such drastic turnover in the sales force. Besides, now that I knew how to sell, I felt I could do better in a different industry.

Going Outside 'the Box'

Moving on, I studied up on the securities business and got myself licensed as a stockbroker. A friend of mine worked for the old Paine Webber, in the Hartford office. I applied there and was hired immediately.

Even as a broker I practiced cold calling. It had gotten into my blood. Several times a week I'd hit the streets with some copies of our latest investment prospectus. My primary targets: physicians and dentists.

The best time to catch them was in the morning, before they'd started seeing patients, or at the end of the day, when they were wrapping up. I had one question for them: "Do you invest in tax-free municipal bonds?" Usually they did. Then I'd say, "Do you mind if I call you the next time Paine Webber has an issue, an investment bond trust?" They had no problem with that.

We would exchange business cards, and I would hand over a copy of the prospectus. Gradually this little system created a hefty file of prospects to call whenever we had some action in bonds.

There were about 40 brokers in the office, but none of them had ever tried an approach like that. It deviated from the profession's genteel self-image at the time. That didn't bother me at all, of course, because it worked.

But selling stocks and bonds never made me completely comfortable. They tried to dress it up with financial planning and such, but the business seemed to lack sophistication. It just wasn't for me. I wanted to be dealing in something more straightforward, a product or service with more substance.

The Power of Being There

For a brief period, I sold direct mail advertising coupons that came out in a packet called The Money Mailer. From there I signed on with a company that installed insulation, where the job as sales rep came with a company car and a base salary, along with commissions.

With each move, as my experience deepened, I learned that if you could sell one thing you could also sell something else. A good product at a fair price was required, of course, but beyond that it was *me* that made the difference – my enthusiasm, my conviction, my genuine desire to help the customer. An enthusiastic sales rep who really cares about his or her customers will blow away the competition. I had seen it happen. Indeed, I had *made* it happen.

But potential clients and customers can't really feel your enthusiasm unless they meet you, and they can't meet you over the phone. You've got to put yourself in a position to meet somebody who will be receptive. You have to at least get up to bat. That won't always happen unless you see people.

Can Any Sales Rep Learn to 'Go in Cold?'

After several years in sales, I grew restless for something with serious, long-term potential. Selling was the occupation for me. That much was clear. But I needed to focus on a specific field where I could develop some real expertise. That's when I discovered a good opportunity in the world of collections – recovering money for a fee.

The business of collecting bad loans and delinquent accounts was totally alien to me, but that didn't matter. Presumably it could be learned. And so I signed aboard as a sales rep with a company called IC Systems, a collection agency with operations all over the country. They put me through a rigorous training program, then gave me coastal Connecticut as a territory and turned me loose.

Tackling that job in my now-familiar style, I walked in cold on anyone likely to have problems collecting overdue debts. You name it and I went after it – banks, law firms, hospitals, retailers – always operating on the "assumptive," believing that people would see me, or would *want* to, if only they knew my program. I worked feverishly to schedule appointments, and by the end of my first year I'd brought in more than 200 new accounts. That landed me in 11th place in a sales force of 150.

Based on that performance, IC Systems transferred me to suburban Philadelphia as the new regional sales manager in charge of Pennsylvania. The Keystone State was the company's sorriest territory at the time, the absolute worst, badly in need of a turnaround.

If there was an upside to the situation, however, it was this: Here was a perfect laboratory – a test bed – to see how my method of selling worked for the new reps I had to recruit. Was cold call selling something that I had a special knack for, or could it be applied more universally? Could any reasonably intelligent salesman or saleswoman pick up the skills necessary for success?

Total Immersion Training

I needed to hire a whole new sales force, get them trained, and send them into the field. It was straight commission work, with no base salary. If you didn't sell, you didn't eat. But even with those tough conditions, nine new reps came on board.

The most gung-ho recruits were fresh out of college, young and hungry and enthusiastic about a new job and a new career. They had no qualms about cold calling. With experienced sales reps, it was harder, because they already had established methods, and cold calling was not among them. They wanted proof that it could be an effective tool before adding it to their repertoire.

GOLD GALLING ADVANTAGE   #2

Cold calling sets you apart from the herd. Your competitors might consider face-to-face prospecting too punishing and reject it as a strategy. But that's precisely why you should consider adding it to your repertoire. Take advantage of something that nobody else wants to do.

When you show up in person, you enjoy a huge advantage. Business dealings today are so arms-length that it's hard to make contact. Company owners and managers inhabit a world plagued by countless voice-mail messages and scores of e-mails on the computer. They're looking for ways to simplify their hectic lives. If you physically appear someplace with a product that fills a need, you make their decision easier. Convenience counts.

Regardless of their background, I put all nine through a total immersion in the art of face-to-face cold call selling, one on one. We'd start off their first week with in-office education on the company itself and our various services. We'd cover some of the basic principles of selling – the importance of prospecting and following up, the need to keep yourself proactive and customer-oriented, the techniques to overcome objections and close a sale.

A day or two later, we'd hit the field together so they could observe me in a variety of sales settings. The pressure was on me, because I had to demonstrate that they could close enough deals to make at least $600 to $800 a week. On top of that, a chunk of my own income was based on their commissions. I stuck with these young troopers until they were ready to fly solo, downloading into them everything I knew about selling.

The typical training week was a crash course, very intense, and by the end of it they'd be doing their own cold calls. I went along as a kind of advisor, lending moral support. Then over lunch, after I had observed the rep's techniques, I would weight in with a little critique. Where could we make improvements? With that sort of no-nonsense training they came out of the gates fast. As a team, in fact, we lifted our territory from the bottom of the IC charts to half way up the stack in just over a year – an impressive turnaround.

Entrepreneurial Drive

After selling collection services for six years, making money for other people, I took stock of my personal situation. I was pushing 40. If I were going to somehow break out of the ordinary, workaday world, and reach for something higher, a now-or-never point was fast approaching.

The entrepreneurial revolution was erupting everywhere, unleashing a contagious surge of energy. Starting a business was suddenly the thing to do, and I got the fever. By taking an equity stake in a new venture, I figured, it might be possible to realize what virtually all sales people want – a stronger sense of financial freedom and security.

A collection business was a logical starting point, given my background. But one vital ingredient was missing. I needed someone who could manage the inside aspects of the operation. A collection agency requires equipment and phone banks and personnel to generate letters and calls to delinquent debtors. Ideally, I also wanted a person with the financial acumen to handle the complicated accounting work intrinsic to the business, leaving me free to bring in clients.

What happened next was an amazing bit of seren-
dipity. I met up with Michael Barrist. A certified public
accountant with extensive experience in the medical insurance industry, Mike had all the financial expertise I could
want, and more. And here's the corker – he needed a sales
guy. Back in 1926, his grandfather had started a collection
agency called National Collection Office, or NCO. When
his grandfather passed away, Mike's mother took over the
business. By the time he and I joined forces, the client base
had dwindled to a little nucleus of about 60 companies.

Thinking with an entrepreneurial bent, however, Mike
saw big potential. In his insurance job, he had dealt constantly with collection agencies. There were thousands of
them, mostly mom-and-pop operations. The whole business
suffered from a sort of shabby, Columbo-like image – the
guy in the cheap trench coat. There was definitely room in
the field for a company with a relatively sophisticated management system.

Mike purchased NCO from his mother, and I came
on board as equity partner and vice-president in charge of
sales. It seemed to us that together we could make some
exciting things happen. After all, this was the teaming up
of the greatest operations guy in the world and the greatest salesman – at least that's what we told ourselves. Even if
it wasn't true, so what? We believed it, right to the core of
our souls.

Building a Company on Cold Calling

Renaming the company NCO Financial Systems, we
set up shop in a cramped little office in Rosemont, a leafy
suburb on Philadelphia's Main Line. We assumed the existing accounts, naturally, but the atmospherics smacked of a
pure start-up. Everything moved at double-time. Mike and
I were in a hurry to succeed. This was our big chance, and
we didn't want to blow it.

Our responsibilities divided cleanly. Mike ran internal operations, and I worked the streets to drum up business. We had no master plan, but as entrepreneurs we were driven to take the company as far as we could.

We certainly had faith in what we were doing. Management of receivables – the money they are owed – is a nightmare issue for many companies. They hate chasing after delinquent accounts. Professional people, especially doctors, lawyers, and accountants, find it undignified to hound patients and clients who refuse to pay their bills. That's not their business. But it was *our* business, and over time we became very adept at it.

COLD CALLING ADVANTAGE   # 3

According to an old saying, there are three kinds of people – those who make things happen, those who watch what happens, and those that wonder what happened. When you cold call, you definitely make things happen. There's nothing in the world of sales more proactive than walking into a stranger's office. It keeps you sharp and trains you to react to all sorts of different situations – the good, the bad, and the ugly. In time, it steels you against rejection and gives you the mettle to keep going in the face of adversity.

From those lowly origins we transformed the company into a dominant force in our industry. During the early years, we made the annual *Inc.* 500 list of the country's fastest-growing private companies four times in a row, a rare feat. We couldn't make it for a fifth time because, by then, we had taken our company public.

After a dozen years of operations, our revenues – that portion of recovered money we keep as our fee – had shot up to about $550 million. A few years later, they went over $700 million. We now employ more than 9,500 people. And from that single location in Rosemont, we've expanded – thanks to a string of acquisitions – to 70 offices across the country, reaching as far west as Hawaii and as far south as Puerto Rico. Outside the country, we have outposts in Canada, England and even India.

With more than 6,000 collection agencies in the United States, the fighting for big, lucrative accounts is ferocious. Still, our client list numbers more than 14,000 and is studded with blue-chip names. We have contracts with many of the country's largest banks. We also provide accounts-receivable services to the likes of Federal Express, Airborne Freight, and Emory Worldwide. In telecommunications, our clients include Verizon, BellSouth, and AT&T. We're even involved in higher education, running down delinquent loans for everything from the University of Pennsylvania to the California Student Aid Commission.

Walking in Thousands of Doors

How did we raise our tiny company up out of the mud and get it positioned to fly so high?

By going in cold.

To kick the business into gear, I walked in thousands of doors during the first few years. I cold called everything from the season-ticket office of the Philadelphia 76ers (and got the sale) to Sun Company, the oil giant (and again made the sale), to hundreds of doctors' offices, hospitals, and medical clinics. I walked into law firms, insurance companies, electric utilities, auto dealerships, retail establishments, and banks.

Sometimes I'd work my way down from the top of a skyscraper, floor by floor, cold calling my way through the entire building, constantly prowling for someone who needed my service.

As our company began to thrive, I hired new sales reps and trained them in my techniques, secure in the belief that old-fashioned face-to-face sales work, sometimes called "the big schmooze," is the most dynamic way to generate leads and get business. Cold calling carries with it a whiff of the unseemly, like there's something wrong with it, but from a sales standpoint there's nothing better.

It's like opening Christmas presents. You want to cold call to see what's inside the boxes. You get some lumps of coal, sure, but you also get some neat presents. It really can be fun and rewarding, in that you get a chance to go find people you can help, and who in turn can help you.

It's hard to imagine that many sales people have gotten more coal than me, or as many presents. I've made at least 15,000 cold calls during my career and closed more than 3,000 sales, plying my trade everywhere from executive suites of the *Fortune* 500 to small-town pizza joints. It's been a fabulous education in salesmanship, dealing with such a huge range of companies and characters. I've learned the importance of humor and determination to success in selling, and I've gained a good understanding of human nature, another intangible ingredient to making it in sales.

The "King of Cold Calls"

I think there are four basic levels of sales ability. You start out "unconscious" and unskilled – a raw recruit. As you begin to find your footing, you are "conscious" but still unskilled. Your approach, your presentation style and your closing techniques aren't yet refined. Then, as you master the art, you become both conscious and skilled.

The highest level, the stage when people call you a "natural," is when you are unconscious and skilled. It just comes. It took a while to get there, but I finally made it – or so people tell me. A few years ago, in fact, *Inc.* magazine profiled me as "the King of Cold Calls."

GOLD GALLING ADVANTAGE   #4

Cold calling gives you experience in dealing with a range of different industries, which in turn opens up numerous "intelligence" channels. There's no better way to get information about the competition than getting out in the field and talking to their customers. Look for a weakness. See if there's an opportunity for you. You'll become smarter, wiser and more sophisticated in your work.

I've had lots of fun with that "title" – that's often how I'm introduced on stage. But don't let it fool you. I haven't written this book because I'm some loudmouthed know-it-all. People like that give sales reps a bad name and give me a rash. There are plenty of books about selling by consultants and academics, but this one comes from a guy who has worn out his shoes in the field. This is from an infantry soldier on the front lines.

It's been a 20-year adventure for me, and in the process I've developed an abiding respect for sales people. As far as I'm concerned, we're the greatest people in the world. We're the ones who keep progress rolling. We bring out the new and improved. We belong to an old and honorable fraternity.

Men and women who can get a customer to put a signature on a contract are worth their weight in gold and diamonds. Without the guy or gal who goes out there and gets the deals – the contracts – nothing else matters, not the computer people, the operations people, the accountants or anybody else.

So my reason for writing this is simple. I understand your plight. I know what it's like out there. And I want to help you make it big in sales.

This book is for those of you who want to make a quantum leap from $60,000 a year to $100,000. Or from $100,000 to $250,000. Maybe even more. I know sales reps who are pulling down seven-figure incomes, so don't ever sell yourself short.

To make a jump like that, it helps to have some sort of a dream. Maybe you've always wanted a vacation house at the beach. Or a ski chalet in Aspen. If you have children, you might want to have their college tuition banked in advance. Maybe you'd like to retire at 50 and sail around the world or pilot a hot-air balloon over South America. It could be anything, as long as you have a goal and the desire to reach it.

You need determination to make good money, because cold call selling isn't a game for the timid or the easily discouraged. It requires drive, persistence, and a sense of purpose (a sense of humor doesn't hurt, either). You need discipline and mental toughness to ride out the dry spells.

Almost certainly, cold calling will be more physically demanding than chasing leads and appointments by means of phone work, direct mailings, trade shows, and the like. For the indomitable sales professional willing to plunge in seriously, however, cold calling can be a tremendous boon. There are diamonds under your feet, waiting to be discovered. You just have to dig them up.

Easing Your Way In

Nobody is suggesting here that you jettison your tried and true sales techniques and switch "whole hog" into cold call selling. The common sense approach is to continue using the techniques that work for you, but add cold calling to the mix. Gradually merge it into your arsenal, but do that in a disciplined, systematic way.

Make it a habit, for example, to get out of the office every Wednesday and meet someone new. Drive into nearby office parks or business districts and start knocking on doors. Or suppose you're selling to a residential market. Let's say you have a landscaping business, or a roofing company. Maybe you're a painting contractor or a caterer. Go out on Saturday afternoons, when folks are at home, and canvass a few neighborhoods.

Introduce yourself. Tell them what you do. Be yourself. Be honest. Ask if there's a need for the service you provide. Take along some testimonials and a list of satisfied customers, including their phone numbers. If you have a cleaning company, go cold call apartment houses and industrial complexes.

You don't know what won't work until you try. Sure, it all takes effort, but do you want to make good money or not? Besides, you have absolutely nothing to lose.

Quick Tip 🏃

Forget the critics

Cold calling has more detractors and enemies than just about any known business practice. Don't believe them. Most people who attack it lack the guts to do it themselves. The real reason so many sales people avoid it has to do with fear of rejection, or laziness, or poor training. There's no rule that says you have to fall in love with cold call selling, but it works. It's a highly effective tool when handled with skill and intelligence. It's also an excellent way to develop yourself professionally.

A Final Word

Cold call selling isn't just an art. It's more like an entire atmosphere. There's a Zen quality to the thing, an aura. It takes spiritual strength to move past the intimidation and fear and actually put it into practice. For some of you, it will require a fresh way of thinking about your business or your job. But you won't regret it.

I've seen many sales folks begin to really take off financially once they incorporated cold calling into their bag of tricks. It was the one piece they were missing. I've watched it work successfully for reps in any number of industries – from transportation to distribution, and from retail and manufacturing to services of all kinds.

My goal in these pages is to get you up to speed on one of the most neglected but most powerful forms of selling. You will find here an assortment of techniques and examples, along with some war stories from the field. Hopefully they will provide inspiration and guidance as you integrate a cold calling system into your own work.

And keep in mind, it's important to have fun while you're doing this. Every great cold caller I know has fun in the field. They turn it into a game. They joke around with the gatekeepers. They delight in the detective work of tracking down live prospects.

So have some fun. And go sell.

Chuck Piola
Iron Horse Farm
West Chester, Pennsylvania

CHAPTER 1

Forget the Experts–Cold Calling Works!

Chapter overview:

- Cold calling gets a bad rap. But the negativism is unjustified and based on misinformation and fear of failure.

- Cold calling is producing prosperity among those who have applied it, stuck with it, refined it, and allowed it to lead them to more and more sales opportunities.

- Many people are loathe to give cold calling a chance because they believe they can't do it. Their fear freezes them out of practicing, persevering and getting past their normal preliminary reluctance.

- The reward of cold calling is that you become more than a salesperson; you are a valued consultant who builds long-term personal relationships. These assure repeat sales while adding to your network of referral sources.

- Gatekeepers will let you in if you present yourself and your product in a way that offers value and meets the boss's needs.

- Following the chain links of a cold call leads to additional sales, new contacts, and collateral networks of prospects.

- Doors open to cold callers who share knowledge about their industry's "best practices" and what's happening on the streets with acquisitions, mergers, vendor affiliations, new products and similar scuttlebutt.

- The experts claim that cold calling is a waste of time. But performed properly, cold calling gets more than your foot in the door. It has the power to generate leads, sales, commissions, and sources of referrals.

During my early years in selling, I grabbed anything that might give me an edge – books and magazine articles about sales, inspirational tapes, seminars and workshops. I devoured it all and went back for more.

One particular seminar stands out. It took place at a hotel in New Haven, Connecticut. The main attraction for me was a session led by a prominent sales and marketing guru. I arrived early and sat in the front row, ready to absorb any wisdom the great man might impart. Surely, I figured, he could supply a few pointers to help me in my work – cold call selling of collection services for a large, national company.

There were about 100 people in the audience, and the guru began by asking how many of us liked to cold call. I raised my hand, thinking he might salute the cold callers in the group as the elite of the sales profession – like Marines storming the beaches in the face of hostile fire.

But I couldn't have been more mistaken. Instead, he singled me out for ridicule in front of the whole group. He said, "What? Are you crazy? Are you a masochist?" I asked what he was talking about. "Turn around and take a look," he said. No other hand was raised.

Everyone in the room was watching me now. I didn't need the attention, but I stood my ground, trying to defend my position. Sure, I had experienced plenty of rejection, but what sales person hasn't? It comes with the territory. Great hitters don't get on base every time at bat, and nobody belittles them for striking out once in a while. And my batting average was pretty good. Year in and year out, I told him, my techniques placed me in the top ten percent of every sales force I joined.

No matter what I said, no matter how powerful my evidence, I could not sway the opinion of this exalted poohbah. For the rest of the session, he treated me as an object of amusement, as though I were a bizarre laboratory specimen or the village idiot.

A few years later, I gave a talk on cold calling at a sales conference sponsored by Minolta Corporation. I was in a downstairs meeting room at a Las Vegas hotel, in front of about 40 sales reps, trying to convince them that true cold calling – the face-to-face pursuit of unqualified prospects – held tremendous power to generate leads, sales, and commissions. We talked about the magic of the "multiplier effect," the ability to thread a sale from one person to another, always looking to find a need for your product. The discussion centered on specific techniques and strategies, and the session bristled with positive energy.

At the same time, upstairs, another speaker was telling his group that cold calling was a waste of time. Those poor souls who did it, he said, were gluttons for needless punishment. It was like a bi-level debate. People kept coming downstairs saying that he was up there attacking the whole idea of cold calling, telling his audience it was for the birds.

The Bizarre Fear and Loathing About Cold Calling

Cold calling stirs up plenty of controversy among the so-called sales experts. For every true believer, there seems to be a critic bent on tearing it down. That has always struck me as odd, because the most inspiring books about sales that I've read were authored by people who practiced cold calling – and got rich doing it. In my first few jobs, except for a year I spent as a stockbroker, everyone cold called. That's how we were trained.

It was the only sales technique we knew, and it was one that I liked, because it worked. It didn't matter if my product was insulation or collection services or advertising space on phone book covers. Cold calling invariably produced great results. In my experience, it was the single most powerful method of identifying prospects. Consequently, I never regarded myself as some sort of a maverick. Far from it. It always seemed to me that I was operating in the mainstream.

But obviously I wasn't. Obviously, some sort of fear and loathing surrounds cold calling. Some sales and marketing "experts" keep coming out against it, propounding their theories at seminars, workshops and conferences.

Cold calling is dead, the experts say. The days of sending a foot soldier into the field to make random sales calls are over. It's too expensive, too untargeted and too ineffective to pay off. According to one statistic, it costs about $500 to send a sales rep on a single industrial sales call, counting salary, travel expenses, benefits and support costs. That's just too much money, goes the argument, to risk on a total crapshoot.

And if you *do* try to make a cold call, the experts say – well, good luck. The person you are trying to reach – the decision maker – is shielded from you and your ilk by battalions of receptionists, secretaries and administrative aides. They exist, in part, to keep you out. Keycard doorways and enhanced security systems also block you from just walking in. If somehow you do slip past the gatekeepers, the experts claim, you face more impediments. With organizations "flattening out" and downsizing, they say, it's becoming increasingly difficult to find someone with the authority to sign a contract.

Nobody likes cold calls, the critics will argue – not the person who makes them and not the prospect who receives them. The people you're calling on don't want what you have or they already have it. Busy people will resent the intrusion – they just don't want to be bothered. A cold call is a brazen gate crash, and it might wreck your chances of ever getting a crack at that particular piece of business – or so say the experts.

Then there's the issue of productivity. "When I ask other sales people why they don't make cold calls, they bring up time effectiveness," says one sales rep I know. "They say you can cover far more ground sitting around making phone calls." There's no disputing that telemarketing can be an excellent tool. But that doesn't negate the effectiveness of cold calling and the network it helps you build. And as I've said before, just because you add cold calling to your arsenal doesn't mean you abandon your other techniques.

The "experts" also insist that cold calling is the lowest percentage sale. You might get lucky on two calls out of a hundred, but you're fighting uphill all the way. Today's business buyers are looking for lasting relationships, not the hit and run tactics of a cold calling sales guy or gal.

Proving the Experts Wrong

After rattling off all these arguments against cold calling, the critics sit back with an air of triumph – case closed. You'll hear these same opinions in classrooms and conference sessions. You'll read them in sales books and journals. You'll find them cited in the sales and marketing articles posted on the Internet. You can't escape them.

With cold calling under attack from so many angles, is it any wonder sales reps give it short shrift. Let's see – it doesn't work; you can't get through; the economics border on the lunatic; you'll feel demeaned; and people will resent the intrusion. It sounds like the business equivalent of a death march.

Fortunately for me, I never paid much attention to the experts. I was always too busy selling.

Let me reiterate a point from the introduction. When my partner and I went into business, our company, NCO Financial Systems, was like any small entrepreneurial start-up – hungry for cash and eager to grow. A dozen years later, we'd turned it into the largest collection agency in the world, with revenues of more than $550 million. We're now over $700 million. Our client list exceeds 14,000 companies.

I know cold calling is effective because that's how we grew the business – by converting cold calls into hot leads and hot leads into sales. That approach worked when we were struggling to get on our feet. It still works now that we're a dominant player in our field.

Remember the old saying, that the streets of America are paved with gold? It's almost true. The gold is there all right, but it's in the ground. There's only one way to find it. You have to dig it out. That's what cold calling is all about.

Call Reluctance – the Big Trap

Let's forget about the "experts" for a moment. When you get right down to it, there's only one true barrier to cold-calling success. That barrier is fear – fear of approaching strangers, fear of rejection, fear of looking foolish in front of others. Fear knocks many sales reps out of the game in the first inning.

I know those fears well. I've experienced them all and I've seen their daunting powers over others. In a cold call, you walk up to strangers in their own workplaces and fight to get their attention. You want them to stop whatever they're doing and talk to you. That doesn't come naturally to very many of us.

The polite name for fear of cold calling is "call reluctance." It's a widespread phenomenon throughout the sales world. One sales management company claims on its Internet site that 80 percent of new sales people get out of selling the first year simply because they don't make enough calls. *Eighty percent!* If true, that's an astounding dropout rate. The company – Opportunity Management, Inc., of Beaverton, Oregon – reports further that 40 percent of *senior* sales folks suffer bouts of call reluctance severe enough to cause them to quit their careers.

The company's Internet site offers a free needs-analysis kit to help determine the level of "reluctance toxicity" in your organization. One of the main symptoms, according to the folks at Opportunity Management, is when sales reps spend too much time preparing and not enough time selling. That leads to panic at the end of every month or every quarter as reps scramble frantically to make their quotas.

When they consistently miss sales objectives, they come under the gun to step up their performance, bringing on stress and anxiety. Beneath it all is the fact that they're uncomfortable making cold calls – even on the phone. In the world of face-to-face selling, of course, call reluctance is magnified many times over. It can range into an outright phobia.

Apprehension is always with you when you walk through a stranger's door. You never know what's on the other side. You might get lucky and go right through to the decision-maker or you might meet some opposition.

It pays to remember that when you finally call on the business where you are welcomed, you can end up spending half an hour in someone's office talking about your families, the colleges you went to, and more. You establish rapport, not as sales person to customer but as person to person. And when you go back for the formal presentation, you're walking into a warmed-up and comfortable setting.

Quick Tip 🏃

Myth Versus Reality

Myth: Cold calling has a low percentage of success at a high cost.

Reality: When you overcome your own "fear barrier," your effectiveness increases daily, building your confidence and leading to positive results. Most of all, you establish a pattern of building long-term relationships that lead to repeat sales and burgeoning contacts for years.

No two cold calls are alike. Each has its own distinct flavor, based on the personalities and moods you encounter. You never know when you're going to strike gold, just as you can't predict when your smiling charm will be met with abject scorn. Admittedly, it's tough to keep going in the face of fear and rejection – to bounce back from the inevitable bummers and press on. If you've been in sales any length of time, you have encountered dry spells. You tell yourself that rejection is all part of the numbers game, that it's nothing personal. But no matter how you rationalize it, rejection wounds the ego.

Quick Tip 🏃

Adjusting Your Attitude

Many sales guys and gals think that cold calling is somehow beneath them. They've heard the war stories, and they don't like the sound of things. I've had people say to me, "I don't know how you can do that! I could never walk in on people cold and have them tell me to get out of their office."

These same folks deal with rejection constantly over the phone, of course, but it strikes them as somehow more stinging when it happens face to face. It offends their dignity. But if you're going to make it big in cold call selling, you learn to deal with the bad stuff and stay focused on the upside. That takes a willingness to persevere, come hell or high water.

When you get shot down time and again, it takes a toll on your self-esteem and self-confidence. That's true even when you're selling over the phone. Eventually, you can get so down and discouraged that you'll quit your job – if you're not fired first.

Every successful sales person first needs to get past fear. The lazy, the timid, and the procrastinators aren't very likely to do what it takes. That's why this book is for salesmen and saleswomen who are serious about making real money. Later on we'll explore the fear factor in greater detail. But for now, rest assured that you can definitely bring it under control.

Remember, fear is nothing more than a head-trip. No one is pointing a gun at you in a sales setting. The fear you might feel in cold calling is mostly self-inflicted. While you might never make it vanish completely, you can definitely minimize its impact with the right approach and techniques. Whenever you feel a ripple of fear about walking in cold, ask yourself this: What's the worst thing that can happen to me? Answer: You don't make the sale. Big deal. There are plenty of other targets of opportunity.

A Case Study in the Right Stuff

In these pages, you will meet a cast of characters who have discovered the same secret I learned early on – cold call selling can turbo-charge a sales career. These folks all share a common trait. I think of it as the "right stuff," that hard-boiled determination to persevere and succeed no matter what obstacles get in the way.

Frank Scaravaglione fits the bill. He sells limousine services for Carey International, the world's largest ground transportation company. It has operations in hundreds of cities in 65 countries. But due to its skimpy advertising, it lacks public visibility.

A few years ago, the folks in its Philadelphia branch – Frank was one of them – decided they needed a higher profile in the local marketplace. They came up with a two-pronged plan. On one front, they joined a number of business associations to help with networking and brand recognition. On a second front, they set up a cold calling program. The strategy called for using business directories to target their face-to-face visits on the most likely prospects.

As the local director of sales, Frank was the point person for the cold calling campaign. He had done extensive cold call selling many years before, when he was with Avis Rent A Car. Over the years, he moved into management jobs and his cold calling skills grew a little rusty.

But Frank was willing to give it a shot, in hopes of advancing Carey's market penetration. If nothing else, it would at least spread around the Carey name – and Frank's name, too. So he began working his way around Philadelphia's Delaware Valley region, focusing on the usual suspects, the sort of companies that form Carey's base – banks, insurance companies, meeting planners, consultants, executive-search firms, and manufacturers of all stripes.

As the program kicked into gear, Frank began making about 80 cold calls a month, usually four or five a day. He didn't really mind his new routine. Sometimes he even looked forward to cold calls because, as he says, "they can be fun." But he wasn't crazy about the reaction he sometimes got. "There's this look you get once in a while," he says. "You walk into an office and you get that look, like you're the dirt of the earth. It's like, 'What do you want? Don't bother me.' Not a good feeling.

"Or sometimes, they'll have these huge No Soliciting signs on their doors and on the counters. And as soon as you walk in and approach somebody, they just point. They don't even speak," he says.

More than once, Frank has been physically expelled from buildings. That's probably the ultimate repudiation – rejection by ejection. "I've done a lot of work in the big office towers," he says. "There was one situation in Philadelphia, where I was in a building on a legitimate appointment. I went up to the 35th floor, and when I finished I went down to 34 to see who was there.

"That was my method – first get inside, and then nose around for other prospects. But in doing that, I had security guards come to get me a couple of times. Obviously, somebody had complained because I knocked on their door. Guards came up and escorted me out."

In the past, a sales rep walking into a high-rise office building had no trouble figuring out which companies were inside. Their names and floors were posted on lobby directories. But as Frank discovered, times had changed. "They don't list the occupants anymore," he explains. "They put them on these little video monitors right in front of the security guard. They will ask you who you're looking for, and if you don't know, that automatically sends up a red flag.

"A lot of buildings – not so much in the suburbs but in large cities – clearly emphasize no soliciting," Frank says. "Even when I have the name of someone to see, the guard very well might call ahead before I'm allowed on the elevator."

Frank's Tactic to Get Inside

For Frank, making it past security isn't much of a problem. A sales person in professional dress can slip unnoticed into an office building with the morning rush, or when a crowd is returning from lunch. He simply avoids eye contact with the guards.

Once inside, he often encounters more hurdles. As Frank tells it: "A lot of office doors are locked these days," he says. "You either have to punch in codes, use an electronic entry card, or call on an intercom. I just buzz them. You can't be intimidated by gatekeepers and locked doors.

"So I buzz, and when someone answers, I'll say, 'Hi, I'm from Carey International. I was just visiting XYZ upstairs and thought I'd ask if you folks use ground transportation services – buses, vans, limousines, things like that.' They'll say no, we don't, or yes, we do.

"When it's a yes, I'll ask to leave some information for the right person. So I get someone to come out, usually a secretary. I hand over the packet and, while I'm at it, I ask whom I should call – who handles travel arrangements? I'd say that 60 percent of the time, you can at least get a name, and then you can follow up.

"They don't all turn into sales, but at least I've established a contact and established a user. And who knows? Down the road, if they get unhappy with the people they're using, you might get an opportunity. I do a little tickler every few months. I'll call and say I'm just checking in to see how you're doing. I'll say that we've grown or we've added these new cities, and if we can be of any assistance, please let me know."

Being escorted out of a building doesn't deter Frank. "When you think about it," he says, "if asking you to leave is the worst thing that can happen, that's not much of anything. I mean, I haven't been arrested or physically hurt.

"Some people might interpret it as demeaning," Frank adds, "and that's what you really have to get over when it comes to cold calling. You can't think you're too good for it, because you'll forfeit a lot of opportunities. It's definitely a viable means of generating revenue and business. There's no question about it."

Who Dares Wins

We'll get back to Frank a little later. But first, let's meet Mark Macrone, another sales guy who has the right stuff.

Mark has been with my company for more than a decade, almost from the start. A super sales guy, he has walked in cold thousands of times. Thinking back to his early days in selling, he says success in cold calling comes down to a matter of guts. It's like the motto of Army Special Forces commandos: "Who dares wins."

"I always believed I was a gutsy person," Mark says, "but all of a sudden, when you're cold calling, you can get a little knot in your stomach. I remember when I first started. About 70 percent of our client base was medical, so I dealt with a lot of doctors. They have a terrible time collecting money.

"I'd walk into a doctor's office, and I'd see a glass reception window with three women behind it, running around like crazy. There'd be 15 people in the waiting room – kids crying, people coughing and sneezing. The place would be busy as all get out. And I'm walking up to the gate there. I'm a sales guy, obviously, and they are look-ing at me as that.

"In some cases, people wouldn't even give you 30 sec-onds. They wouldn't hear you out. They'd be rude to you. If you were new to selling and that kind of thing happened a lot, you might say, 'To hell with cold calling. I'm not doing business that way. I don't want to get beat up like that.' "

Right from the beginning, I told Mark – and every other sales person I hired – that cold calling takes guts. I said you have to let rejection bounce off you like BBs off a bulldozer.

That sounded okay to Mark. After all, this was his first job out of college, and he liked the idea of selling because he could control his own income. As his mentor, I put him through cold-calling boot camp. The day he started with us, I took him out in the field, and we walked in doors together.

After two more days, he was doing it on his own, and I'd team up with him once a week to work on the finer points. He was a quick study who seemed to have the essential ingredients required to flourish in face-to-face selling: self-starting personal drive, thick skin and relent-less optimism.

In teaching him, I emphasized that he could not become me. "You can pick up my verbiage and mannerisms," I told him. "I want you to study my eye contact, my inflection, my hand gestures, the way I let a word drop before continuing. Watch it all. You can take pieces and incorporate them into your own style. Learn what I say, but don't get so pat with it that you lose your spontaneity and freshness."

Overcoming the Initial Nervousness

Certain aspects of cold calling came easily to Mark. He was always the class clown, the joker. He had no trouble relating to people, and they liked his sense of humor.

Still, during his first few months on the job, he felt intimidated making formal presentations to physicians or bankers or business owners twice his age. But once he developed his own style and built up his confidence, nothing could fluster him. In a room with 15 corporate executives, with all attention trained on him, he would be a little nervous, but it wouldn't show. He projected self-assurance, because he knew exactly what he wanted to say and how to say it.

Mark was becoming a player. "There will be times when it's going to be real hard, and you're not going to feel comfortable," he says. "You just have to go ahead and do it anyway. If you're apprehensive, just go in and fake it if you have to. Never let them see that you're nervous."

Cold calling is a numbers game, and Mark put up big numbers, often making more than 30 calls a day. He discovered that for every ten cold call stops, he would get one appointment to give a presentation. And given the chance to sit down and lay out the NCO program, he closed half of those deals.

So, on average, he needed to make 20 cold calls to sign up a new client – a five-percent "hit" rate. The experts might call that "low percentage" selling. I don't. It worked well enough that, by his third year, Mark was earning $80,000. From that point on, his income climbed into six figures.

Despite that level of financial success, Mark has encountered plenty of skepticism along the way. "I've met some very nice sales reps before," he says, "people who obviously had good personalities for selling. But they could not believe we were going to try to grow our company by cold calling. They said it was too expensive to do it that way. They said we'd fail.

"I think people shoot down the idea because, one, they've never tried it, and two, they personally don't have what it takes to get in front of someone cold. To disguise their own deficiency, they turn all of cold calling into a negative – 'Why the hell would you do that? That doesn't work.' "

Mark quickly found out differently. As he puts it, "What's so valuable is that cold calling builds up your overall confidence, and you meet people you would never have met by picking up the phone.

"A lot of the edge is the networking and referrals," he adds, "which is where a lot of our business came from. If I didn't have personal contact with people, I wasn't going to get referrals from them. Cold calling made it easy to follow a sales lead from one person to another. I'm not saying it can't be done in other ways, but it happens automatically with cold calling. Once you're in front of someone, you usually get somewhere with them."

The Knack

Let me give you one more example of a sales rep who cut his teeth on face-to-face cold calling and went on to great success.

As vice president of sales at NCO Financial Systems, it was my responsibility to build up an effective sales force. I liked to assemble a batch of recruits and run them through my program, and see which ones survived.

I recall one class of seven sales people who came on board at the same time. Our company was small then, about 35 folks, so we couldn't afford a generous compensation package. The new people were paid on a straight-commission basis – no sales, no money.

I took each recruit into the field for three or four days of cold-call selling – my usual crash course. Let's say we were canvassing center-city Philadelphia. They could watch me work my way through a hospital or skyscraper. They'd see me get shot down. Between calls or over lunch, we'd talk about technique. And on that last day together, they'd make some solo runs – not dress rehearsals but actual calls – while I looked on as coach. Then they were cut loose. "Don't come into the office," I'd tell them by way of final advice. "Just go out and sell."

At the end of six months, only one of those seven reps remained. The sole survivor was a young man named Tim Kleppick. Tim had come to us straight from college. It was his first real job, and he just had the knack. "Starting in grade school, I knew I wanted to go into sales," Tim says. "I always had fairly good confidence knocking on doors and talking to people. So it came kind of naturally to me."

Even so, Tim didn't become an adroit cold caller right off the bat. I told him you can't just dabble at this a few times and then drop it if it doesn't work instantly. It *won't* work instantly. Nobody becomes a skilled cold caller in a month or even three months.

"It took me a good year to feel completely and truly comfortable, where I had my confidence, where I could speak intelligently, and where I was used to the cold-call process," Tim says. "Before that, I was just trying to be a nice guy – I was trying to get somebody to sit down with a nice guy, which also worked."

Tim got enough people to sit down – and sign contracts – that he enjoyed a promising first year. From that point, he was off and running. Today, as one of our top account executives, he's still out there knocking on doors.

"If you can cold call, the hardest technique of all, then you can sell anything," he says. "It's also the most profitable and most rewarding way of selling. You'll get a much bigger reward if you're able to make cold calls, and your income is going to reflect that.

"I've always tried to keep the financial upside in mind," Tim adds, "because some people definitely look down on cold callers. It still bothers me if someone treats me like some sort of cheeseball. But it also motivates me, because I know I've been successful doing it. Not everybody can hack it, though. Not everybody can brush off rejection and keep going. I could, and that's why I was the only one of those seven guys in my training class to survive here."

Why the "Experts" Hide the Truth

Tim Kleppick's last point there cuts right to bone. Not everybody can hack it. They just can't get past their fear; they can't handle rejection. And that, my friends, is the real reason that the so-called experts badmouth cold calling. And it explains why they have to fog the debate with high-sounding arguments about gatekeepers and economics.

They are hiding the naked truth – cold calling is just too tough for lots of folks. The "gurus" know how hard it is to find sales reps willing to try it – or, if they do try it, who are willing to stick with it. So they attack it with "studies" and "reports" and shoddy research that somehow never gets to the heart of the matter. Why insult the people who buy their books and pay to attend their seminars?

Their audiences like it when the experts fuzz the facts. It makes them feel better about themselves – less guilty. They know deep down that they should be out there, prospecting in the field. They suspect that maybe they're a little lazy. The experts provide a perfect cover: Why cold call when all the "authorities" talk it down?

But the fact remains: most people who reject cold calling as a sales strategy simply lack the courage to try it and the guts to persevere. They're not *warriors*.

But let me tell you, sales managers love it when they find a guy or gal experienced at it. I've trained people who later left our company for one reason or another. When they went elsewhere and let it be known that they always cold called for leads and appointments, their new employers were ecstatic. They could not believe they had someone trained in this skill.

One young man left us to sell long-distance telephone services, and he consistently landed in the top ten in a sales force of 400 people. Why? Because he had been schooled in the most effective ways to generate business.

In fairness, it must be said that cold call selling isn't a perfect fit for any location or in every industry. The optimum scenario involves a commonly used product or service in a well-populated area. Our company has headquarters in Horsham, Pennsylvania, a large suburb of Philadelphia. The whole metropolitan region is alive with commerce and brimming with opportunities.

"I could literally *walk* from my office and find at least 50 businesses that I could cold call," says my colleague Mark Macrone. "It's very possible that some of the people who shoot it down can't do that. Or they might be dealing with a very specific market. Maybe they're only going to sell to big telecom companies, and there are only three of them in Philadelphia and two in Baltimore. I can see how they'd say, 'There's no way I'm cold calling.' But in my business and lots of others, I can play the numbers game. That how I built my business. I'm able to walk in 40 doors a day to any business that extends credit to customers."

If people tell you that you can't cold call in your industry, you better be damn sure that's true, because in most cases it isn't.

What's Wrong With Conventional Methods?

Your primary mission as a sales person is to generate new business while keeping existing customers satisfied. New business is the lifeblood of your company, so you always need to be on the alert for fresh prospects.

If you rule out cold calling as a means of developing your business, you're limited to the traditional techniques. You work the phones. You send out direct mailings. You try to build up your business with existing customers or through referrals. You advertise. You network and join business groups – the Rotary, the Lions, the Elks – to get your name around. Those are the most reliable ways, the experts declare, to generate leads and sales.

Obviously, those methods are widely used, and they are fine as far as they go, as long as they deliver the goods. But let's consider their limitations, when contrasted with the advantages of going in cold.

Direct mail pieces are usually just another scrap of paper coming in the door. Almost everybody sends them. Our mailboxes are perpetually crammed with brochures and come-ons. Out of a thousand mail recipients, a small number of people, maybe two or three percent, will respond with some degree of interest. These few responses are leads – there's no guarantee that any of them will bring a sale. Meanwhile, it's expensive; and it's *passive* selling. You're waiting for the phone to ring or for the mail to bring in requests. You'll never make a big splash in sales waiting for a potential customer to make the first move.

Telemarketing – "dialing for dollars" – is an equally dubious approach. The calls can be effective in the hands of a superb sales rep. The problem is that it's just so tough to make telephone contact with people today. Most business people hate getting these calls, so they don't take them. With voice-mail systems, answering machines and services and caller ID, getting through to the right person is harder than ever. Sure, you can leave a message, but the chances of getting a callback are slim to none. They don't know who you are or what you have, so why bother?

If you are lucky enough to reach a live human being, most likely you'll be dealing with a receptionist or other gatekeeper who is proficient at deflecting sales calls. The phone is a gatekeeper's power base, and he or she knows how to defend it. They can cut you off in a split second. If you ask to speak with someone in authority, the person is inevitably "in a meeting," the universal dodge. The secretary will take a message, of course, but again the odds of getting a return call from the boss aren't good.

Cold Calling Advantage

Being There

Imagine a sales person standing right there in your office. Are you going to be so swift to send him or her away? Probably not. Most people are friendly enough to give you a few minutes to explain yourself, even if they are just being polite. In fact, they might even welcome the diversion. In today's technologically based, impersonal business world, there is still something in our psychological makeup that connects with a living, breathing sales person who walks in the door.

There are exceptions, for sure. If you've been dazzling on the phone, you can win over an advocate for your cause. When a secretary warms to the tone of your voice, finds you likable, and decides your product or service deserves at least a look, he or she might go to bat for you. In that case, you'll be able to get some worthwhile information. Does that company use the kind of service or product you represent? If so, who's in charge of that particular area? You'll be able to get names, titles, and phone numbers of the people you need to reach. But by and large, if you make a cold call over the phone without a specific name of someone to ask for, you won't get far.

If you've ever taken a call from a telemarketer – and who hasn't? – you know how easy it is to say "no" over the phone. A quick "no thanks" and then you hang up. You have no problem getting rid of the caller quickly because it's just a voice on the phone.

Remember, you're not asking anyone for a huge chunk of time. The goal of any sales call is to get the sale, of course, but the cycle often starts with scheduling an appointment. You should have a one- or two-minute drill locked, loaded, and ready to go. All you need to deliver on that first pass is a quick description of what you and your company do. Then, if you have sparked some interest – if you have found a need – arrange a time to come back and explain your program.

For a cold caller, the question is: Will they *make* the time to see me? I've made more than 15,000 cold calls, and I'd have to say, in general, yes they will, provided you come in with a friendly attitude and some sensitivity to their job pressures. If you walk in the door and are like a breath of fresh air, you're not an infringement on their time. They'll make room for you. But if you come across as pushy or aggressive, forget it. Nobody wants to deal with that. Just be natural. Sales reps can get so slick with techniques that they forget to be nice, regular people – but that's what sells.

The marketplace is crowded. You need to cut through the noise and get results. In my view, going face-to-face with potential customers consistently delivers a payoff seldom matched by more conventional styles of selling.

You're Not Just a Cold Caller. You're a Sales Consultant

There's no reason to feel defensive or apologetic about going in cold. As a matter of fact, the sharpest company owners and managers don't regard a face-to-face call as an imposition. Quite the opposite – they see it as an opportunity to gain competitive intelligence.

Because sales people call on so many different people in various industries, they become good consultants. They can tell you what works and what doesn't work in like businesses. The savvy cold-calling sales rep comes in the door with a wealth of information for the prospective customer. And the customer may want to know: What is the competition up to? What are people in my field doing? What is the best possible solution, or the most economical in my circumstances?

You bring a lot to the table when you arrive with a very positive attitude: I am a resource for you; use me. I see how company owners and managers handle problems. I pick up on the "best practices," the most productive ways to run a business.

That's valuable information for you to share with your prospects and clients. Just like an MBA management consultant, you come bearing ideas and cutting-edge methods to improve their operations.

You bring real value, even though you're only at step one, the initial meeting with a potential customer. If you come across as friendly and helpful and if you hit the right "buttons," you might be well on your way to making a sale. If nothing else, you will have established yourself as a go-getter, and you might get some referrals.

Rewards for Go-Getters

"I think people give you extra credit when you walk into their office," says my associate Tim Kleppick. "Now, obviously, some people don't want to deal with you. But when you come across those who appreciate you, it's very rewarding. There's a feeling of accomplishment. Even when they don't buy from you, they respect what you're doing. They respect you for doing it.

"For me, the biggest upside is not the money," Tim adds. "It's the feeling you get by walking in, meeting somebody, and selling an idea or a good product. That's a great feeling, going in there and forging a new relationship with another person, another organization – totally from scratch. And who knows where that's going to grow? That's how you broaden your market. It really helps with referrals, because when you do a good job for one person, they're more likely to supply the names of other prospects, and then vouch for you."

Every relationship has to start somewhere. In Tim's view, there's no better setting than a cold call. "You can establish so much more credibility in person, immediately, because you're face to face with somebody. You never know when two different personalities are going to click," he says. "And if you can schedule an appointment on a cold call, your chances of converting it to a sale are pretty good."

On the other hand, he says, appointments set over the phone don't convert at nearly the same rates. By Tim's calculation, about three quarters of the sales he closes start with a cold call. But when a relationship begins with a telemarketing call that wins him an appointment, he's lucky to close half the time.

"They all hear the same presentation about the same product," he says. "The difference is the credibility and trust that exists because you've met before. You've already broken the ice, so when you walk back in, it's a lot more comfortable. That creates a whole different atmosphere."

Gatekeepers Don't Bite

To hear the "experts" describe it, you'll never break through the first line of corporate defense – receptionists, secretaries and administrative assistants. They protect the boss the way offensive linemen protect a quarterback. They block and, if necessary, they "hold." According to the sales gurus, your odds of penetrating into the backfield are pretty low.

Frankly, the experts are wrong. Gatekeepers are there, of course, especially in large and mid-sized companies. In smaller, entrepreneurial companies, you find a much-reduced protective squad. Because cold calling is fairly rare nowadays, most companies have lowered their guard to a degree. I've seldom had trouble reaching the person I needed to see, although not always on the first try or even the second.

That doesn't mean you run roughshod over the receptionists or try to bully your way past them. You don't want to fight the system; the idea is to make the system work for you. Your goal is to talk with Mr. or Ms. Big – a company owner, a president, or perhaps the head honcho of some division you're targeting.

We've already seen what happens when you try to get through on the phone. You stand a much better chance of success when you meet someone face to face – not only the boss, mind you, but also the gatekeeper. This is where your personality, your honesty, and possibly your "charm" come into play. Do you have a winning way with people? Are you quick with a joke or a friendly word? Use whatever "people skills" you have.

Gatekeepers are ordinary folks, and if you come across as polite and sincere, you'll be fine. The magic is in your approach. No canned spiel; no fake "sales" personality – people will see through that very quickly, dooming your chances. Be yourself – that's key. You have to make some small talk, but you have to mean it. Small talk is a big thing in cold call selling. It can open the door.

And why shouldn't it? You mean no harm. The product or service you're selling – a copier, say, or a retirement plan – has real value. Your business has excellent reasons why someone should buy from you. If you're dealing with a gatekeeper, you have to make clear what is unique about your company – why you're special, and why the boss needs to hear more about it.

A competent secretary or admin assistant will decide if you have the company's best interests at heart. If you do and you seem genuine, the assistant will get you in for a few minutes with the boss. It might not happen immediately, but it will happen. So don't believe the experts when they say the gatekeepers are there strictly to keep you out. They can be your ticket to a meeting, then a presentation, and then a sale. They can provide valuable assistance by organizing the whole process and moving it along. (More on this point later.)

There's No Better Way to Meet Potential Customers
As for the financial argument against cold calling, most of it is sheer nonsense. No one is suggesting that you fly all over the country to make a few cold calls. That *would* be crazy. But most sales reps have time in the course of a day to knock on a few more doors.

If you're already at an appointment in an office complex or a downtown district, why not try to meet some new people? After your appointment, walk into a few nearby offices and introduce yourself. Ask to see the person in charge – the owner or manager. You have absolutely nothing to lose. You're already there. You've already paid for transportation and parking.

Extra calls cost you nothing, and they can be worthwhile even if they don't directly lead to a sale. The more calls you make, the more you spread around your name, your brand, and your service. In sales, you're always better off when you know a lot of people and understand their business, and when they're familiar with what you're all about.

When you stop in somewhere, make sure to leave your business card, and never leave without getting theirs. At least they'll know who you are and how to reach you. It's good exposure, and you never know how it might pay off. I've had people call me and say, "You were in here three months ago, and I'm ready to talk to you now."

Quick Tip 🏃

Tactic: The Leave-Behind

On a cold call, ask the gatekeeper if it's okay to leave a packet of information for the boss. If you come across as friendly, polite, and sincere, nine times out of ten, the gatekeeper will help you. While you're at it, ask for the gatekeeper's card, too, and make some small talk. Have some fun.

When you do that, you have a perfect excuse to call back, even by phone. "Hi, Marie. This is Chuck Piola. Remember me, from NCO Financial? I left some sales materials with you last week." She always remembers. "Did Mr. Smith get a chance to look at them?" If he did, could you speak with him for a second? This is the moment to go for the appointment, and frequently it works. It works because you have physically been there. That gets you extra credit, and very often it gets you in to see the decision-maker.

Using The Cold-Call Domino Game

Walking in cold sets in motion what I call the "multiplier effect," a powerful feature of face-to-face sales work. In business-to-business dealings, you meet people – in the elevator, the hallway, the reception area – and everybody you see is a resource. It's a natural way to network, and that's what makes a cold call so interesting. You can't predict the direction it will take. Each call is a new adventure and you just go with it; it maximizes your contacts.

The more folks you meet, the greater your chances of finding someone who needs your product or service. I've been in plenty of places where the prospect wasn't interested in my service, but they knew somebody else who *might* be interested. I follow the string from one point to another.

Quick Tip 🏃

Following the Thread
The myth is that cold calling is one-shot and doesn't work. The reality is different. Like "Six Degrees of Separation" (someone who knows someone who knows someone), the multiplier effect threads sales and contacts from one person to another. One cold call reaches into many pockets.

Many of the best sales I ever made came at the end of a string of contacts. For example, I've threaded my way through the bureaucratic maze of a large bank or insurance company until I found the office where the buck stopped. Other times, I'd follow a trail leading from one business to another. This is a huge advantage of cold calling – the ability to leverage personal contacts as you pursue a sale. You won't get this kind of critical spin-off action from a direct-mail campaign or over the phone.

A Secret Benefit – Gathering Intelligence
Given the emphasis on getting through to a decision maker, sales reps frequently speed past one of the natural values of cold calling. It's a terrific way to collect information – a useful tidbit about a competitor, a name, a current bit of news, anything that can strengthen your position or give you an edge. I'm not talking about corporate espio-

nage. You'd be surprised by how much you can learn simply by exercising your powers of observation.

A case in point is a fellow named Jack Deal. A former cold-calling sales guy, he runs the Deal Consulting Group, based in Santa Cruz, California, ideally situated on Monterey Bay and now considered part of Silicon Valley. Deal advises clients on Internet linkage, Web design, e-business and other aspects of information technology.

That's a crowded sector of the consulting world, so he sometimes uses cold calling to discover what his competitors and potential clients are doing. He compares it to "management by walking around," a concept promoted by Tom Peters, co-author of *In Search of Excellence* and other popular business books.

"When I first read that, I thought, well, if you could manage by going out in the plant and walking around, I could do the same thing in my business," he says. "When you cold call someone, you are just tuned into everything as you walk in. Your senses go on alert. So I can walk in cold and come away with all sorts of information – what kind of software they're running, where the inventory stands, who makes the decisions, how they manage. I can also find out at least parts of their sales and marketing plan.

"You can pick up all sorts of things in 15 or 20 minutes," he says, "if you know what you're looking for. None of this is illegal. You're not stealing hard drives. You're just watching what people are doing. You might get some of that information on the phone, but not much. You can't do it on the Internet. There's no real substitute for being there when you're out to collect intelligence, and you can usually get it or find out who has it.

"If you get out of cold calling, you can very quickly lose touch with what's happening at the real, kind of street level," Deal says. "So it's valuable for education, and boy, you really get some life experiences. It makes you flexible, and you need that because you never know what you're

going to find. You get screamed at and yelled at and sometimes threatened, but very often also you are welcomed
and given the company tour. You make a game of it and
see how far you can go."

COLD CALLING ADVANTAGE

Building Your Sales Base

Myth: Cold calling will beat you down.

Reality: Cold calling builds you up by supplying a
growing list of clients, referrals and word-of-mouth
entrée to others. But you need to learn the techniques.

All told, Deal concludes that cold call selling has been
an enormous benefit in building his clientele. "Not only
does it get business," he says, "it also teaches you the side
things, like how to collect intelligence. You can learn about
all kinds of industries. It absolutely works in a lot of different fields, and you can learn an incredible amount of
things by doing it. I still do it, and I like to do it."

Like Golf, It Takes Time to Learn

It's not a perfect analogy, but in some ways cold calling resembles playing golf. In my experience, charity golf
tournaments are always fun, and they provide an enjoyable
way to meet new people and do some networking. There's
a built-in camaraderie, because you automatically have
something in common – the game at hand.

Golf is a difficult sport. The first time you line up at
the tee with a driver in your hand, you're hacking at the
ground or smashing the ball into the woods or the next
fairway. Sometimes you top the thing and it scuttles along
the ground. You suffer through hooks, slices, and whiffs.

Then you have to learn how to swing your irons. How far will a seven-iron shot fly? From a hundred yards out, should you hit a pitching wedge or a short nine? All of it requires "touch" and course management. Finally, there's putting, one of the toughest things to do well. You need to master all of the essential tools of the game to be a decent player. It can take years.

When you walk into someone's office on a cold call, you have a driver in your hand – that's the big, bold stroke. Then you pull out a long iron for that second shot that gets you past the gatekeepers. Once you get in front of the decision-maker, it's your putter, your finesse club, that matters most. This is where artistry comes in, the thing that separates the pros from the weekend hacks. In golf, you need the savvy to read the green and its subtle breaks, just as in selling you need the deftness and empathy to read all different personality types.

Cold calling involves a whole set of skills. As we'll see, each one plays a vital role in the course of face-to face sales work. Nobody masters these skills overnight. You can't become a low-handicapper by golfing a few times a year, and the same applies here. These things take time to learn.

If you want really convincing results, you have to practice. You have to get out in the field and meet people. Find customers where they live. Make it happen. Getting in front of people gives you a chance to learn by experience. It's also where you can make your first hundred mistakes and where you can learn to take rejection and move on.

The more "prospects" you meet, the more comfortable you'll feel about doing this. Each new call you make adds to your self-assurance. Your confidence keeps building while your fear is diminishing. This is how you learn: Which approaches get you in the door? Which sales techniques are the most reliable?

Gradually, your whole method will fuse into a "style" that fits both your personality and your market. It takes effort, but if you do work hard at cold calling, you're practically guaranteed to expand your universe of contacts in a big way. Don't forget: It's a numbers game. You're playing the percentages. And when you stuff a lot more action into the funnel, you're bound to close a lot more sales.

Capitalizing on the Networking Dimension

Remember Frank Scaravaglione from an earlier example? He's the salesman for Carey International, the big ground transportation company.

A few years ago, Frank and some others came up with a new marketing plan centered on generating sales by deepening Carey's brand identity. To provide instant market presence, it called for extensive work in the field. Frank and the other sales reps were expected to make many cold calls.

"The idea was to cold call on the phone or go in face to face – stop and meet the receptionist and see where you could go from there," he says. "That was the game plan, and cold calling appeared to be the most direct way to spread our name around and begin penetrating the market."

Frank launched into it with conflicted emotions. "I was very pessimistic – I'll be the first to admit that," he says. "I wasn't all that confident that cold calling would work." But he got in his car and began a pace of about 80 calls a month or about four a day. To avoid wasted effort, Frank carefully targeted his calls toward the business categories most likely to contract for limos and vans and buses. Rather than make his first move by phone, he preferred walking in cold.

"It was a more dynamic approach," he says. "It gave you a way to really delve into your market and do some fact-finding. Phone work just was never as productive. You can get the names of a company's top officers from business directories, but you won't get those people on the phone. And in my case, I didn't need senior executives – I wanted the people who made their travel arrangements. In this business, the decision-maker, the buyer, is usually an executive aide or secretary who doubles as travel administrator. You can usually get those folks on the phone, but you lose that networking dimension that comes with a personal visit.

"So I'd go into a large banking corporation," Frank says, "and I'd try to find the travel administrator for the chairman of the board. It might turn out that Mr. Jones, the chairman, uses a competing service and wants to stick with it. But because I was standing there, in the flesh, I could ask about the other company's other travel administrators. Were they booking services for their bosses? Who were they, and how could I reach them? More often than not I'd get some names, and then I could network my way from one person to another.

"In our field," Frank says, "it's seldom a consolidated buy. Ground transportation can be a personal thing. In a company with ten executives, each one might use a different service. That always provided me with multiple entry points inside the same company, and any one of them could bring a sale.

"The CEO's aide might say, 'We're very happy now, but we'll keep you in mind.' But then you'd walk into the controller's office, and an aide would say, 'You know, I'm glad you stopped in. Let's talk.' No matter how a call turns out, though, if you're there in person, you can always leave a packet of information and ask for a name so you can follow up."

That's essentially how Frank got my business.

Here's how he remembers it: "I stopped by Chuck's office one day, a pure cold call," he says. "A receptionist referred me to his office, but he wasn't around, so I left some information and a note explaining the purpose of my visit. A week or two later, I followed up with a phone call, but got no answer. And then one day, out of the blue, he called me. And he switched from a competitor he seemed satisfied with and came over to us."

Frank didn't know this at the time – he found out later – but I switched because he had cold called me. I admire the moxie it takes to walk into a stranger's office and ask for their business. It didn't matter that I wasn't there. What mattered to me was that *he* had been there. That kind of initiative deserves to be rewarded. It gave Frank a big leg up on the competition, and then the terms and conditions of the deal sealed it.

Was Frank's cold calling program worth all the aggravation and rejection? "Absolutely," he says. "My pessimism quickly gave way to enthusiasm because I had some very decent successes. I signed up at least five customers that are generating $80,000 or more in business for us each year. They all came from cold calls. Cold calling turned out to be a very effective means to build our clientele and enhance our visibility in the market."

Frank's cold-calling program paid off quickly. In just over a year, he expanded his business base substantially. And that's another point: You don't need to keep at this for the rest of your working life – unless you want to.

'Where Everyone Learns How to Sell'

Cold calling is a great way for young reps to get up and running. After building a substantial base, they leverage existing customers to gain referrals. Without cold calling, many sales careers end in failure. If you really want to learn about business, there's no substitute for cold calls. Without them, you give up sales and building networks; and you give up a valuable education. There's no better training ground.

Even some of the experts agree about that.

"Cold calling is the place where everyone learns how to sell," says Jim DeForrest, of Sales Consultants, Inc., as quoted in *The Houston Chronicle*. In an article headlined "Is Cold Calling a Gold Mine or Mine Field for Salespeople?" there was no question where he stood. "Cold calling – where you make a call, either by phone or in person, to a person or company that has not contacted you in the past – is where you learn the ABCs of selling," he says. "It's Basic Sales 101."

DeForrest spent more than 20 years as a sales rep, so he knows the real world. "Cold calling requires two key traits," he says. "First, you need to be able to deal with people, face to face, the first time you meet them. The second trait would be patience or persistence, because it can take a lot of calls to produce a sale. And remember," he says, "cold calling is only the prospecting part of the cycle. Once you get in front of the person, then you still need sales skills to perform a needs assessment, you need qualifying skills, and you need to be able to listen and present yourself well."

Cold calling, DeForrest says, isn't rocket science. Anyone can learn to do it effectively. "There's nothing mysterious about it," he says. "It's the process of relationship-building with people and companies whose needs you can fulfill with your products or your services. It comes down to a matter of identifying needs. If whatever you're selling can solve problems or meet those needs, you have a chance to make a sale. If you don't have something that matches needs or solves problems, it's over."

The bottom line: Don't trust the experts when they dismiss cold calling out of hand. The pessimists have never done it themselves, maybe because they lack the courage it takes. You're in sales to make money. You have what it takes. And cold calling, within normal parameters, is one of the most effective ways to establish a successful sales career. Believe in yourself, because you can do it.

CHAPTER 2

Setting Up Your Cold Call

Chapter overview:

- Good field preparation is invaluable. It reduces the fear of cold calling.

- Knowing key elements about your customers and prospects before going in increases your chance to make the sale.

- Knowing your material – what it is and how to cover it – makes a huge difference in the level of self-confidence you exude to help you win over prospects.

- Design and use a helpful "script," but let interruptions and questions flow spontaneously to keep your presentation conversational and convincing.

- Your opening moment could be your last unless you deliver your message quickly and cogently.

- In cold calling, you make your own breaks – through homework, planning, and paying close attention to each prospect's situation.

- The timing of your call can be as crucial as any other element. Consider the advantages of off-hours: no screen, undivided attention, and the camaraderie of hard workers.

- Likely prospects are in your own backyard – if you're aware and take the initiative.

- Money is to be made in the field, not in the office. It's up to you to manage your time and devise creative ways of putting yourself in front of potential buyers.

That first cold call is something no sales rep is likely to forget. Mine feels like it happened yesterday, although it was more than 20 years ago. While nothing can fully prepare you for the emotional impact, you can maximize your chances of success by planning your attack.

On my first cold call, butterflies the size of bald eagles were turning somersaults in my stomach. Fear and doubt flashed warning lights: What if I forget my script? What if the guy gets mad and kicks me out? The first faint trace of perspiration was breaking.

The setting was a gloomy old industrial section of Bristol, Connecticut. The whole area, it seemed, had been bulldozed for urban renewal. It was one of the bleakest and most dismal places I'd ever seen. I felt stiff and queasy as I approached my "target," a storefront retail business called Bristol Auto Parts. I didn't want to do it. I'm basically a shy person. But I had no choice – my family was counting on me.

"Chuck," I self-talked, "nothing is going to happen unless you go in there. You just have to do it." Besides, I reminded myself, my product was nothing to be ashamed of.

I was selling advertising space on plastic covers for telephone books. There was nothing spectacular about it – it wasn't like advertising during the Super Bowl – but it represented good value for a small business. People hang onto those covers for years. The ads weren't big, but they showed your logo, your phone number, and maybe a short motto.

I entered and asked to see the owner. "Just tell him Chuck Piola is here to see him," I said. The owner came out of his office and asked, "What can I do for you?"

This was my moment. I had to grab him with my opening lines. "My name is Chuck Piola," I said. "I'm with a company called National Merchandising Corporation. We're doing a program here in Bristol, and I think you'd like it. We market a service that will have a big impact on thousands of households right around here. I can only deal with one auto parts company, and there are 25 of them vying for business in this area. The purpose of my stop here is to make an appointment to see you today or tomorrow."

I paused for a second before hitting him with the big question: "Would two o'clock be okay, or is tomorrow better?" Then I stopped, cringing inside, waiting to get blasted for wasting his time. Instead, he asked quietly, "Well, can you make it three o'clock?" You could have knocked me over with a feather – that's how relieved I was. I would have met him at midnight, or even underwater. "No problem," I said.

I asked for his business card, wrote 3 p.m. on it, and gave him one of mine. "Fine," I said. "I'll see you then. And by the way, usually with what I have to talk about, people bring along a partner or colleague to hear my presentation. Is that the case with you?" (My training had drilled that line into me.) To which he replied: "Sometimes I like to have my wife listen in on these things." I asked if she could be there at three, and he said sure.

Working Towards the Close

So far, so good. The owner seemed like a decent sort. And having his wife there would be helpful. Most prospects feel more relaxed talking with a sales rep when they have a trusted associate in the room. It gives them a little more confidence to make a decision.

But I wanted his wife there for another reason. My sales trainer was adamant about making qualified presentations – try to be sure all of the decision-makers are present before you give a presentation. Otherwise you're giving the prospect a way out. They'll say, "I'll have to talk it over with my partner." That can be a deal-killer.

When I returned that afternoon, I gave my first-ever presentation. Again, I was nervous – the featured performer playing to a small but attentive audience. I started by thanking them for meeting with me. Then I distributed samples of the plastic phone book covers we'd already produced. That way they could see the actual advertising spots and be reassured that National Merchandising was for real.

Then I started talking. I had the presentation down pat – exactly as role-played during training sessions. And if they raised objections, I was armed with the successful rejoinders pioneered by my predecessors at National Merchandising.

For a visual prop, I had flip charts set up like a tent to face them. Each page listed three features and benefits of my advertising program. As a former teacher, I liked visual aids because they emphasized my message. Talking to somebody is one-dimensional; when they can hear and see, it adds a dimension and keeps their minds from wandering.

As I proceeded, they asked me questions. I generally had the answers, but just as important was this: Each break from my practiced pitch gave me a chance to talk with them in a normal, conversational way. That made the whole atmosphere much more relaxed.

Quick Tip 🏃

Involve the Prospect

Let the customer touch the product, hold the spec sheet or make notes on your brochure. The earlier in the presentation you engage the customer with props, the more likely you will close the sale.

As I was coming to the critical closing question for the first time, my heart pounded. (Adrenaline flows in the most practiced salesperson when approaching the closing.) Everything I'd done up to that point was leading to that question. I had to say it with conviction, not apologetically but as a routine part of the process: "Do you have a logo, or would you like to see what our art department can come up with?"

Then I stopped. That was the question we were trained to ask. And once asked, they told us, stop. Don't oversell. When the customer is on the verge of buying, just shut up!

The next 30 seconds seemed like an eternity. He fingered the material again. Then finally he looked at me and made a face. "Let's see what your art department can do," he said.

We had a deal! I was flying but tried to act calm as I pulled out a contract. What's the formal name of your company, I asked. What about the address and phone number? Do you have a title, and how do you spell your name? I started to write and didn't look up until I came to the money part. "Would you like me to write this up for 50-50 – half down and half on delivery – or do you want to take advantage of our cash discount?"

He went for the 50-50 option. I completed the contract and slid it across the table for his signature. As I handed his copy to him, I said, "Okay, I need a check for $275, made out to National Merchandising Corporation." He wrote it without hesitation.

I thanked him heartily for the order. And before leaving, I asked for referrals. Are there other Bristol business people I should be talking with? Is there a local car dealer who should be on this cover with you, as a kind of tie-in? How about a pizza place that advertises a lot, a really good one? He'd been in town a long time and knew everybody, and I walked out with three or four solid recommendations. He even said I could use his name as a reference.

I was floating. My first cold call and already I had a sale and some nice leads. With a good Beatles song pumping on my car tape deck, I drove away shouting to myself, "It works! It really works!"

Research Lays the Groundwork

Don't get the idea that my successful first outing was purely beginner's luck. I almost *expected* to make that sale. It's true that I felt some fear and nervousness walking into Bristol Auto Parts for the first time. That was normal. All the other salespeople had warned me about "the jitters." But I had done my homework. It isn't really walking in cold when you do the advance work right.

Before each call, I'd muster all the ammunition I could find. I looked for facts and figures that would lend rational authority to my opening argument – the appointment clinchers. Equipped with that kind of information, I could position my remarks to address each situation. It didn't matter if the prospect was a dry cleaner, a restaurant or a hardware store. Each business sector had its own hot buttons. I wanted to know in advance what they were and how best to push them.

My years as a teacher had impressed on me the value of good preparation, whether in the classroom or for a cold call. I had to know what I was going to say, how I was going to say it, and why it was important to my audience.

First, I had to know my material inside out, so I could present it effectively. That's not to say that every cold call has to or can be carefully mapped in advance. You don't always have the time for that. But you're always better off when you have some background on the company you're visiting.

Quick Tip 🏃

Preparation Matters – Sales Pros Agree

Some years back, Inc. magazine published the results of a sales survey taken by Dartnell Corporation, a Chicago firm. More than 1,500 sales managers and reps were asked to rank 14 basic skills in order of their importance to long-term success. The clear winner, with 54 percent, was pre-call planning. The next three: approach and involvement, qualifying prospects' needs, and time management. What's interesting, reported Chris Heide, who conducted the survey for Dartnell, is that "the top four tie into activities that are done before you meet a prospect face to face."

In cold call selling, you must know your stuff, because you are there alone, exposed and vulnerable. That takes self-assurance, and a big part of that comes from having confidence in your material. The objective of the prospecting call is to get the appointment. If you know your subject matter backwards and forwards, you won't be at a loss for words when you come face to face with a potential customer. You don't need "the gift of gab"; you need a firm grip on your product or your service and the to ability articulate it. On top of that, you need a sense of timing – knowing when to make your calls for optimum results. And you'll need an organized plan of attack. There are ways to prepare for all of it.

Coming Up with a Script

Cold calls generally fall into two categories. One is the blind call, in which you walk into someone's office having no idea what business they're in, let alone who to ask for. You are flying by the seat of your pants, with only your wits and judgment to guide you.

These are the purest of cold calls. I've made thousands of them, especially during our formative years at NCO Financial Systems. And it worked, as evidenced by the growth of our customer base, which rose from 60 clients at the outset to 1600 in a few years.

The second category includes "strategic" calls, meaning you've conducted research beforehand. You might know the decision-maker's name and you've determined that company XYZ (or at least companies like it) could use the product or service you sell. This more targeted way of prospecting is useful because you've winnowed the field to the top candidates, thereby improving the odds that every call you make will meet your client criteria.

Whether your cold call is category one or two, one part of preparation is essential: You must know what to say. When you get down to the moment of truth – your opportunity in front of the decision-maker – you need to express your message quickly and effectively.

As a rule, business people take less than 30 seconds to decide if they're going to listen to you. That's especially true of cold calls over the phone. Face-to-face encounters give you more latitude, because at least nobody can hang up on you. But basically, you have half a minute to convey the features and benefits of your product or service – the things that make you special. The opening is the most crucial stage of any cold call. You are being judged by what you say and how you say it.

Start by grabbing attention. Humor can be a fine ice-breaker, especially when it's in good taste. When you can make people laugh or smile, most will be more receptive. Whimsy also works. Pranks and capers can work for some salespeople, at least some of the time.

Later, we'll describe some advanced opening lines and creative gambits that veteran cold callers employ. But until you get your cold calling "sea legs," better to start with the basics – like developing a script.

Quick Tip

State-of-the-Art Opening

- Be prepared to state the purpose of your call in the first 15 seconds.
- Boil it down to four or five sentences. Time yourself.
- Use the next 15 seconds to talk about your competitive advantage.
- Condense the distinctive features and benefits to essences.
- Convince the prospect that your product or service has genuine value by highlighting the aspects that will likely benefit this client the most.
- Avoid sounding like a robot. Keep your remarks conversational in tone, even if you have rehearsed them to the nth degree. If you come across as sincere, open and informative, most folks will give you the chance to explain more at a later presentation. Or maybe right there on the spot.

Getting Straight to the Point

A good script sparks interest and entices prospects to want to hear more. It's the sizzle that precedes the steak. The goal is to win a chunk of someone's valuable time – the appointment. You want to come back for a full-blown presentation. So you have to give prospects a good reason to see you again. You won't have much time to break the ice after you've introduced yourself and shaken hands.

Asking for the Appointment

In Dale Carnegie's famous bestseller, *How to Win Friends and Influence People,* he nailed a keynote: "A person's name is to that person the sweetest and most important sound in any language." True! The most reliable way to get someone's attention is to use his or her name, preferably more than once.

During introductions, take the initiative. Offer your name first and wait for the other person to offer his or hers. Now use that name whenever it seems natural. Don't overplay it. Slip it in where it makes sense. The same goes for receptionists, secretaries, and assistants. You should treat everyone you meet with respect. Get their names, write them down, and use them.

I came across Carnegie's wisdom on name usage when I started selling collection services, and it seemed so perfect for cold calling. My script was direct – "Hi. My name is Chuck Piola, and I'm with IC Systems." Most of the time, I'd get a similar greeting – "Chuck, Jack Harris," or something like that. If no name was volunteered, I would simply say – "I'm sorry. I didn't catch your name." When you say this in a friendly way, people will tell you.

Getting a name set the stage for the rest of the script. "Mr. Harris," I'd begin, "the reason I'm here is because my company has decided to expand its sphere of business in your area. Over the next 18 months, we plan to double the size of our local presence. We're hiring people who know how to go after delinquent accounts, and we specialize in businesses like yours. Mr. Harris, I know you're probably using one of our competitors already," I'd say. "However, we're making a big financial commitment to being the number-one company of our kind in your market. I think you'd like our service. So I'd like to come back and give you a presentation. Would tomorrow be okay, or is Wednesday better?"

Just that fast, I would go for the appointment. Then I'd stop and wait for the reaction. If the prospect agreed to a presentation, fine. But I was prepared for the reluctant response: "Well, I'm not sure I want to talk to you yet."

"Oh, I'm sorry. I don't mean to come on too strong," I'd say. "It's just that I'm really excited about what we're offering here. Maybe you haven't heard of us, Mr. Harris, but we work for companies like" – and here I'd mention two or three respected players in the prospect's field. "We've done a lot of innovative planning and creative work with them, to make them more successful. I'll be in the area for the next few days, and I'd really like the opportunity to give you a presentation. It only takes about 30 minutes, and I think you'd find it interesting." And I would ask again for an appointment.

You can't win them all, but I never gave up without a second try. If I was still nowhere, I'd use my ace in the hole: I asked if anybody owed him money. "Everybody has accounts in arrears," I'd say. "Do you have any of those, Mr. Harris? I might be able to give you some advice. I've seen so many situations." And he might say, "Oh, I've got one. There's a client who owes me $5,000 that I can't collect."

That's all I needed to hear. I'd get him to tell me about it. Then I'd ask, "Do you have any others?" From there, we'd often get into a 15-minute dialogue about the people and companies who owed him money. Sometimes the prospect would pull out the files and we'd scan them together.

Each file had a story. People can get very emotional talking about money they're owed, and I'd always be sympathetic. "You know, Mr. Harris, it's really incredible," I'd say. "You did work for these people. You drilled a well (or fixed their car, catered their wedding, filled a tooth – pick one), and then, when you bill them, they stiff you. How about if I take a few of these accounts back with me to the office? I'll walk them into our system by hand, and we can get started working on them."

Very often, the prospect would say, "Okay, I'll give you a try. You can take ten accounts." I'd then ask for an even dozen. Once he gave me the accounts, I had the sale. He hadn't signed a contract but I knew he'd sign later. Those first dozen accounts were a test. He hadn't made the major decision yet. But he would see that I could get back at least some of that money. Then, all of a sudden, the paper would start flowing and we'd be in business.

Notice how my script had multiple layers. The initial burst got across the rationale for the call and a thumbnail sketch of my company. Expecting at least one wave of resistance, I had written and memorized a "second opening," providing more information to reinforce my message and give it more zip. When the next barrier was raised, I resorted to a third level of appeal. Your script isn't finished after that 30-second entrée. You need to anticipate the most common objections and script a lively counterattack. Never leave without conveying your most persuasive material.

Brainstorming for Effective Openings

How do you create those magical words that differentiate you from the competition, the ones that will make the person *want* to see you again? I've always found brainstorming sessions to be productive, whether my product was advertising or insulation or collection services. I'd meet with my manager and a few other salespeople, sometimes over a beer, and we'd talk about the best, most compelling things to say to break the ice, to open a presentation, and to counter objections.

These lines were our "greatest hits" – the "hooks" and techniques that landed the most appointments. We put them all on the table and swapped ideas. If two heads are better than one, six were better yet, and afterwards we all felt more confident about our opening remarks.

If you need help writing up a script, sit down with your manager. He or she is there to make you more successful – or should be. Bring in other sharp folks from your sales force. Talk about everyone's favorite opening lines. Set a friendly, collegial tone and welcome any ideas. To get the creativity flowing in this session, agree that no negative remarks are allowed.

One of those random ideas might spark a dynamite statement that everybody can use. Stitch together the best lines to formulate a great script, fine-tuned for those initial calls. Write it down so you can polish it as you go along. Memorize the script, put your own spin on it, and make it sing.

This takes practice. Don't wait until you're standing before a prospect or you'll be fumbling for the right words. Before "going live" with your script, try it out on your sales teammates and your friends. Get their honest reactions. Your script will become fluid if you rehearse it, role-play it, and give it a rigorous shakedown cruise.

Each time you do it, you'll become more proficient, more conversational, more relaxed and comfortable. Every now and then, review the written script to refresh your memory. When it becomes second nature, you won't forget it under pressure.

Questions That Get to the Fundamentals

To be effective, you need to deliver your opening remarks sincerely, and framed to require a response. If you engage people, it's possible to stretch that initial meeting from 30 seconds to five minutes. That's usually long enough to establish basic rapport and learn everything you need to proceed. Let's see what you need to know.

Prospecting has two basic elements – identification and qualification. Identification is finding potential customers who have the need, desire and ability to buy your products or services. Qualification helps you decide which prospects merit your time, energy and resources. You have to assess their level of interest and determine what obstacles you might encounter. The information you need is:

- Who are the decision-makers?

- Do they want or need to buy right now?

- Is my timing right in terms of their buying cycle?

- What is their decision process?

- Who are they currently buying from?

- Under what conditions would they consider changing suppliers?

Incisive questions can save you time by cutting to the chase – is this a live prospect or not? Is it worth following up? Questions that get quickly to the fundamentals will give your first encounter a crisp, businesslike tone. When you focus on business issues, it shows respect for the other person's time.

Quick Tip

Controlling the Call

I've always believed that the person who asks the questions controls the conversation, and the person who talks the most dominates it. It's better to be in control, because you'll be more at ease, and you can direct the flow and pace of the dialogue. Your ability to get information through questioning is vital on both blind and strategic calls. The would-be prospect has no idea who you are. Strangers constantly judge our intelligence by how well we speak, and of course you want to make a favorable impression. When you ask bright, perceptive questions, you come off as a sharp individual – someone to be reckoned with.

Consciously avoid talking too much. You're there to learn, so let your prospects talk all they want. By listening carefully, you can pick up terminology that insiders use in that business. When you go back to make a presentation, use that special vocabulary. Knowing the lingo might help you hit the right button to make a sale.

Nothing But the Facts – A True Story

Can you explain succinctly why your widget is better or faster or cheaper than the other guy's? People are always looking for reasons *not* to buy. But if you have the facts on your side and the poise to make them clear, you can spin around even the most hostile of prospects.

During my first year of selling ad space on telephone book covers, I sold an advertising spot to a prominent real estate broker in a suburb of Hartford, Connecticut. We became friendly, and one day he invited me to lunch at his Rotary Club.

He introduced me to several important business people in the town, telling them, "You've got to do business with this guy." One of the members, named Jimmy, urged me to talk to "Ray" – not his real name – a fellow Rotarian who owned a high-end auto dealership. In the spirit of the moment, Jimmy even phoned Ray and set up an appointment for me the next morning.

I approached the meeting with high expectations. After all, I had an inside track on this one, a personal connection. But when I showed up at his office, Ray seemed aloof, even a little hostile. He was a classic controller with an ego bigger than Texas. "I only agreed to this because Jimmy said I should talk to you," he said by way of a greeting. "So let's make this quick. What do you have?"

I skipped my usual warm-up and dove right into my presentation. Inside of three minutes, Ray said abruptly, "I don't have time for this shit." He grabbed my materials out of my hands and threw them across the desk with disgust. "I don't need this kind of crap."

Things weren't looking good, until suddenly Ray gave me an opening. Trying to impress, he said, "Look, I advertise on *The Tonight Show*. Why do I need this kind of nonsense?"

Thinking fast, I asked what time his television commercials aired. "Right after Johnny Carson's monologue," he said. "I'm on the local affiliate. They cut away right after the monologue and my commercial comes on."

Three days earlier, I had been reading in my sales manual about the limitations of other types of advertising. For local business owners, it said, one of the problems with television and radio advertising is that it goes far beyond their market. They spend a lot of money to reach places they don't need.

But in Ray's case it was worse than that. My manual, handily enough, contained the water usage table for the Hartford metropolitan area. This gave me some competitive ammunition. In scanning it, for instance, I had noticed a huge spike in water usage at 11:45 p.m. That was right after Carson's monologue, I figured. People were in the bathroom, flushing the toilet before going to bed.

That was the fact I needed, but I hesitated to bring it up, thinking I might further unsettle this blowhard. I was scared. Then I reminded myself that I had nothing to lose. So I said very softly, "I hate to tell you this, sir, but nobody is watching your commercials."

He looked at me as if I had just landed from Mars. "What the hell are you talking about?" he snapped.

I pulled the water chart out of my briefcase and held it up. "Let me show you something," I said. "Do you see this big spike at 11:45 every night? People aren't even in front of the TV then."

Agitated, he snatched the chart out of my hand. I walked around behind his desk – entering his space now

– and pointed to the precise spot. I said, "Look here. See how water usage goes way up just about the time Carson's monologue ends? People are in the bathroom. They're not watching television. Nobody is seeing your ads."

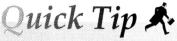

Quick Tip

Tactic

Slipping in a telling fact at the perfect moment can devastate even the most belligerent objections. The more of these facts you have at your fingertips, the more appointments you will get.

The news did not sit too well with Ray. For a moment, he pondered the horror of what he was hearing – all that money almost literally poured down a toilet. Then he flew into a wild, stuttering rage. He stomped around his office, steaming, all red in the face, and roared to somebody, "Get me that advertising SOB in the phone!"

Then I went to close. When he had calmed down enough, I said, "Sir, I have an appointment this afternoon with another fine-car dealer down the street. I don't want to go to him. I want to put you on the phone book cover, right next to Jimmy's ad. This will give you good, affordable advertising, and people will see it all the time. I just need your okay on the bottom of the agreement."

My heart was pounding as I spoke. But I got the sale. He actually bought two ads – a double spot.

I can't say I ever "broke the ice" with Ray. I never even finished my presentation. But in this case, none of that mattered. I had pulled from memory the one unassailable piece of information that nailed the deal.

A lucky break? No doubt, some luck was involved. If I hadn't had that one decisive fact, Ray would have thrown me out. But in cold call selling, you make your breaks. I had taken the time to study my material, so I could draw on it if and when I needed something. Thinking on your feet, knowing when to make your move, and having the courage to stand your ground when you know you're right are all part of the sales game. But these soft skills work best when the facts are on your side.

Do your homework. This is your livelihood. You want to be able to argue your case on the basis of facts and logic, so you have to keep abreast of the competitive arena. Fighter pilots call it "situational awareness." Whether you're selling medical equipment, insurance or aluminum siding, somebody else will be gunning for the same business.

So do your market research. Read the trade journals and business dailies to find out what's happening in your industry and in your customers' industries. When time permits, study up on the company you're targeting. Then you can place the prospect in context and your opening remarks will have a lot more "grab." It shows you know what you're talking about. And if you do manage to win extra minutes on your first pass, that background information could make the difference between rejection and winning an appointment.

Using Facts to Strengthen Your Story

Getting stoked for the first cold calls of my life, I boned up hard on my target town – Bristol, Connecticut. I knew I wanted some auto parts companies as advertisers on my phone book cover. So I studied the city's demographics and collected some useful intelligence that would enable me to make a strong argument. I used those facts and figures to help me get past blockades.

"Mr. Jones," I'd say, countering the first rebuff, "the average American family spends $900 a year on auto repair – tires, batteries, and all. That's according to the federal government. Three thousand houses in your town are going to receive this phone book cover. Three thousand times $900 comes to $2.7 million. There are 25 companies like yours competing for that business. I can only take a couple of them and then my program is closed. I'd like it to be you. I can significantly increase your market share. I could come back later today, or sometime tomorrow."

It wasn't elegant, but it garnered appointments. You have to give people a reason to see you, so do your homework first. To be nimble on your feet, you need a working command of your subject matter, not just the core material but also surrounding issues. You never know when some bit of industry background or a competitive detail will rescue your call.

Getting the Names You Need

After you've fueled up your knowledge bank with a good script and some industry context, you're ready to talk to somebody. But where do you start? Do you need the name of a specific prospect, or can you walk in cold on practically anyone?

The answer depends on the nature of your business.

If your company does residential landscaping or driveway sealing, you can walk through neighborhoods with your brochures and price lists and letters of reference, and ring the doorbell of any house with a lawn or a driveway. Looking around, you'll see if the grass and shrubbery need attention or if the driveway needs a new coat of sealant. You don't need to know who lives there to make the call. Many businesses, ranging from insurance companies and retirement planners to janitorial services and the suppliers of spring water, enjoy a similarly broad market.

Mark Macrone, one of the premier sales guys at my collections company, has built a lucrative career by working the same way. Almost all companies have a certain number of customers who won't pay. He offered a solution to a generic problem, so every business was fair game.

"I just park my car and start walking in places," he says. "As long as I have my business cards and my calendar, I'm fine. Occasionally I might have some idea of who's there, but I could count on two hands the times I've gone in someplace with a good idea of who I needed to see. I'll ask for the controller or the vice-president of finance, but I never have their name.

"I never try to get tricky," Mark explains, "because people see right through it. My attitude is to be up-front and honest. You can't act as if you know who the person is, when you don't know. I'll walk in and say, 'I wonder if you could help me out. My name is Mark Macrone, and I'm with NCO Financial Systems. We do collection work. I'm here to see if anybody owes you money that we could help you recover.'

"You can't be more straightforward than that. In ten seconds, I get across who I am and why I'm standing there."

But if your business isn't universal, this is where market research counts. You can't afford to waste time on calls where you have no chance. Before you visit a company, you need specific information to identify the most promising prospects.

Research comes in many guises. In the case of my phone book cover ads, my first task was to figure out which local businesses liked to advertise. So I gathered intelligence the way I'd been trained. I looked on outfield walls at Little League fields – they always have advertising banners. I looked in newspapers, in church bulletins, and on bowling alley score sheets. I looked anyplace where advertising might appear, even on shopping carts. That's how I got the names. Granted, it was a primitive way to identify prospects, but it was all I needed, because once I had the names, the Yellow Pages provided the rest.

Example: Finding Information that Qualifies Prospects

Most sales people today have sophisticated resources at their disposal, thanks largely to the Internet. If you use a computer with Internet access – and who doesn't? –you have a mine full of data to help you draw up a list of promising prospects.

Remember Frank Scaravaglione, the salesman for Carey International? In designing his cold calling campaign, Frank first needed to identify which Philadelphia-area businesses were likely to sign up for Carey's transportation services.

"We know the kinds of companies that traditionally use our services – ground transportation by limousine, van, bus and so on," he says. "We do a lot of business with financial companies, meeting planners and consulting firms. Our plan was to find businesses in those same sectors and then cold call on them."

But Frank had to know whom to call on. He relied primarily on two resources to find suitable prospects. First, using the local Yellow Pages, he was able to obtain the names of companies by category – all the convention organizers, say. And second, when he had the company names, he accessed hoovers.com on the Internet.

Hoover's Inc. publishes business directories. When the Internet took off, the company launched Hoover's Online: The Business Network, an impressively rich Web site, providing information on thousands of public and private enterprises worldwide.

Much of the material on the site is free, and subscribers can gain access to more comprehensive corporate reports for a modest monthly membership fee. A full-blown Hoover's profile includes a company's history, a list of key officers and employees, along with a detailed look at its products, its competitors, its financial statements, and related research on operations.

"It's very helpful," Frank says. "You can get a good four- or five-page rundown on a company. You could put that together without Hoover's, I guess, but having it all on the Internet makes it fast and easy. When you can read up on a company before walking in cold, you have a clearer idea of where the power is and what to expect."

Contact Information Abounds on the 'Net'

Hoover's doesn't have a monopoly on information like this. More than a dozen companies offer this kind of corporate information via the Internet.

At the industry's highest end is OneSource.com. This outfit offers two different programs – an "entry level" version called Company Browser, and the more comprehensive Business Browser. Both product lines offer "all-you-can-eat," unlimited smorgasbords of timely information on more than one million businesses, public and private. They integrate data from about 30 information providers, who in turn draw on at least 2,500 sources of content.

Using OneSource service, you can create prospect lists by industry, company size, or geographic area. Each entry comes with names, addresses, and contact points.

In preparing for a sales call, it's sometimes crucial to get a heads-up on a prospect's financial standing, its business operations, or its organizational structure. One-Source provides analytic capabilities in all those areas, as well as biographical information. If you want to review the career of an executive you're scheduled to meet, it's here. What's more, you can monitor moves made by your key clients, their competitors, and even your own competitors. For a complete rundown of features, visit the Web site at Onesource.com.

OneSource doesn't come cheap. The annual Company Browser fee for a single subscriber is $10,000. (It might have changed, so check.) But the price drops dramatically when clients sign up for multiple usage. For ten people, the total tab is $20,000, and for 50 people, it's $35,000. There's also a quarterly option at $2,700 for an individual user. As stiff as those prices might seem, most OneSource subscribers opt for the more expansive Business Browser version, at $21,000 per "seat," or $31,000 for ten.

Like a good sales rep, OneSource's Chris Robinson distinguishes value from price. "It's not an inexpensive product," he allows, "but what separates us from probably most of the other companies in this field is that OneSource licenses data from over two dozen sources of company and industry information. If you wanted to subscribe to all the sources that we incorporate into our product, it would cost you hundreds of thousands of dollars. The sum of those parts is an astronomically high number."

Many other companies trade corporate information electronically, but I'll rest with these two – Hoover's Online and OneSource – to make my point. We're swimming in a sea of information, and the Internet, in a quantum leap of efficiency, puts it all at your fingertips. With the click of a mouse, you can obtain the names of potential customers and much, much more. You can slice and dice your market any which way. For a cold calling American sales person, it's a great time to be alive. You're operating in the wealthiest and most dynamic economy on Earth, and the Internet brings it right to your office. Consider yourself lucky.

Timing Your Move

As a cold calling sales rep, you'll be fortunate if you get through to the decision-maker on half of your calls. You can always leave a note and some product information, get the boss's name, and come back another day. But if you want to dramatically increase your chances of seeing the right person the first time, go in during the off-hours, when there are no assistants or secretaries to fend you off.

If you're out in your market by 7:00 a.m., you frequently can catch a company owner or president in the office before the staffers arrive. He or she might be setting up for the day or reading *The Wall Street Journal* over coffee. Before the pressures of the day kick in, you are more likely to get a few minutes, long enough to explain who you are, what you're all about, and to take a crack at getting an appointment to come back.

And who knows, your early-morning industriousness, your work ethic, might be impressive enough in its own right to give you a better shot at a sale. Other hard workers might respect your dedication.

The same holds true at the end of the day. Many of my sales have come after everybody except the CEO had gone home. And the boss, with the pressures of the day subsiding, might be more disposed to give you a little time. You also should think about trying to get through on Saturdays or legal holidays. Lots of owners and managers show up on those days to clear their desks. There's a more relaxed ambiance when the office is quiet and mostly deserted. On a day without phones ringing and meetings to attend, the person you need to reach will be more accessible.

True Story – Finding the Owner Working Late

One wintry night, I decided to make one last call. It was dark when I wheeled into the prospect's parking lot, but the lights were still on inside. The door turned out to be unlocked but the receptionist was gone. Nobody was in sight, so I boomed, "Hello! Hello! Is anybody here?" And from somewhere deep in the building came a reply. "I'm back here. Come on in."

It was the owner himself, sitting at his desk. He glanced up at me, curious and a little surprised. Who in the world was this guy walking into his office, with his dark topcoat and leather briefcase, at this hour? "Excuse me, sir," I began. "I'm very sorry to disturb you. My name is Chuck Piola. I'm with NCO Financial Systems, and I'm trying to find the person in charge of receivables management."

He said, "That would be me."

I walked over and shook his hand. "I won't take up your time right now, but I'd like to come back and see you," I said, and proceeded to give him a 30-second rundown on our collection service. He took off his glasses, leaned back in his chair. He looked interested and thoughtful. And he didn't mind taking a break from his paperwork.

Matter of fact, my 30 seconds turned into five minutes as he peppered me with questions. I had gone in with the hope of an appointment, but he suggested a full-blown presentation on the spot. We ended up talking for an hour. I left there, incredibly, with a signed contract. That business grew, and he turned out to be a terrific long-term client.

Chalk that one up to good timing – after hours, with no clerical screen.

When you are selling to a specific industry, you obviously have to know its tempo. Most companies follow a natural cycle of daily activity. The trick is to identify the peak and slack periods, and then time your calls accordingly. When you can do that, your batting average is bound to rise.

A friend of mine, for example, sells heavy-duty kitchen equipment to the restaurant trade. When he started out, he cold called restaurants at random – whenever he pulled up in front of one. He soon discovered that the owners didn't want to talk to anyone but their customers during meal times. That ruled out the three hours over lunch – eleven till two – and anytime from five o'clock until closing. But there was a natural lull in the action at mid-morning and again after lunch. He learned to call during those calm periods.

If you're selling to more than one sector, balance the calls with their cycles – for example, retailers early or late, restaurants at the lulls. To make this point at it most basic, you wouldn't try selling to an accountant on April 15th, the last day to file tax returns; but the two weeks after that might be the ideal time to get a hearing.

Outside the Box – Better than Par

Great military leaders don't fight every battle. They take on only those fights that advance their objectives. Their key to success is in deciding how to deploy their forces.

As a sales rep, you need to consider prospecting along those same lines, strategically and tactically. Your goal is to bring in new clients, and the success of your mission depends on how efficiently you marshal the resources under your control – time, energy, ingenuity, and know-how. You have to go where the business is and plan an avenue of attack. Even when you're operating in a target-rich environment, you might have to think "outside the box" to make the most of it.

True story: Shortly after my company acquired a firm in Detroit, we joined them for a day of golf. They were hosting a social outing for 50 of their best clients, at the Pontiac Country Club. I flew in the night before and saw that I was scheduled to play in a foursome with some of the largest customers.

The next day, I decided I wasn't going to play golf. I knew from experience that it wasn't the best use of my time. I knew I would meet only the people in my group and most likely end up going to dinner with the same people.

I announced my decision at the course that morning. "I don't think I'll play today," I said. "I'll just drive the cart around." Although this did not please the event planner – he had carefully balanced the foursomes by handicap – I apologized for the inconvenience and stuck to my plan.

I zoomed off in the cart, taking another sales person with me. We had a blast cruising around the golf course and dropping in on each foursome. We not only met all the players; we met them two or three times at various holes.

If the beer cart skipped somebody, we'd hunt it down and bring back a few "cold ones." We had extra sleeves of balls in our cart, and we handed them out like goodwill ambassadors. During lulls in the action, we'd pull up beside some of the folks to swap jokes and "war stories." Those extra touches made them realize subliminally that "these people are okay – they are sensitive to our having a good day."

Back at the clubhouse, during the post-game festivities, I table-hopped and made some appointments. So did the sales rep who had been in the cart with me. He scored a meeting with the top executives of a major customer, eventually landing a larger share of their business.

One account I personally wanted was a large Detroit bank that had switched to one of our competitors for some collection work. We still had a piece of the action with the bank, but I thought we should have a lot more. Three of the bank's top officers had been out on the course, where I'd run into them a few times.

By the end of the round, we were all laughing and chatting. It was just so natural. I tried to keep the talk light and casual so as not to distract from the game. But I had told them, in passing, about some of the other banks we did business with and a bit about our track record.

At the post-game cocktail party, I saw these three fellows again. "Gee, guys," I said before we sat down to dinner, "I'd like to come talk to you, because we should be working for you." I left it at that. At dinner, we sat at different tables, but before they left, one of the vice-presidents pulled me aside and said, "Chuck, give me a call in a month. I'd like to do business with you."

When I got home, I sent him a letter saying that I'd enjoyed meeting him and his colleagues, and I enclosed our annual report. I was scheduled to be back in Detroit the following month, and I told him that I'd call beforehand to set up an appointment.

Everything went as smooth as butter. There was no need to break the ice when I went to see him. We already had some common ground – golf – and we rehashed the "tournament" for a few minutes before getting down to business. In the end, we came away with a much bigger piece of the bank's collection work.

Chances are none of that would have happened if I had played golf that day.

Breaking Precedent

Occasionally, it's okay to ignore protocol. While you never want to do anything unethical or unscrupulous, you can't worry too much about social decorum when you're hustling to make sales. You just do what it takes to get business, and if your methods sometimes stray beyond conventional etiquette – well, that's okay.

Our culture has unwritten and unspoken rules of behavior and of doing business. If I approach someone in a business setting and say, as I do – "Hi. My name is Chuck Piola, and I wonder if you can help me out?" – am I breaking the rules? Not many people act that intrusively anymore, and I think this is one of the biggest hang-ups when sales people contemplate cold call selling. It seems socially awkward.

You can't let that stop you. After all, your livelihood is at stake, so don't be reluctant to deviate from traditional norms. I'm not talking about being rude, disrespectful or behaving like a social misfit. Thinking with creativity and innovation – that's the point.

Speaking at a business seminar one time, I took off my jacket and rolled up my sleeves. I picked up a chair, set it down in the middle of the room, and perched on the back of it. Then I said, "I've been on the road for 20 years. Let's cut to the chase and get down to the core of selling. Instead of my giving a prepared presentation, let's go to the question and answer period. Just tell me where you need help."

It worked wonders. About 50 people were in the room, and for 90 minutes we let it rip. It was the most energized seminar I had ever done. It created such a buzz at the conference that the organizers asked me do it again the next day. When you break protocol, you can engage people in positive and productive ways.

Dare to be a different. It makes your work life so much more interesting. Every day, we all experience situations that offer a chance for fun. All it takes is a little imagination and a sense of humor, and you can to turn an ordinary moment into one with a special twist. The most serious obstacle in cold calling isn't the gatekeeper who won't let you in or the prospect who gives you a hard time. The biggest problem is sales people who lack creativity, who shun risk, and who don't know how to have fun.

You have chosen to be in sales. If you make it fun, you will find that fun is contagious. That's how to make the most of cold calls.

Hurrah for Pigs – Breaking Protocol Big-Time

When it comes to breaking with common protocol, it would be hard to top a guy I read about in *The Denver Business Journal*. The story was written by Jeffrey Gitomer, author of a book called *The Sales Bible* and president of Business Marketing Services in Charlotte, North Carolina. It concerned a salesman who combined creativity and high risk to break through "the wall" to reach certain people he needed to see who had previously declined to see him. He made a list of these high-value prospects and returned to the scenes of his previous rejections with an astounding prank.

One day a week, he cold called these same people again, but this time he brought along his potbellied pig. That's right – a pig. He'd walk up to the receptionist and say, "Could you tell Fred that Bill and his pig are here to see him?" Imagine the gatekeeper announcing that news: "There's a guy out here with a pig who wants to see you."

Most of the time, Gitomer reports, Bill would be escorted straight back to the boss's office. Who could resist something so unusual and amusing? "Look at the principles of cold calling that Bill executed successfully," he writes. "He got in where others (including himself) could not before. He gained the prospect's interest. He will never be forgotten. He was having fun and creating smiles for others."

Yes, it's not "professional" in the usual sense, but remember the first objective of a cold call: Get in the door.

Crazy Bill probably wracked his brain for good ideas before hitting upon the pig stunt. He had to decide that it would work and that it wouldn't be so bizarre that he'd put people off. It turned out to be a masterstroke. He needed a flamboyant opening move, one sure to win attention, and he came up with something unique. If people still refused to see him after he'd walked in with a potbellied pig, well, it was time to move on.

Yet, no matter how original or colorful you can be, you'll never get through to Mr. or Ms. Big 100 percent of your attempts. When you come up short, ask: Is this prospect worth approaching again, or should I cut my losses? There are always plenty of other places to try. But you never want to quit too early. It's been said that most sales reps give up after one attempt, but more sales come after five tries. It's hard to know if that's true, but I do know that it has sometimes taken me five or more visits before getting through to someone I really wanted to see.

'Decide' is the Key Word

In selling, you're constantly making decisions that affect your income. You have ten or so hours in a business day. How you manage that time is what counts. If you're not making decisions that will move the company forward and increase your commissions, you are wasting precious time. The decisions you make will affect the entire flow of the day. They will determine whom you will see, whom you will present to, and where you will go.

Each and every day, ask a potential customer one simple question, such as: "What do we have to do to get going?" or "How can we get started?" or "Where do we go from here?" – something to push the process along. If you decide to ask a question like that to four prospects every business day, it would total at least 100 questions a month. If only ten percent of the prospects respond positively, that could still translate to ten new clients a month, or maybe hot leads. Decide to ask.

When you set your mind on succeeding in sales and swing your attitude into a "can do" mode, you're halfway there. Get into the field and go for the gold. And be smart about it. Focus consciously on making productive decisions. Be creative and don't worry about breaking some unspoken sense of protocol. Our friend with the potbellied pig surely didn't.

A Cold Call Rookie Learns the Ropes

Cold calling – the very words struck fear in Denise Manniello. The thought of being cold conjures up images of chattering teeth, frostbite, and freezing weather – a hostile environment. All those unpleasant associations hit Denise like an avalanche when her boss suggested that she start cold calling – or else.

Denise was a rising star at JDR Recovery, a collection company based in Ramsey, New Jersey, 15 miles west of New York City. While developing, building and running JDR's client service department, she also did some selling. It was telephone sales, mostly to existing clients, and she excelled. "I was outselling any sales person we ever had," Denise says. There was no questioning her drive. While working full-time, she put herself through business school. And that's when things changed.

With her newly minted MBA, Denise hoped to curtail her sales activities to concentrate on marketing and client services. But her superiors at JDR had other plans. They were so impressed by her performance in sales that they wanted her to do selling and nothing but selling, MBA or not. Denise protested, but management held firm. "Denise," they told her, "this is what you already do. It's the same thing."

"I didn't have a choice, " she says. But it wasn't the same thing. Gone were her comfortable days of "upselling" to customers she already knew. Her new role required her to bring in new clients and fresh business, and it didn't go well. "I had a ton of contacts, but a lot of problems," she says. "The worst of them was all these people hiding behind their voice mail. That's a huge obstacle today for anybody trying to sell over the phone, and I was on the phone almost exclusively."

She tried to be creative. She'd hit the pound sign during a voice-mail program, switching the call to a secretary or operator, hoping they would put her call through. She would dial one digit off, like 2112 instead of 2111, hoping an associate would pick up the phone, since most companies share a family of numbers. And of course she left message after message, but only one person in 50 ever called her back.

"I was really flopping," she admits. "It came to the point where the gentleman I work for finally said, 'You have to sell something, or else it's goodbye.' If I wanted to save my job, he said, I should get out in the field and start cold calling."

Denise was stunned. "Once the idea was suggested to me, all the fear came flooding in." But she dug in nonetheless, methodically doing a demographic search of the five Zip Code areas in and around Ramsey. That produced a list of prospects. But she was scared. "I didn't know how to cold call," she says, "and it just seemed so intimidating."

About that time, my own company acquired JDR Recovery and folded it into the NCO Group, our umbrella name. As usual, I told the new staff members to call me if they needed help. Denise took me up on the offer.

I drove up to Ramsey and spent a day with her in the field, showing her the ropes in a one-day cold calling boot camp. Denise had a list of four companies to hit that day – a mortgage firm, a coaxial cable manufacturer, the U.S. headquarters of a foreign camera manufacturer, and the credit division of a huge retail chain. We handled the first three calls as a team, then I watched from a reception area as Denise did the fourth one on her own.

"The idea was to incorporate cold calling into my repertoire," she says. "It was the one piece I was missing."

We had fun making the rounds, as I showed Denise how to get past the gatekeepers with the help of some offbeat opening lines (which I'll report in a later chapter). I showed her how critical it is to get in the door and the importance of winning a prospect's attention.

She could see that it worked – by the end of the day, she had lined up three appointments. One of them was with an executive at the retailer's credit division. Denise had telephoned the woman four times before and received no response. On this day, in person and determined, she got through.

Every one of these calls was within five miles of Denise's office. She was smack in the middle of a target-rich environment. You don't have to go across the country to find prospects, I said. Just dig the diamonds in your own backyard.

Confident that she had at least rudimentary skills, Denise proceeded to make scores of cold calls. In fact, she exhausted her local area and began searching for fresh hunting grounds on Long Island, elsewhere in northern Jersey, and in eastern Pennsylvania.

Taking the Chill Out of Cold Calling

Like many seasoned sales reps, however, Denise still feels anxiety about going in cold. To overcome those feelings and enhance her probability of success, she usually tries to warm up her calls a little.

"I think it's better to strategize ahead of time, and at least get their names, rather than walk in totally cold," she says. "When Chuck started in the business, anything and everything would fly at the company. Now we have goals, forecasts, structure, and specific objectives and numbers to meet. I have to spend my time wisely. A deal has to reach a certain size before we'll accept it, so I have to quantify and qualify and make sure I'm spending my time on the right people."

Her system, as she describes it, involves common sense, tenacity and follow-up. "First," she says, "I identify who I want my prospect to be. That takes some qualification work. I will go into that high-rise and I'll know in advance whom I need to see. I try to find out who handles delinquent accounts over the age of 30, 60 or 90 days. If they give me the name of a supervisor, I'll say, 'No, I really need a decision-maker.' And typically that's somebody at a vice-presidential level. They will give me either a director or a vice-president."

Example: Denise At Warm-up Work

"I get information by befriending receptionists and operators on the phone," explains Denise Manniello, super salesperson. "I'll start out by saying, 'I was wondering if you could help me today.' I always use the word 'help,' because that's a key indicator for people.

The receptionist says, 'Oh, I don't know, I'm just a receptionist here.' And I'll come back with this: 'Don't say that. You have a wealth of information. I'll bet you can help me. Here's what I need.' And sure enough, 90 percent of the time, they can help."

Denise goes for three pieces of information – the decision-maker's name, phone number, and e-mail address. "Once I have that," she says, "I call the person. The challenge is always getting someone on the phone. If I can't reach a person that way, I'll leave a voice-mail message or send an e-mail. I just say who I am and why I need to see them. And it's interesting. Only two percent of my phone messages get returned, but 12 percent of the people respond to an e-mail. I guess it seems less personal. I've even faxed people – 'I have been trying to reach you. Please call me.' That sort of thing."

When all else fails, Denise puts together a package of material, personalized to the prospect, and drops it off. "There's a lot of value in seeing anybody in that company," she says. "Even if I can't get through to the person I need to see, I'll leave a card, and maybe a note, and my information. Now, somebody there has heard my story." With every attempt at contact, Denise softens up the target. The prospect at least knows her name, her company, and her business. Some of the chill is gone.

"Chances are that when I call back later," she says, " they will pick up the phone, because I've been to their office, and I've left voice-mails and E-mails. That's the benefit of persistence. It might not be an instant benefit, but it will pay off when you get on the phone. Once you have some dialogue and there seems to be some interest, I'll say, 'You know what? I think we can help you. Why don't I come over to give you a full presentation?'

"So I'll go for the appointment. I need to get in front of the customer," Denise says, "because when I can present to them, 98 percent of the time I'll get that sale."

If the idea of walking in on someone stone cold makes you break out in hives, try using Denise's approach. Warm up the call. If you've pinpointed your prospect, then use your ingenuity to learn the vital statistics about him or her. Receptionists in large companies can generally help you. Some will go out of their way to steer you in the right direction. Use the Internet – the prospect's own Web site, if possible – to fill in the blanks. Or talk with someone who is familiar with your target company.

Learn everything you can; then send the prospect an e-mail or fax or leave voice-mail messages. Or better yet, send a letter, and enclose a brochure about your product or service. Staple your business card to the top. Mention that you'll be stopping by in the near future.

Each step you take defrosts that deep freeze a little. You will feel more confident and comfortable when you walk in a few days later, because even if your prospect can't remember the letter, it gives you a reason to make the call. You have paid your dues to earn a few minutes of his or her time.

Use that face-to-face time wisely. Ask for the appointment. If you go in well prepared, with a strong script, a mastery of your material, and maybe a little twist to your approach – you'll be surprised at the results.

Denise Manniello certainly was. "It was amazing to watch Chuck get through to people I'd been calling for a month," she says, referring to that day of boot camp. "Part of the secret is in being yourself and making people feel comfortable around you. People want to do business with people they like."

And finally, find the fun of it and make it a game you like to play.

CHAPTER 3

They're Buying You

Chapter overview:

- Good salesmanship begins with your attitude and what you project about yourself in person.

- Every potential customer sizes you up – your polish, diction, body language, clothes and attitude – from the moment you cross the threshold. Learn to look like a winner.

- Integrity enhances everything you do in the sales process – how you feel about yourself, your company and its products, and how your customers feel about you.

- Learn how to build customer trust, the bedrock of long-term relationships, through shared personal experiences.

- Cultivate the magic of enthusiasm for generating long-lasting "special effects" on everyone around you.

Somewhere in your sales training, you've probably heard one of the basic rules of the profession: You can't sell anything until you sell yourself first.

Nowhere is this rule more important than in face-to-face cold calling work. Regardless of what you are selling, *you* are the real product, from the instant you walk through the potential customer's door. Everybody you meet, from receptionist on up, is making a snap judgment about you. You've got to become real to them, so they see you as something than just another business dude.

If they buy you as a worthy individual in your own right, you're more than halfway to winning an appointment or a sale. One great way to accomplish is by finding a common interest or experience, then talking about it with friendly enthusiasm.

I'll give you an example:

During my days of selling collection services, I really wanted a certain dentist as a client. He had a thriving practice with six examination rooms in a beautiful brownstone building in Pittsburgh. By all accounts, he was a wonderful fellow, but he did not like talking to sales people. Three of my reps had already approached him, but not one had advanced past the gatekeeper.

As manager of the Pennsylvania territory, I decided to give the good dentist one more try, so I dropped by his office. In the waiting room, I immediately noticed several handsome framed photographs of Mozart's house in Salzburg, Austria. By amazing coincidence, I had taken almost identical photos of Mozart's home during a trip to Europe a few years earlier.

I introduced myself to the office manager at the front desk and asked to see the dentist. Impossible, she said. I pressed on. "I just need to see him for 30 seconds, between patients, to arrange an appointment," I told her. But she stood her ground. "There's no chance you can see him today," she snapped. She was a tough one.

Just then, the dentist himself came walking in my direction, going from one examining room to another. I had five seconds to decide if I should approach him. In a flash, I reasoned: What do I have to lose? The office manager will get angry, but so what?

"Excuse me, doctor," I said. "Did you take those pictures of Mozart's house?"

He stopped. "Yes, I did," he said. "Why?" I told him I'd taken the same pictures when I was in Salzburg for a Mozart festival. He asked who I was. "I'm Chuck Piola," I said, "and I'm here on behalf of IC Systems. We do financial recovery work for medical and dental professionals. I'd like to arrange an appointment to come back and see you."

His response left the office manager speechless. "I'm tied up right now, but if you can wait in my office for 20 minutes, I'll have time to talk." No problem, I assured him, as the gatekeeper shot me a hostile look.

The Salzburg Connection

When the dentist returned, the subject was Salzburg. He had been there as a traveling dentist with the Pittsburgh Symphony. We chatted about what it was like touring Europe with an orchestra, and we reminisced about visiting Mozart's birthplace. We'd both noticed the finger-worn keys on the piano where the great prodigy had learned to play.

I told him about my days of teaching music appreciation to kids in junior high. I told him how I'd met Leroy Anderson, composer of "The Syncopated Clock" and "Sleigh Ride." Music was his hot button. It melted the ice. Now he saw me as a fellow music lover, not just another sales guy.

Eventually I turned the conversation to business. "Doctor, I know you're busy," I said. "Let me tell you quickly what I have here." He listened as I outlined my program. I knew he had some problem accounts, because virtually all dentists do. As professionals, however, they consider it unseemly to play hardball to collect their fees.

Quick Tip 🏃

The 'First Look' Test

As the saying goes, you get only one chance to make a first impression. The image you project in the first few minutes is crucial, because if you can't pass that "first look" test, the call might be terminated right there. You need to reach stage two, where you get a chance to explain yourself and your work.

When I pledged to him that IC Systems specialized in "discreet" recovery work, he began to perk up. Yes, he had some long-overdue bills, he said, and most of them, it seemed, would have to be written off.

Before giving up completely on those debts, I said, why not give us a chance? "Don't worry; we'll be sensitive about recovering fees for you. Many of our clients are dentists and doctors," I told him, "and we handle awkward financial situations with a tactful touch."

I left with a signed contract to collect his delinquent accounts. That cold call opened a gold mine. He became a good client and so did 18 other dentists in the Pittsburgh area. He had deep roots in the community, and he referred me to his colleagues. "You can use my name," he said, ending our meeting on a cheery note. We had already established the sort of affinity usually reached after several visits.

Look for Something – Anything – To Establish a Bond

Why was I able to land that account after three of my reps had failed? Had I caught the dentist at a weak moment? I doubt it. Was my service any different? Not really. Had I simply been lucky? Sure. It was lucky that I'd been to Mozart's house.

Without that shared experience, I might not have gotten through. The whole topic of music might never have come up. When it did, we had a natural bond. Less than five minutes after shaking hands, we were deep into a discussion that had nothing to do with business. After ten minutes we were talking like fraternity brothers.

But if it hadn't been Mozart and music, I would have looked for something else to talk about – maybe his antique desk or the Persian rugs gracing his office. And there's always football. What about those Steelers? With luck or without, I would look to establish rapport with the man. Because in the end, he wasn't just buying my service, he was buying me.

Quick Tip

Nothing Beats Sincerity

Whether you're making an initial cold call or a return trip for a presentation, your attitude can profoundly affect the outcome. You need to be not only friendly and considerate but also sincere. Forced or phony affability turns people off.

To thrive in cold calling, you have to genuinely like people and let it show in your enthusiasm. When you are confident and spirited, you send off positive vibes. When you're sincerely fired up about your product, prospects sense it. It's contagious. That's how you start building rapport and trust. And once you have established a foundation of trust, most of the battle is won.

It's odd to think of yourself as a "product," but that's how the prospect views you at first. Who cares what you're selling – what do you look like? Your physical appearance is a crucial part of the package. Unless you're selling T-shirts at heavy-metal concerts, you had better look neat and professional.

The prospect will pick up additional signals from your body language – your posture, your eye contact, your facial expressions, the way you shake hands. And once you start talking, what you say and how you say it matter. Verbal dexterity is key – your ability to speak convincingly and with the right pitch, volume, cadence, punch and pause.

Your attitude is an underlying force that governs whether or not the emotional "buy" takes place. Since people prefer to do business with someone they like, smart salesmanship suggests that you treat everyone with friendliness and respect. They will usually respond in kind.

All of the external cues, from the cut of your hair to the excitement in your voice, combine to form the "you" that customers have to buy before they'll do business.

Personal Packaging

Early in my sales career, I read *Dress for Success*, a popular book stressing the importance of looking professional. Even if you're not making much money, it said, look prosperous. In the business world, people respond more favorably to someone who seems successful. It puts you on equal footing.

The image you project is absolutely crucial on a cold call, because you have only an instant to convey that you're a person of substance and quality. During that first blush, when new prospects are shaking your hand, they are taking your measure.

With a limited clothing budget, you can adopt the basic uniform – one dark blue suit, several white shirts, conservative ties, and a pair of conservative shoes. Clothing trends come and go – sometimes casual is in, sometimes not – but a polished, professional appearance is always in style. When you are meeting people, you want to look like a winner.

On the other hand, be smart about it. If the client advises you before a presentation that folks will be casually attired, dress down a tad. You can never be faulted for looking "too professional," even if the audience is sporting sneakers and jeans; but neither do you want your appearance to detract from what you're saying.

Quick Tip 🏃

Dress for Successful Image

As a new salesperson right out of college, my associate Mark Macrone quick discovered that personal grooming had a lot to do with his success.

"Our sales force was mostly young guys," Mark says. "Ninety percent of us were cold calling doctors' offices, and 99 percent of the office managers were middle-aged women. You want them to look at you like you're their son, because they're going to take care of their son. They will give you the business and help you out.

"If they see a clean-cut young man walking in wearing a suit, with his hair combed and his shoes shined, it dispels negative notions about the collections business." He says. "We looked like investment bankers. I'd stick out my hand and say, 'How are you, ma'am? My name is Mark Macrone. I'm with NCO, and I just wanted to see if you had a minute.'

"It was a rare call when you couldn't make any headway. As long as you were polite, respectful and looked decent, they'd cooperate and check the schedule for a time when you could meet with the doc."

When you're looking your best, your confidence soars. Part of achieving the aura of successful cold calling is to keep yourself as comfortable and pumped as possible.

Clothes and appearances may open the door, but they can't make the sale. The real you must be sharp, too. As a sales person, your stock in trade is the power of your words. You need to be clear-headed and well organized, because a new prospect will watch not only what you say, but how you say it – the empathy in your voice, the conviction, the eye contact. You want to be at the top of your game.

Conditioning for Competition

The ideal is to be fit. If you seriously want to succeed in selling, you need to gear yourself for competitive combat. Competition comes at us from every direction – from abroad, from across the country, from across the street and from the Internet. Every year, thousands of new companies pop onto the scene and thousands of others perish. The drive for profitability is relentless.

Only the fittest survive in this environment. It's easier to deal with this level of pressure if you're in shape.

Mental fitness and physical fitness go hand in hand – I think Plato said that. And there's no doubt that it's true. A physical workout is a great way to get rid of stress, and the benefits of conditioning will flow in your favor every time you walk in cold. A three-mile run or an hour of tennis will give you a healthy glow. When you're in shape, you'll sleep better, you'll have more energy, you'll think more clearly, and you'll look and feel better.

On a side note, it's a bad idea to drink the night before hitting the field. At the very least, it will impede your thought process and make you sluggish. At the worst, it will leave you hung over and bleary-eyed. Yet, plenty of sales reps finish up the day in a bar. It's bound to sap their efficiency the next day. There's no great harm in having a glass of wine or a couple of beers when you're out for dinner. Just don't overdo it.

Jump-Start Your Day

We still joke about the Great Elevator Race. One day, standing with one of my sales reps in the lobby of a highrise and waiting for three elevators, I spontaneously pulled out a dollar bill and said to my sales rep, "Okay, I'll bet my elevator beats yours." He accepted the wager with a flourish, whipping out a buck and waving it.

A well-dressed woman standing between the two of us seemed amused by our antics, so I said to her, "You've got the third elevator, the one in the middle. A dollar says mine comes in first." She was a good sport – she laughed and pulled out her wall. "No," she said. "Mine's coming in first."

It soon became a game for everyone waiting with us. All eyes were glued to the wall display, tracking each elevator's progress. Every time one of the cars made a big downward move, a little cheer erupted. Then, in one big rush, the middle elevator dropped 20 stories and came in first. As the doors opened, we both congratulated the woman on her big victory and gave her the money. It was smiles all around.

My rep and I boarded the elevator and went up to start making calls. And guess what? The same female executive was at one of the businesses we visited. She was in the front lobby of her office when we walked in, telling the receptionist about these two crazy guys and the elevator race. I couldn't believe it and neither could she. "All joking aside," I told her, "we really have to see you," and she showed us back to her office. We ended up getting an appointment.

It was a cold call with the ice already melted. Instead of being as serious as everyone else standing in the lobby, we had decided to have some fun. It was a way to pump ourselves up for the work ahead. The impromptu elevator gag set the motivational tone for the whole day; it gave us momentum and confidence. We eliminated our jitters by taking control of the situation.

How you feel every time you enter the field bears on your performance. While you can't control everything, you *can* control how you start the day. Focus on positive thoughts and get charged up by reminding yourself that you have value, your company has value, and what you are selling has value to your customers.

Start every day with a fresh, positive outlook. You'll have more spring in your step. You'll be in a better mood. That sense of optimism will give you a great attitude when you get in front of a potential customer. You want to come across as your irresistible self.

Staying Upbeat

Like many people, I used to start my morning by reading the daily paper over coffee. But why burden yourself first thing in the morning with bad news? Instead, cancel your subscription and read a good book or chat with your mate. Sing in the shower once in a while and see what happens to the rest of your day.

The same goes for your car radio. If you drive around listening to an all-news station or a talk show, you're exposing yourself to external problems, and that subliminally darkens your perspective. Forget the news. Cold calling is tough enough by itself. Try playing some music that makes you feel good. If your car is essentially your office, keep it spotless. Before you head out to make sales calls on Monday morning, cruise into a car wash. Spend the extra buck for the "hot wax" treatment. Clean the windows and toss out the trash. No matter what year or model your drive, keep it clean and you'll feel better starting out fresh.

Similarly, make sure your sales materials are in good condition. Don't show people dog-eared stuff with coffee stains. Everything has to be crisp, because it is a reflection of you and your company. In your corporate office, surround yourself with upbeat personal items such as pictures, mementos, art objects, golf clubs – things that give you peace and make you happy.

Selling With Conviction

When customers buy you, they are buying your honesty, sincerity and positive attitude. They are trusting that you have their best interest at heart and that you can deliver the goods. What you should be seeking isn't just a sale, but a win-win result – a successful outcome all around – because the benefits live on. When you genuinely care about your customers, they'll give you repeat business, referrals and favorable "word of mouth," the foundations of long-term success.

It can all start with a cold call. In the moment you get with the right person, you must project absolute faith in the product or service you represent and that it has great value to your customers. This is the touchstone of your credibility.

If you have doubts, they will be reflected in your level of confidence and enthusiasm, and prospects will pick up subtle signals. When they sense anything less than complete conviction and fervor on your part, it can poison the impression you make.

Product Integrity

Honesty means facing up. If you're peddling an inferior product or service, why do it? Why beat your head against a rock? Let somebody else sell the junk.

If you're determined to earn good money, put yourself into the best possible selling environment. Your results will be healthier if your product is terrific. When you can totally get behind something, you're able to plunge into your work with gusto, because you know your cause is righteous and fair.

You need a certain comfort level to cold call effectively, and that comes naturally when your product or service is top-notch. In my own career, moving up from one company to another, I always avoided employers who seemed even slightly suspicious. I wanted to be with the best. Quality becomes your ultimate advantage over the competition, a decisive factor no matter what you're selling – payroll processing, insurance, office furniture, house painting services, even beer.

Believing in His Beer – the Cold Calling of Sam Adams

Samuel Adams is the name of an upscale microbrewery. Maybe you've heard of it. Its founder, chairman and CEO, Jim Koch, launched his business by walking in cold.

With an MBA and law degree from Harvard, Jim could have taken a plush job in law or management consulting. Instead he became an entrepreneur. He produced the beer and he sold it, and nobody believed in his product more than he did. Based on a family formula, the beer was made with only the finest ingredients, in keeping with the strict German standard of quality and purity dating to the 16th Century – the Reinheitgebot.

Jim walked into bars across the country, always confident that the virtues of his brew would win out. In time, they did. In 1985, when Jim's company was a year old, Samuel Adams Boston Lager was voted "the best beer in America" by several thousand brewers, beer writers, and beer enthusiasts. By 1986, it was stocked aboard Air Force One and at Camp David.

When Jim started, however, his beer had zero name recognition. More critically, he had no pull with distributors, the linchpins of the delivery network. By law, they controlled beer sales to bars, restaurants, package stores, and the like. Somehow, Jim had to identify the most promising outlets for his beer in order to stimulate the demand side.

"It was the ultimate cold calling," he says. "I'd walk into a bar where I didn't know anybody, and I'd look behind the bar to see what brands they had on tap and in bottles. If they had a significant number of imported beers, I'd know I was in the right place."

Jim estimates that 40 percent of his calls turned up someone – a bartender, a manager, or an owner – who played a deciding role in the beer selection process. When he got his brief hearing with that person, he was straight-forward. "Hi, I'm Jim Koch, and I make a beer called Samuel Adams Boston Lager. Have you ever heard of it?" If they had, he followed up with another question: "Oh good. What have you heard about it?" That opened a dialogue.

"The worst thing you want if you're selling," he says, "is to be standing there giving a pitch. Nobody wants a spiel. So I wouldn't do that until I knew they actually wanted a pitch. For someone to stock Samuel Adams, it should be because it's in his best interest. He might have tried it twice before and it never worked. He might reject beers that cost more than 'x' amount, because he has to maintain a certain pouring cost. Those are legitimate blockades. But you'd get other objections that could be dealt with – nobody's ever heard of it, it won't sell, nobody drinks amber beer, and so on."

Quick Tip

Follow the 80/20 rule. Spend 20 percent of your time talking and 80 percent listening. And I mean really listening. Most prospects will tell you what you need to know, if you ask the right questions. Be interested in customer needs, selling them something because it's good for them.

Jim moved on when he couldn't satisfy legitimate objections. He accepted that his beer was too pricey for some establishments. It had to be properly positioned. He wasn't going to push it someplace where it wouldn't move. As he says, customers would carry it out of self-interest – the win-win result that would yield steady sales. That approach worked. By 2002, 17 years after he started, his company was posting revenues of more than $120 million.

As a smart and ethical purveyor of his own fine beer, Jim Koch imbued his sales force with similar respect for product and market. Intentionally, he avoided hiring experienced sales reps. "They have too many bad habits," he observes, "like talking too much, not being truthful all the time, viewing their relationship with the company as a game to be exploited."

Instead, he recruited for his sales team waiters and waitresses he'd met in bars and restaurants. "I also ended up hiring some people who were our customers. I knew they liked the product," he said.

Make Sure Your Job Is a Good Fit

Jim Koch succeeded because his beer tasted great. There was nothing like it on the market, and it found a niche. He also succeeded based on honest dealings. Customers could tell that he had unqualified faith in his product. His habit was to carry a couple of "cold ones" in his briefcase so he could pour samples on his cold call visits and get managers and owners to try it.

Before you dedicate yourself to cold calling, be sure you believe in the product.

Further: What about your company? Do you trust its honesty? Does your sales manager play it straight with you? Does the company stand foursquare behind you and honor the promises it makes to customers? Is your employer an upstanding corporate citizen? Are you proud to be associated with the company and its owner?

If you can answer yes to those questions, great. But if your company is not ethical, it's probably time to find a company that will treat you fairly and back your play. To make a switch, consider calling the national sales manager of a company you admire. Explain that you want to sell for that company.

If he says, "We're not hiring right now," you come right back with something like this: "I don't care. I'm going to be your number one salesperson. Matter of fact, if you have no budget for me, put me on straight commission. You have nothing to lose. The reason I called you is because your company has a great reputation, and I want to sell for a company like that. Because if I can sell for a company with a good name, based on the way I sell, I'm going to make six figures."

If that sales manager doesn't listen to you, take your appeal straight to the company president. And if you can't make headway there, move on to the next best company on your list. Keep going until you find a good fit. When you're selling good products for a reputable company, you're going to make more money. And you'll sleep at night, secure in the knowledge that everyone is better off because of your work. You can maintain your personal integrity and thrive.

The Magic of Enthusiasm

If you asked me to boil down the secret of cold calling success to its essence, I could tell you in one work – enthusiasm. During my early days in the sales business, my manager recommended the certain book, *How I Raised Myself from Failure to Success In Selling.* Originally published in 1947, its principles are timeless.

The author, Frank Bettger, had been a minor league baseball player, starting out in 1907 in Johnstown, Pennsylvania. He thought his talent would carry him to the top, but to his shock he was released in his first season. When he asked why, the manager told him he was lazy. "You drag yourself around the field like a veteran who has been playing ball for 20 years," he said. "Why do you act that way if you're not lazy?"

Bettger explained that he was so nervous and so scared that he acted nonchalant to hide his fear from the crowd and the other players. The manager offered only advice: "Whatever you do after you leave here, for heaven's sake, wake yourself up. Put some life and enthusiasm into your work."

When Bettger landed a try-out with another squad, he made up his mind to be the most dynamic player that team had ever seen. "From the minute I appeared on the field," he wrote, "I acted like a man electrified. I threw the ball around the diamond so hard it almost knocked our infielders' hands apart. Once, apparently trapped, I slid into third base with so much energy and force that the third baseman fumbled the ball and I was able to score an important run."

In the newspaper the next day, a sportswriter described the game in glowing terms. "This new player, Bettger, has a barrel of enthusiasm. He inspired our boys," he reported. "They not only won the game, they looked better than at any time this season."

Within ten days, Bettger's fanatical play caught the owner's eye, and his salary jumped from $25 a month to $185. "Nothing but the determination to act enthusiastic increased my income by 700 percent," he wrote. "I got this stupendous increase in salary not because I could throw a ball better, or catch or hit better, not because I had any more ability as a ball player. I didn't know any more about baseball than I did before." A few years later, he made it to the St. Louis Cardinals. His income had multiplied by 30 times. "What did it?" he wrote. "Enthusiasm alone did it; nothing but enthusiasm."

'The Biggest Single Factor in Successful Selling'

Later in life, Frank Bettger applied the same theory to the selling of insurance and became one of the top salesmen in the country. "The magic of enthusiasm began to work for me in business," he wrote, "just as it had in baseball. I firmly believe enthusiasm is by far the biggest single factor in successful selling."

Notice how it didn't matter how he actually felt. "When I force myself to *act* enthusiastic," he noted, "I soon *feel* enthusiastic."

After reading that book, I threw myself into selling with prodigious passion and vigor. I don't mean that I barged into peoples' offices and pounded my fists on the desk like a wild man. I still tried to empathize with my customers, to understand and be sensitive to their needs, to know when to talk and when to listen. But there was a change that came across in my mood, the friendliness of my approach, the conviction in my voice during a presentation. If you feel strongly about your product, whatever it is, you can create an infectious excitement about it. Like a force field, you can transfer your enthusiasm and energy to everyone else in a meeting and rev up the atmosphere.

Enthusiasm is at least 80 percent of the formula for successful selling. It's even more important than knowledge. When you're fired up about your product and believe in it, your enthusiasm will be genuine and contagious.

Case Study: Enthusiasm At Work

Some years ago, I spoke to 60 sales people for New York Life Insurance Company. The speaker right before me was Max Carey, a former Navy carrier pilot turned entrepreneur. An intense and energetic speaker, Max talked about pushing the envelope when you're flying an F-14 Tomcat, and the audience was spellbound. At the end of his talk, he gave out Top Gun hats to the top five sales reps.

I wondered how in the world I could follow an act like that.

The best defense, I decided, was an enthusiastic offense. After the coffee break, I was introduced as "the king of cold calls." There was a polite ripple of applause. From the back of the room, I made my entrance and started thundering, "Get up! Get up!" I yelled at the top of my lungs, coming up the aisle. They stood up and I said, "When I come into a room, I'm used to a standing ovation *before* I give the talk."

Was I nervous? You bet. Max was watching me from the back. Then I said, "Now sit down. I'm going to walk out that door and we're going to do it over again, because that wasn't good enough." And when I came back in, they were actually standing on their chairs, cheering.

That did it for me – I was on fire. They had piggybacked on my enthusiasm and given it right back to me. I told them straight out, "I'm very excited to be here, because I am with my kind of people. We're the ones who make it happen, and you are making it happen big-time. You are financially independent because you went into a profession that people pooh-pooh – 'Oh, you're in sales' – and they're trying to cut your commissions or cut your territory, and you're still making it happen anyway. You're the greatest people in the world." At the end of my talk, they did give me a standing ovation – and invited me to dinner to continue the discussion.

Enthusiasm makes you feel better about yourself while making those around you feel good, too. They will want to do business with you.

Creating a Sense of Trust

During my career, I've made 15,000 cold calls, given 6,000 presentations, and closed 3,000 sales. Closing one sale for every three presentations is considered outstanding, but I've been able to close one out of two.

It didn't happen right away. In the seasoning process, I developed core skills and learned something of tremendous value: No matter what I was selling, the core product was trust.

That was the foundation of every deal – trust in my company, trust in myself, trust that I could deliver what I promised. If I couldn't get a prospect to believe in me, the sale wouldn't happen. To succeed, I knew I had to do everything possible to engender a sense of trust and responsibility in all my business dealings.

Quick Tip

How to Build Trust

- Put yourself in the customer's place. Make sure that you have the customer's best interest at heart.
- Be certain that your product or service represents unquestionable value – if not always in price, then in performance.
- In every conversation you have – before, during, or after a sale – make it clear that the customer comes first. If you stay consistent in that, the truth comes out, and your and your ability to connect with your customers rises to a new and empowering level.

You can begin building trust during that first encounter, but you absolutely must establish an atmosphere of trust by the time of your presentation. That can start while you are breaking the ice. The opening conversation about sports or literature or the weather during the first five minutes in someone's office can set the tone for everything that follows.

While giving a presentation to executives of a large company in Richmond, Virginia, I started by saying that I loved Richmond for its history. I mentioned that I had walked into a venerable local landmark, the Jefferson Hotel, and that the staircase in the lobby reminded me of the one at Tara, in *Gone With The Wind*.

They jumped right in and agreed – it was indeed the one that inspired the staircase in the movie. One of the salespeople started talking about his wedding reception at the Jefferson, and somebody else elaborated on its storied past. We talked about that hotel for five minutes, then switched to Richmond in general.

I steered the talk to how we were expanding our business in the area. I told them that Virginia Electric & Power Company was already a client. And as a reference, I said, I can give you the name of someone there to call. Or if you'd like to call a few banks we're working for, I added, here are the numbers. They were writing down all the information. This preceded the presentation, but I was already building trust, and eventually we closed the sale.

I've gone so far to establish trust that I've actually delayed a sale for six months or more. When my company takes over the handling of a client's accounts receivable, the issues can be complicated. When the client is large, many people are involved and lots of information is exchanged.

To make sure that the data streaming into NCO is pristine, I've told customers, "Let's hold off until we're certain that all the data is accurate. I want to avoid any snags." Sometimes we miss start dates because the client needs to reexamine its own processes. They always apologize, and I say, "That's okay, because when we turn the key and go live, I want you to sleep at night. I don't want you ever to doubt that you made the right decision."

When you postpone a sale to ensure that a transaction flows smoothly, the trust factor skyrockets. You are showing that your company has high standards and that you're in this for the long haul. You are the real deal.

Adding Value to the Equation

How do you handle a prospect's question about your competition? I've always replied that we don't have competition. Sure, there are other collection agencies that do a good job collecting money, I would say, but they're not proactive. They don't come to you with ideas. If I can show you a way to reduce bad debts by ten percent and increase your cash flow significantly, I am going to own you.

That's what I say. It's bold, it's powerful, and it works. I am promising to add value, because many companies today don't want just a "vendor," they want a partner on the team, and that's what my company is all about. We partnered with our customers before it was trendy, because I realized that we could revamp a client's entire billing process to identify problems earlier and save them more. We operate like an adjunct of their business. That's all part of my presentation, because I know we'll live up to that and more.

Sometimes I'll offer advice. I have to stand out from the crowd, and the best way to do that is to add value to the relationship. When I can do that, I add trust, too. The whole relationship becomes more simpatico.

Quick Tip

Observation

Forget the old adage, "under-promise and over-deliver." Instead, always aim to promise a lot and deliver more. When you give your customers high expectations and then exceed even those lofty goals, you gain their trust.

Trust-Building Tactics

Use the Golden Rule for salesmanship guidelines. That is, treat your clients and prospects the way you like to be treated. Specifically:

- Show up on time for every meeting. Leave extra time for traffic or anything that might slow you down. Call if you're going to be late.

- Prepare thoroughly for every appointment, presentation and follow-up action. Anticipate the client's questions and concerns, and stand prepared to supply accurate, timely and relevant answers.

- Own up to your mistakes and take full responsibility for any errors made by your company. Do it promptly, before the client calls you. When you dodge responsibility, blame somebody else, or fail to admit a mistake, you diminish trust.

- Make sure your own company is handling the transaction correctly. If your customer is going to deal with your technical support people, your customer service department, or your delivery personnel, take time to educate these folks. They need to know about the nature of the relationship. Be certain they understand every promise and commitment you've made.

- Avoid surprises. Keep your customers fully alerted to any issues that will affect them. Provide as much notice as you can. Never allow them to be blindsided.

- Show appreciation for a client's business, and never take it for granted. Make that client feel like the center of your universe. Stay in touch before, during and after a sale, and meet every obligation 100 percent of the time.

Building Trust in Relationship Selling

If you've ever sold to large companies, you know it can be a prolonged, multi-stage process. We began running into this on a regular basis as our company grew and we started gunning for big-name clients.

One time, I remember, I had worked for two years to land a deal with a major credit-card company. That's how long the sales cycle can be for a big contract. I understood that this company wanted to initiate some innovative actions to manage its accounts receivable – actions that nobody in the financial-services business had ever tried before.

The competing candidates had been culled to a handful of finalists. When it was our turn to present, we went as a team of three, facing a committee of eight people. Instead of talking about our company, I talked about my partners and myself as individuals, and how we had each been proactive all our lives.

I explained that we had taken a risk by starting our company and that as entrepreneurs we were accustomed to saying, "Why not? Let's try it." I said we did not shy away from bold, progressive ideas. "We're right in step with you," I said. "You know what you want, and we're that way, too. Most people like to stand pat and avoid risk. You, on the other hand, are talking about deploying your assets in a way that can add millions of dollars in cash flow to your company. You have the pioneering spirit, which I think is phenomenal."

I appealed to their sense of adventure, their willingness to take a calculated gamble. I could sense it. Trust was setting in. We were kindred spirits. I began to close the sale; then my partner covered the operational side of the deal and the mechanics of how it would work. We had formulated an entire plan.

We won that contract not just because of our diligence, but because we shared the same values. They wanted to do business with people who could take their unconventional concept and run with it, and we were the obvious choice. They were risk-takers, and so were we. On some emotional level, we had connected and established a bond.

So, what is it that customers are buying when they buy you? All of it – personal appearance, level of enthusiasm, sense of rapport, trust, and faith in you and your business. It's a complex formula, and it takes plenty of practice to get it right. Meanwhile, you can do the one thing that comes naturally every time you walk in cold: Be yourself.

CHAPTER 4

Getting In: The Tools of the Trade

Chapter overview:

- Proven techniques to help you make the most of every selling opportunity.

- Effective opening lines – and how to use them to best advantage.

- How to finesse a gatekeeper without ruffling feathers.

- Using the "ripple effect" to track down new prospects by exploiting the interlocking threads of who knows who.

- How a sense of urgency and a truckload of patience and persistence can keep you going.

- How understanding basic personality types can help shape your presentation and channel buying action.

- A crash course on gate-crashing – Denise Manniello goes cold calling

- Timing yourself – the 60-second sales pitch.

- When you look like you know where you're going and what you're doing, no one is likely to stop you.

Your goal in cold call selling is to reach someone who can make a decision to buy. This means that it's imperative to penetrate the front line of receptionists, secretaries and assistants. That's not nearly as tough as you might think. Let me tell you a little story.

Back when my company was small, I flew to Pittsburgh for a morning meeting at Mellon Bank. We collected the bank's delinquent credit card debts, and I was trying to get a larger share of the business.

The meeting ended hours before my return flight, giving me time for some random cold calls. I looked around the neighborhood and spotted a target – the 30-story headquarters of a prominent, super-regional bank holding company.

I was just a sales guy from a small company at the other end of the state, but I decided to make an approach. I told myself I had nothing to lose. So, briefcase in hand, I walked into the bank's lobby, taking care to avoid eye contact with the security guards. A quick glance at the directory on the wall told me that the senior vice-president in charge of credit policy, a man I'll call Ed, was on the top floor. I hopped on the elevator, pushed 30, and went up. Dressed conservatively, I blended in with the bank officers.

I asked the receptionist for Ed. I had just missed him, she said, but his secretary was in. Here I was, in the rarefied atmosphere of corporate power, the executive suite, and she wasn't going to insult me by asking my name. After all, I was calling Ed by his first name – she probably assumed we knew each other.

Without even being asked, she picked up the phone and called Ed's secretary, who said she'd see me. The receptionist pushed a buzzer, and I walked through the glass doors and down an elegant hallway until I saw Ed's nameplate.

I greeted his secretary with my standard line – "I wonder if you can help me out." She seemed very friendly as I explained what I was doing. Ed was not the man to see, she said. My best bet was "Don," down on the eighth floor. She called up Don's secretary, said she was sending a "gentleman" to see her, and then gave me directions. I thanked her and was on my way.

Wrong guy again. Don's secretary directed me to "Margaret" in consumer collections, but warned me that I'd need to make an appointment through an assistant named "Chris."

Chris was at lunch, however, so I asked a secretary for Margaret. She was just walking by with a cup of coffee, and she overheard me. "I'm Margaret," she said. "Do you need me for something?"

In this kind of 30-second situation, you must be ready to say the right thing to make someone want to see you. "I hope you can help me out," I began. "My name is Chuck Piola. I was just over at Mellon Bank, one of my clients. My meeting ended early so I thought I'd make a call here, and someone told me that you're the person to speak with about my business."

Margaret perked up at the mention of Mellon Bank. "Do you know so-and-so over there?" she asked, naming her counterpart. I told her yes, I'd just come from there. My credibility had just shot up in Margaret's estimation. Margaret said she was busy, but she wanted to talk to me and asked me to wait for ten minutes while she finished up.

We ended up talking for an hour. She was the vice-president in charge of the recovery department. We discussed not only credit policies, but also current events and philosophy. She was delightful. She slapped me on the back as I left and wrote down the name of the person I needed to call – Roger. "I like everything you've said," Margaret told me, "and I'll tell Roger to expect your call."

Despite the security guards, receptionists and secretaries, I had managed to successfully navigate my way through that bureaucratic maze without being stopped, all because I looked like I knew what I was doing.

I had done nothing sly or dishonest. I had merely asked, "Can you help me out?" The upshot was that I got Roger on the phone and we set up an appointment. A few weeks later, I flew back to Pittsburgh and made the presentation. It was fast and clean. Two days later, we got the word – the bank had decided to give my small company a try. The "trial run" went well, the trust factor rose, our dealings with the bank grew steadily, and the bank remains a good client to this day.

Would I have ever reached Margaret or Roger with a phone call or a piece of direct mail? Not very likely. Once in a blue moon you might get lucky, but nothing beats being there in person.

Leveraging Your Luck with the Multiplier Effect

I've said it before, but it merits repeating: Every person you meet can be a stepping stone to your goal, and you never know which one will provide the big break. I call that by-product of cold calling the "multiplier effect."

In a nutshell, the multiplier effect involves maximizing your market exposure to multiply your chances of success. The more time you spend in the field making contacts, the better your odds of finding somebody who needs your product or your service. You can pick up the thread and see where it goes, using the name of the last person in the "chain" as a reference. By creating a network of people you know, you'll be able to leverage those contacts to generate more business.

When my partner and I teamed up to revive NCO Financial Services, we inherited a core group of 64 clients. Four years later, we had more than 1,600 accounts. The multiplier effect gets the credit for a major part of that buildup.

New business is your lifeblood. Each time you knock on a prospect's door gives you a shot at picking up a new customer. It's the only way to grow. Without new customers, at best you are just treading water. It's important to take care of existing accounts, of course, because they constitute your base. But for your personal financial success, as well as the overall health of your company, it's imperative that you bring in new business. Salespeople who constantly hustle to cultivate new customers can move, all of a sudden, to a nicer house or drive a better car. New business put them on the road to financial security.

Quick Tip 🏃

Opportunity knocks all the time, but you have to be there to hear it. And when you're working out in the field, you can actively listen for it.

Multiplier-Effect Corollary: The 'Accidental' Sale

An effective sales person has a spider web in his brain, all laced together, and it contains a file on all the people he or she knows. Obviously, a network like that is vital to getting referrals and recommendations, the pillars of growth. When you're knocking on doors for a living, you can constantly add new names to your mental hard drive. You are open to new opportunities.

And simply because you are where you are – out on the streets, meeting people – sometimes success drops right into your lap. It's as if the harder you work, the luckier you get. That cliché has a lot of truth.

One day I stopped at a lunch counter and stuck up a conversation with a young fellow sitting next to me. We chatted amiably about the Philadelphia Eagles and then about business. He confided that his father owned a major national trucking company.

My sales antennae perked right up. After explaining what my company did, I talked about the trouble companies often have in getting paid. We traded horror stories, mine from the collection side, his from the creditor's side. That created an instant bond.

He seemed so curious about how collection agencies worked that I actually did a mini-presentation over lunch. I ordered coffee for both of us and gave him a ten-minute rundown on our company, our track record, and the way we operated. It piqued his interest enough that he offered to arrange a meeting for me with the credit manager of his dad's trucking company.

Bingo! This is the fascinating thing about the multiplier effect – you never knew when or where you'll find the first link in a sales chain.

We traded cards and made a plan. But before we left, he warned me that the credit manager was a gruff, abrasive man who wasn't crazy about sales people. I sensed a tough sell, picturing myself going up against the irascible manager, and this is where instinct came into play. I knew I might need an ally, so I asked my new friend if he could be in the room for the full-blown presentation. He assured me that would be no problem.

True to his word, he ushered me into the meeting a few days later. My presentation to the credit manager included the standard set of fee options. But before I could move into a closing stage, the credit manager cut me off. "I know about this collection business," he snapped. "It doesn't work. We don't we need it."

The owner's son saved the day. "Are you kidding?" he said. "We have 50 customers right now who haven't paid us for six months. What do we have to lose by spending a thousand dollars with this guy?" I was watching the manager's body language, looking for a signal. He was pondering the situation. "Okay," he said at last. "I guess it's worth a try." I came away with his signature on an agreement, and the company became a very good client.

Now, if the owner's son hadn't been there, the credit manager would have brushed me off like a piece of lint. But because I had spent ten minutes over lunch on that mini-proposal and then taken 15 extra seconds to ask the son to be there for the meeting, I had multiplied my chances for success.

Crash Course in Gatecrashing

As a sales manager, I always put my troops through a cold calling boot camp. As our company grew and made acquisitions, I tried to help the new reps we had inherited. One of them was Denise Manniello. You remember Denise, the sales person for JDR Recovery, a collection agency based in Ramsey, New Jersey.

I got a call from her one day. "I'm supposed to go out there cold calling," she pleaded with me, "and I don't know how to do it."

I offered to spend a day with her in the field to show her that with the right attitude and approach, she could be successful and have fun doing it. Given the depths of her career-threatening sales slump, I needed to demonstrate that cold calling was her ticket to job security and rising productivity.

Before going in, I gave her one of my trade secrets: "You can get away with anything as long as you're being honest." And so the day unfolded.

Call 1 – A Riot

"The first call was a riot," Denise relays. "Chuck had warned me he was going to push this call as far as possible. Two women sat at the front desk. Chuck walked up and asked for Jeff, whose name I had gotten earlier by phone. They asked Chuck who he was. 'I'm from WABC news radio,' he said, 'and Jeff just won $10,000 in our cash-giveaway game. He just has to answer one question – who's buried in Grant's Tomb?'

"They looked at each other and at me, and I just smiled. Chuck said, 'Jeff just won our big prize, and my associate and I are here to interview him and present him with the money.' These two ladies looked like veterans, and they weren't falling for it. 'Okay,' one of them asked, 'who are you two *really* with?' I confessed and told them we were with NCO Financial and that we needed to see Jeff for a minute.

"We all laughed, and the two women played along with the gag. They called Jeff and asked him to come to the lobby – there were two people he had to see. While he was on the way, one of them said, 'You know, you're right on the money, because he's been buying lottery tickets for years. And tonight is the big drawing. You ought to stay with your line.' They were getting a kick out of our prank.

"Jeff walked in asking 'Can I help you? He was huge, like six-four, even taller than Chuck, with long salt and pepper hair.

"Chuck shook his hand and said, 'Yeah, I'm Chuck Piola from WABC radio. We're doing a story on the lottery, and we understand you've been buying tickets since the beginning. Tonight is the drawing for a big jackpot. On the off chance that you might win, my associate Denise and I want to interview you before and after. We'd like to do an interview.'

"We all looked at each other, and I thought, 'Oh, we're going over the edge here.' Jeff was interested but skeptical. 'This is a joke, right?' he said. But Chuck stuck with it. 'No, it's true. This could be your big day, and we want to talk to you.'

"After a few minutes of this charade, Chuck admitted the truth. 'We just wanted to get your attention,' he said, 'because we have this terrific product you need to hear about.' Jeff listened for a minute, then said 'Hold on. I'm not the right person, but I'm going to get her for you.' And he brought the vice-president of the division we needed to deal with. We gathered in a conference room, and she spent 20 minutes with us. When I asked for the appointment, I got it.

"On that call, I learned how to get past the gatekeepers. We overcame any objection they would have raised by saying we were from WABC and had the big prize. Nobody minded that it wasn't true. Jeff was a good sport to appreciate the humor. I also learned that if people like you, they will go above and beyond for you. People want to do business with people they like. If you're comfortable with yourself, you will make other people comfortable with themselves, and they will open doors for you.

Call 2 – A Dud

Denise and I pressed on. I'll let her tell the story:

"Our second call was to a company that made underwater coaxial cable. The people all wore pocket protectors and big plastic goggles. The woman behind the desk was past age 60 and severe looking.

"Chuck said 'Watch this' and walked up to her. There was no funny business this time. It was a more straightforward approach. Chuck tried a few friendly lines on her, but the woman wouldn't budge. They didn't use collection agencies. They had no interest. She was not allowed to let anyone through, and she wouldn't provide any names.

"The lesson here is that some companies are as tight as Fort Knox. You have to know when to stop, move on, and look for a better opportunity elsewhere. We did."

Call 3 – Another Bend in the Road

The third call on Denise's schedule was to Minolta's corporate headquarters. I lit up when I heard that. I had known someone there – I think he was a chief financial officer. We hit it off, but I could never get to first base, so I gave up on them a few years ago.

Denise recalls:: "At the front desk, Chuck started befriending the receptionist, who happened to be new. He said, 'I used to know a gentleman here, but I forget his name. I think he heads up the finance area.' She offered the name of the CFO but that didn't ring a bell.

"Then she called another receptionist, the one she had replaced, and handed the phone to Chuck. 'I'm in the building,' he told the other woman. 'Matter of fact, I'm standing right by your old desk. If you went straight down the hall, who was the man on the right, in the back corner office? She knew the name instantly. It was Howard.

"Chuck calls him up. 'Howard, Chuck Piola here. I'm in your front lobby. I'm training a new sales rep, and I told her you'd come out and see her.' Five minutes later, Howard appeared.

"When he came out, we sat in the lobby. They talked about old times before Chuck brought the conversation current. He talked about our service and what we could do for them. I also chimed in about a project we were doing for Xerox, their top competitor in the copier business. It's an automated system that reads the copy meter on leased machines and sends the bill. Howard said, 'We'd be interested in talking about that. Call me for an appointment.'

"I called back two days later and he was dodging me, so I sent him an e-mail message. He answered that he had no need for the meter-reading service in his area – he managed their major national accounts. But he referred me to someone in the mid-market commercial accounts division. And that did result in an appointment.

Call 4 – Denise on her Own

"By the fourth call, Chuck wanted me to fly solo," Denise says. "The company was named Hubco Shoppers Charge, and Chuck gave me my final instructions: All you have to say is, 'I wonder if you can help me out. And don't take no for an answer.'

"But there was a security guard sitting in a bulletproof Plexiglas cell – very intimidating. I had a package and had everything filled out for a woman named Rose. I had called her four times and had never heard a word back, but I knew she had responsibility for handling bad debts.

"I said to the guard, 'I need to give this package to Rose.' No problem – he would make sure got it. I said, 'No, no, I have to give it to her myself. I have to hand-deliver this.' But he was adamant. 'If you don't have an appointment,' he said, 'I can't let you in.'

"Desperate, I leaned closer and practically whispered, 'See that guy on the sofa?' He looked over at Chuck. I said, 'I have never done this before. This is my first day ever cold calling, and he is evaluating me and deciding whether I'm going to have a job or not. If I can get past you, it means I'm going to have a check coming into my family next month.'

"He softened up. 'If anybody knows I'm doing this for you,' he said, 'I could get fired.' I assured him that nobody would ever know. 'Take the elevator to the second floor,' he said. 'Just ask someone there and they will let you in.'

"So I went up. A group of people was going through an inner door, and I just scooted in with them. I went up to a nice-looking guy and said, 'I wonder if you could help me out. I'm trying to find Rose.' He pointed to an empty office. 'She sits over there,' he said. 'Let me see if I can find her. Who are you?' I told him I didn't know Rose, but I had this package for her.

"He finds her and waves me over. I said, 'Rose, I'm Denise Manniello.' She looked at me for a moment, thinking. 'Denise,' she said apologetically. 'I've been meaning to call you back. I am so sorry.' I told her that was okay. 'I figured, heck, you're only on the other side of the mountain, so I might as well drive up here.'

"Rose asked how I got in. I said it was a long story that I'd tell her some day over lunch. Talk turned to business, and I left after 20 minutes with an appointment. Meeting her set off a chain reaction. There was a convention that week in New Orleans, and we discovered we were both going. Matter of fact, she ended up on my flight, and we arranged to sit together, so we actually struck up a relationship. She even took me as her guest to a party thrown by one of our competitors. All my prospects were there."

You never know where things may lead.

Four calls – that's all it took to give Denise the confidence to start knocking on doors by herself. She went on to make scores of cold calls, landing dozens of appointments. Each time she walked in on a potential client, she felt more self-assured.

Given her planned approach, every appointment has high-quality potential. Denise takes care to target a specific company, and then zeros in on the appropriate decision-maker – all ahead of time. With the prospect clearly identified, she goes in knowing exactly whom she needs to see.

"I just try to be myself," she says. "I always use the line, 'I wonder if you can help me out.' " Winning an appointment with the right person is like gold to her. "If I can get in front of you, if I can present to you," she says, "98 percent of the time I will get that sale."

Penetrating the Defenses

Almost always, when you're trying to reach a decision-maker, you must deal with one or more persons who control access. In large corporations, you can expect to face several echelons of resistance – security officers, receptionists, executive assistants.

Critics of cold calling say you'll never make it through this defensive shield.

But gatekeepers aren't monsters; they're regular people, a lot like you. You don't want or need to fight these folks. The key to getting through to the boss is to make the system work for you. Think of each person you meet not as an adversary but as a potential ally, a possible stepping-stone. You need to win them over to your side, so it's important to start each new relationship on an up note. Walk in with a cheerful attitude; take time to banter with receptionists and secretaries; show respect, courtesy and a sense of humor. Good manners never go out of style.

Sales people tend to underestimate gatekeepers. Very often, these people know nearly as much about the business as the executives for whom they work, and some are empowered to make decisions and appointments on behalf of their bosses. It's to your benefit to treat them as important individuals. If they like you, they will give you a fair hearing and try to help you.

Getting In, Getting Past

Security guards: In most large office buildings, uniformed guards man the front desk. They can appear as intimidating as the lobby, with its imposing marble and glass. You're the intruder here, and a diligent security guard will stop you for questioning.

To avoid that, enter under the radar. Walking in, be as innocuous as possible and never make eye contact with the guard. Don't stand and stare at the tenant directory on the wall. The last thing you want to do is draw attention to yourself, so look like you know what you're doing. Dress like the natives. Time your arrival when other office workers are coming in, and then blend in with the crowd. Hop aboard the elevator and head upstairs. If a guard does stop you, you have to know what to say.

If you have no idea what companies are in the building, just say you're going upstairs to see somebody. If pressed, tell a plausible story: "I need to see a law firm here, but

I couldn't reach them by phone. I'm in town today and thought I'd stop in."

It's preferable to get the name of one or more companies located in the building you plan to approach. That way, you can state a destination. It's even better if you have someone's name.

Receptionists and secretaries: Plan a positive approach to those guarding the inner sanctums. Make sure the receptionist or secretary knows that you are going to help the boss, not hinder or hassle anyone. In essence, you are in a sales situation involving your credibility as a person, as a vendor, as a product. In that first minute or two of the initial contact, you need to come across as courteous and good-natured. The best thing you can do is to set a comfortable, respectful, non-threatening tone.

One way to do that is by opening up with a very innocent-sounding question – "Excuse me, Ma'am. I wonder if you can help me out?" That line applies anywhere and everywhere. It's a technique that can evoke empathy. Most people *do* want to be helpful.

Then follow up with an introduction, explaining the reason for your visit. If circumstances permit, try to engage the person in conversation. It can be about anything, as long as it helps make you real to them. Try connecting as a parent, a sports fan, an observer of the local scene, so you can start building a relationship.

Everybody's the Boss

Cruising the Internet one day, I encountered an article entitled "Everybody's the CEO," by Sam Parker, at www.justsell.com. Parker writes: "In the last three days, have you treated each person with whom you've come in contact as the CEO of the organization? I'm talking about the person who answers the phone right on through to the person who can sign off on your deal. If you have, do us a favor and send in your resume – we need you. If not, start making it your practice and you'll never have to be concerned about your monthly bills again."

When you treat each individual like the final decision-maker, he says, it has tremendous bearing on the success of your mission. "This doesn't mean you have to make a full presentation to every person you meet. It just means you recognize their importance within an organization and as an individual. This is the foundation to successful rapport and relationship-building within a potential client's organization."

Finally, Parker includes a tip to get you in the right mindset. "On the outbound call or just before you walk through the prospect's door, take a second," he writes. "Internalize the thought that the person you'll be talking with is the CEO and has final authority on signing the contract. Own this thought. I'm talking about complete visualization of it being fact – recall the last time you talked with a CEO and tell your brain you're about to do it again. Sometimes, it may actually be the case. Have you ever been talking with a prospect and later learned that they were in fact the CEO or the final decision-maker, when you thought they were the gatekeeper or influencer? If you haven't, give me a call and I'll tell you some stories."

Traditionally, the relationship between sales rep and prospect has had an adversarial aura. You, the sales person, are driving towards a deal. The customer, however, is wondering how to get rid of you as painlessly as possible, with his wallet intact. This creates discomfort that is detrimental to your effort. You want to begin defusing that tension right away, with the first person you meet.

When you show genuine interest in a gatekeeper or a prospect and a real desire to understand that company and its needs, you're demonstrating respect for that person, and stress is diminished on both sides. When you ask intelligent, open-ended questions that induce the customer to do the talking, you can sit back and learn.

Few things are more effective in opening doors than a sense of merriment. Even when you're playing it straight, it pays to throw in a quirky line. I used to introduce my company and myself, and then add this: "The president of my company asked me to stop in. We need to gather some information for a proposal we're going to send you. I need to see your chief financial officer."

It was true. I wasn't lying or even bending the truth. The president of my company did ask me to stop in. In fact, he asked me to stop in to *every* company. You can use that line even if you're the president of your own company. When you say that, you feel great, because you have the right kind of words.

Opening Gambits for Fun and Profit

If you're a natural comedian, breaking the ice with humor will come easily. If not, feel free to use any of my lines or let your imagination run freely. Welcome to some of my favorite ploys:

- "We're doing a survey of receptionists," I said to a young woman at the front desk, "and we're trying to find trends. How many sales people do you see in the course of a day, and how irritating are they?" She chuckled and a minute later we had an appointment to come back.

- One day, I approached a receptionist and said, "I'd like a Big Mac, some fries, and a Coke. And my friend here will have – Mark, what do you need? – a chicken sandwich."

- Another time, the secretary was on the phone when we walked in, and obviously having a stressful time. I said, "Isn't it a pain? Can you get out of here a couple of hours early, and we'll beat the crowd to happy hour?" And she'd come back with something like, "Oh boy, could I use that!"

- Don't forget the old standard: "I wonder if you can help me out?"

- My sales rep Mark liked this one: We'd go into an office and right away they'd ask, "What are you selling?" I would start fishing through my pockets, putting keys and spare change on the desk. "I'm selling used lottery tickets from last night," I'd say. "They're half price." And it would take the people a moment to realize that they were worthless. Then they'd start laughing, and once they were laughing, we had them. When you get people to smile, they will listen to you for a minute.

- Another of Mark's favorites: "Chuck had a great line he liked to use in medical offices. Before we approached the reception desk, he'd fill up a little paper cup from one of those big water bottles. We knew the people were probably watching us. Chuck would take a sip of the water and act like he was tasting it, like it was wine. He'd make a face. Then he'd walk up to the receptionist and say, 'Do you know there's vodka in your water?' She would look puzzled, like what the hell is this. And Chuck would say, 'Yeah, I can taste vodka in here,' and he'd take another tiny sip. Then I'd start laughing, and he'd laugh, and he had an air about him that when he laughed, everybody around him started laughing, too. And right there, you knew you'd at least get an appointment."

- Another: "I used to tell people that I was just getting started in sales," Mark says. "It made people more willing to help me." When someone asked him how long he'd been selling, then he'd admit "14 years" and get a big laugh – and greater receptivity.

Workable Alternatives

After you've loosened up the atmosphere with humor and made the gatekeeper feel comfortable with you, then small talk becomes a big thing. Ask if they've been on vacation or are planning one. Little inquiries mean a lot, because few people make them.

Have some laughs while you're cold calling. It dissolves tension. It brings in fresh air and helps establish you as a likable person.

If I can't get to see the head honcho on that first try, I sometimes lower my voice and say to the receptionist, "I'm going to leave you some material. I have a good company that can really help you. Would you please make sure that the boss gets it? Tell him a nice guy came by to deliver it and that the nice guy will call in the morning."

Then I'd phone back the following day and say, "The nice guy is calling back. What did the boss say?" She might say, "It looks like you'll be able to get in." So all of a sudden, the gatekeeper is helping me.

Never part company with a secretary or receptionist until you have accomplished three things:

- First, make sure that the person you're trying to see is, in fact, responsible for signing the contract. Job titles can be misleading, especially in large corporations, so make certain you're on the right track.

- Second, ask the secretary for the boss's business card. Explain that you need his or her name, address, phone number, and an e-mail address because you're going to send some information.

- Third, ask the secretary for his or her own business card. This can be very flattering.

Keep Track of Details

- Build a dossier on the prospect. Write down any pertinent facts about the decision-maker you learn from the gatekeeper. What's the best time to call? When does the company usually buy services – is there an annual or quarterly or monthly cycle? Will the boss see you without an appointment, or is an appointment imperative?

- Jot notes for yourself about the gatekeeper's personality, where she went on vacation, what you talked about – anything to help you remember the conversation. You might be dealing with "Julie" five or ten times before you ever see her boss.

- Later, enter all that information on your computerized contact-management system. A software program like Goldmine is designed specifically to handle that data and keep it easy for you to retrieve as needed.

In dealing with people who hold the keys to getting in, it never hurts to bring token gifts – pens, letter openers, note pads, an extra T-shirt from your company's softball game. That's a nice gesture, and you want the gatekeeper to think you're a nice guy.

Executive Assistants – the Final Hurdle

When you're trying to make contact with a top officer at a large company, the last gatekeeper is an administrative assistant or executive secretary who coordinates everything. As far as you're concerned, that top aide is the second most important person in the organization. He or she deserves the same degree of courtesy and respect you would extend to the CEO.

Assume, for starters, that the executive aide is on top of everything from the boss's travel schedule and lunch dates to the company's strategic goals and current needs. He or she probably is as knowledgeable about the organization as the boss and might very well have the authority to speak for the boss.

People in these pivotal positions provide a rich resource for you, so take full advantage. If they like you, they can tell you everything you need to know. They can make it happen for you. They can be entrusted to convey your message to the boss with accuracy and fairness. Just as with receptionists and secretaries, you need to come across as friendly, considerate and good-natured. You need this person as an ally who can provide the inside track to a meeting with the decision maker.

Stay focused on your goal: You're here to see the boss or to schedule a meeting with the boss. To do so, you need to win over the chief aide.

Tim Kleppick, one of my company's top salesmen, says that small talk often leads to big things. In his words: "You never know which direction it will take, but if you keep talking, you might mention something that sparks interest – your product costs less, has superior features, or can cut operating costs – whatever distinguishes you from the competition. In that brief face-to-face moment with an executive aide or even with the prospect, always get across that one benefit, that one feature, that will win an appointment."

Tim continues: "Most people have time to talk to you. The key is asking the right question of somebody who handles what you're trying to sell. You have to create a reason for someone to want to talk to you. You can do that by asking that extra question or being a little more persistent, in a pleasant way."

Personality Types—Knowing What Makes Customers Tick

Selling is a multifaceted discipline that requires an array of skills. When you are with a gatekeeper or potential customer, you are a performer and an artist. The art of selling has aspects as complex as psychology and sociology. Every sale has a unique "culture" – its own set of personalities, atmospherics, obstacles, and opportunities. You need to be able to read a situation and then play to its dynamics.

After you've broken the ice, channel the talk back to business. You demonstrate professionalism when you steer the meeting to the issue at hand – getting the appointment. You'll be more successful in doing that if you understand four different personality types: dominant, easy-going, formal, and informal.

- **Dominant-informal** people are drivers and promoters. They tend to control conversations, and they're not steeped in convention. They are all-out competitors, the so-called "alpha" males or females. Their strongest need is to be in charge, and they will maintain control by whatever means necessary, including insults and intimidation. These people like to feel like the boss, even when their job or title doesn't reflect that. You often find them in middle management, but sometimes they are the top dog. Remember "Ray," the auto dealer who gave me so much abuse when I went in to sell him advertising space on those phone book covers? He was a classic driver.

- A **dominant-formal** individual is a controller. They dominate conversations, and they stand on tradition. Not much casual levity and joking in this bunch. Bankers and lawyers are usually dominant and formal.

- **Informal and easy-going** people are supporters. Supporters, sometimes called "amiables," don't like negotiations and don't like to make decisions alone. They want a committee to make a decision and they'll go along with it. They feel a need to arrive at conflict-free, "consensus" solutions. They don't like confrontation or high-pressure tactics.

- People who are **formal and easy-going** are analytical.
  They tend to be more structured people who are fluent with data. You will find many accountants in this
  category, because they have lots of rules. Be ready to
  feed them the facts, figures and documentation that
  their logical minds thrive on. Unanswered questions
  or fuzzy details make them nervous.

These four classifications are not ironclad. We all
lean toward one of them, but we can float among them,
depending on the circumstances. In a business setting,
however, most people gravitate to their basic nature.
Remember this when you practice the art of the cold call.
When you walk in, you should be able to discern within
a few minutes what sort of personalities you are dealing
with.

Sometimes, you can tell quickly if they are formal
or informal just by the way they sit. Controllers are hard
to sell to sometimes because they think they know more
than you do. They create confrontation. They want to go
to the price issue right away. If they are dominant and
controlling, they'll tell you to hurry up. They can be difficult people to sell.

Personally, I prefer to deal with promoters, because
I'm a promoter. I understand them. But a salesperson
needs to be a chameleon at times. You need to be able to
appeal to many different personality types, from control
freaks to supporters and analysts. Subliminally, you have
to read the atmosphere and mirror it. If the person is
quiet and reserved, I am quiet and reserved. If the person
is outgoing, I am outgoing. If the ambiance is formal, I
am formal. And what happens? The prospect will like you
without even thinking about it.

When you are selling to a large organization, sometimes you have to orchestrate the sale. There might be
seven or eight people you have to sell and they all have

different agendas and their own reasons to buy or why they don't. Sometimes you have to sell one and then go to the next. Or you meet with three of them one day and four more the next. Or you might have to sell them all in one fell swoop.

Let's say you have a few of these personalities in the room. You are pressing for the deal. You can assume that the chief financial officer or the comptroller is going to be formal, but he or she might also be analytical and controlling, too. The billing person could also be analytical and controlling. Someone from purchasing could be dominant and informal, and the computer specialist would likely be analytical and informal. The owner of the company could be anywhere, but typically falls on the dominant side.

In your remarks, you have to say something to make everyone happy, but you have to give tons and tons of data to those with an analytical bent. You have to strike just the right balance, and that comes with practice.

Incidentally, you can learn a lot about the personality of the decision-maker before you meet by paying attention to how an assistant reacts to your cold call. Watch for the clues. The more helpful an assistant is to you, the better the relationship that person has with the boss, and the more influence. In my experience, the friendliest secretaries and office assistants will also be the most willing to offer suggestions about how to influence their bosses. Usually, these bosses are easy to work with.

When the secretary is hesitant or timid about arranging a meeting or even a conference call, however, she might be afraid of the boss. Maybe the boss is a domineering type. That's good to know – forewarned is forearmed. If the secretary tells you the boss always keeps his or her own schedule, you could be dealing with a suspicious type, someone who's tough to pin down.

Keep Multiplying Your Contacts

As a salesperson, you need to take the initiative by looking for ways to start the process that leads to productive relationships. The multiplier effect won't kick into action without a push. To put yourself in a position to meet somebody who will be receptive, you have to talk to people – many people – without fear. Just remember: You have nothing to lose by engaging in casual conversation. You never know where it may take you, or how far.

In pursuing AT&T as a potential account, I threaded my way through the organization until I identified people I could deal with, and each person I met led to another one higher up the chain of command. During my journey through the corporate bureaucracy, I dealt with 18 different executives before finally making contact with the folks who mattered. You need patience and the gift of gab (or the right questions or rehearsed script) to score in a labyrinthine system like that.

The sales cycle can take weeks or months, and the multiplier effect can be a powerful tool to get you closer to your goal. Everybody you meet along the way is a potential ally, and you never know where your big break will come from.

A true story: When I was selling advertising on plastic phone book covers, I wanted an ambulance company in the Hartford area as a client. I stopped by to see the owner several times, with no luck. The fourth time, the dispatcher told me that the owner was *never* there – except around midnight on Saturdays. He liked to work the radio on Saturday nights, because there was a lot of action.

"By the way," the dispatcher added, "bring him a hot fudge sundae. He loves them."

The next Saturday, just after midnight, I walked in. "Who are you?" he asked from his post behind the radio. When he heard my name, there was a flash of recognition.

"Oh yeah," he said with a nod. "I hear you've been looking for me."

I said, "I sure have, and look, here's a hot fudge sundae, because someone told me you like them. I figured it would give me a better shot to talk to you." He laughed and dug directly into the ice cream. I gave him a presentation that night, during gaps in the radio action, and at 1:30 a.m. I got the sale.

Under normal conditions, you probably won't need to do anything like that; but you *do* need to attack the market with intensity and a determination to get through to the decision-maker. It's in your best interest to cultivate a sense of urgency.

We're in sales because we need to support ourselves, raise a family, and pay the bills. But you're reading this book because you want more than that. You want a nicer house, a bigger boat, or a carefree retirement. Take a look at your income situation. Are you in the top 20 percent of the sales force that brings in 80 percent of the orders? Or are you in the bottom 80 percent?

If the way you sell today won't win you the lifestyle you want, you need to make a change. When you step out into the realm of cold calling with an optimistic outlook and the persistence to get through to somebody who matters, you're only one deal away from becoming a superstar.

The 60-Second Sales Pitch

Here's one of my all-time favorite "ice-breaking" acts. It comes from a colorful character named Matt Hessian. I was doing a workshop on cold call selling, and he approached me afterwards. He handed me his card – his title was "head honcho" – and told me that even though he was president of his own company, he cold called constantly.

Hessian realized that his target customers were too busy to make time for a standard sales call, so he came up with a nifty solution – the 60-second sales pitch. Once he got face to face with a prospect, he would ask for "just one minute." Then he'd take off his watch to time himself. "They think it's fascinating," he told me. "They say to themselves, 'Hey, the entertainment just walked in.' "

His company, Key Medical Supply, sold or leased medical equipment such as wheelchairs, and Hessian's customers were pharmacists, whom he hoped to sign up as allies. He needed to be able to drive down the highway and make 15 or 20 cold calls a day. He couldn't afford to have people say, "Leave your card and I'll call you back." His company was doing about $3 million a year, and Hessian said he was experiencing "entrepreneurial terror" about keeping it afloat.

In 60 seconds with a pharmacist, he'd describe his program, which cost nothing and took up little time. A minute later, he'd say, "My time's up. I want them to know that I'm a person who means what he says. They're impressed that I manage to pull it off."

A week later, he would call back to see if they had read over the contract. Everybody remembered Matt, the one-minute man, and an amazing 90 percent ended up as customers.

I've always admired Matt's gambit. What an irresistible way to get in to see a prospect and break the ice. It combines so many of the elements for a successful first meeting – honesty, humor, sensitivity, and respect for the person's time. In that brief period of 60 seconds, he gets across the essential features of his program, and in such a tantalizing fashion that people come aboard.

CHAPTER 5

Once You're In

Chapter overview:

- More on breaking the ice – finding common ground by establishing a personal connection.

- Warming up the call by finding the customer's "hot button."

- Winning the prospect's trust by coming across as an honest expert.

- How mastering the lingo of specific industries gives you an edge over the competition.

- Questions guaranteed to start a conversation.

- Learning to spot buying signals by watching the customer's body language.

- Looking for the "windows" in the sales process when you can close a deal.

- More proven questions to close the deal.

No two cold calls are identical. Each one is virgin territory where you survive by your wits, your verbal skills and your resourcefulness. The dynamics and degree of difficulty can vary tremendously.

You can't always know what sort of situation you'll face. No matter what it is, though, you've got to generate some positive energy. It's all up to you. As you walk in cold on somebody, you've got to be putting out good vibes. When you break the ice in just the right way, the "close" can start with the handshake.

The Warm-Up

The first time you meet a prospect in person, time is short. Your job is to get an appointment and move on. But it sure helps when you can squeeze in a nice comment or two to warm up the atmosphere. It gets the relationship off on a positive note. You might talk about the weather, the diploma on the wall, or the football game. But when you get to the reason for your call, use your rehearsed script and you ask for the appointment.

Later, when you go back in for a formal sit-down, it is absolutely vital to find some common ground. That not only breaks the ice, it creates a bond. If my typical presentation lasts 45 minutes, I'll usually take an hour, because the first ten or 15 minutes are the "warm up" phase.

You should never be stumped for a topic. If nothing jumps out at you from the surroundings, you can always start with some open-ended questions:

"Where did you go to school?" I ask that one a lot, because it leads in all sorts of unpredictable directions. You get into discussions about various universities, the caliber of today's students – any number of things.

And then there's one of the most surefire conversation starters that I know. You say, "I've always been fascinated by this business. **How did you get involved in this line of work anyway?"** Most folks like to talk about what they do for a living. It's a great way to learn something about their past and how the business works. And many times, the person will say something in passing that you can glom onto.

One fellow, for example, in talking about how work intruded on his home life, happened to mention his kids' scout meetings. I homed in on that like a heat-seeking missile. I was a scoutmaster when we started the business. One of my kids was a Boy Scout, and I kept the troop for four years.

This made for classic icebreaking, because we talked about scouting for 10 minutes. I told him I'd found it to be a fantastic thing, not just for my son but also for me, because it forced me to go on camping trips and really escape from work. It made me stop and do something at my workbench to build a car for the "pinewood derby."

We spoke as one parent to another. He even picked up a picture of his kids from the desk and told me a little bit about each one. I reciprocated by pulling out my wallet and flipping through some photos of my children. All this gave him a chance to see me in a different light, not as just a salesman but as a decent guy and a good father. We built a foundation of trust, and I eventually made that sale.

Looking for "Hot Buttons"

When you show up at a prospect's office on appointment, begin looking for something to talk about. It can be anything – a set of golf clubs in the corner, the view, the weather. It might be something you notice in the reception area, like a picture or a plant. It gives you a chance to focus momentarily on something other than business.

Astute business people understand that they're being warmed up. But if you come across with a sense of honesty and freshness, and you're talking about neat things that they like, they won't feel manipulated.

Whenever possible, you want to talk about something you know. This is where your background, your life experience, and even your personality come into play. How interesting are you as a person? Can you talk about a lot of different things? Do you have hobbies? Do you coach Little League, belong to business groups, or play a musical instrument? Are you a sports fan, a gardener, or a private pilot?

You never know where the customer's hot button is, but when you find it, you're golden. Hitting the hot button can turn a five-minute cold call visit into a half-hour conversation and get you positioned to make the sale.

Sometimes, hot button clues are in plain view. I remember walking into one manager's office and spotting a copy of a Tom Clancy book, *Executive Orders*, on her desk. I had read it myself, and I asked how she liked it. She thought it was great.

She had read all of Clancy's books. I said, "So have I. He's tremendous." And we talked about Tom Clancy for five minutes. It was a fabulous way to break the ice. She responded to me on a personal level, not as salesman to customer, and when we finally settled into the presentation, we were already on good terms.

Sales people gravitate to marketing majors in college. Oriented as I was toward teaching, I majored in history and took a double minor in English and philosophy. It turned out to be an ideal background for sales, because it was really an education in people. It gave me insight into human behavior and motivations. When you study philosophy, you study psychology – the reasoning behind things. Then you couple that with history, where you study all the forces that make people do what they do. The study of English, of course, gives you a stronger command of the language.

Such a broad education trained me to be conversant in lots of areas. Later on, I expanded my knowledge through travel and reading. The more things you can talk about, the better, and you never know when they will come in handy.

You're the Expert, So Speak Like One

The most important words you say are the ones that benefit the customer. Focus on the prospect's point of view. Talk about the strengths of your company only in terms of how they can help the customer. If you bring along supporting documents or graphics, they should highlight and emphasize the benefits to the customer.

You want to speak in decisive, commanding language, using action words and the power of positive suggestion. When you project energy and conviction, you create a kind of charisma that draws people in. A good presentation should align with the prospect's goals, and those goals should be mentioned several times, and phrased to bring an affirmative answer – "You want to reach more people with your advertising, don't you"; or "You want your company to have the best retirement plan you can afford, right." A "yes" answer moves them closer to the sale.

You want potential customers to see you as an expert in your product or service. Words like "maybe," and "I'm not sure" should not be in your vocabulary. If you sound unsure of yourself, you won't inspire much confidence. Try instead to use absolutes like "never" and "always." "You should always go with a house painter who has good recommendations." Or, "In my opinion, you should never go without disability insurance."

Use the word "you" repeatedly. This applies to everybody you meet, from the frontline guard troops to the buyer in the corner office. Studies have shown that advertising with a "you" in it draws double the response. It just seems friendlier, more personal.

Let's say you're selling for a pest control company, talking about your quarterly service to get rid of mice or moles or how to keep squirrels out of the attic. You could say, "Our maintenance visits are timed to when pests usually appear. That's been effective in the past."

Think how much more convincing this would sound: "When you use our service, you can count on us to be here at the best time to handle the problem. We know these pests inside out. We'll know your specific concerns, and we'll address them promptly. We're gonna hit those moles hard for you."

Buying involves emotion. Make it work for you. And work on your phrasing.

Above all, be honest in everything you say. When you speak from the heart, with genuine conviction, clients can sense it. And when your voice is alive with enthusiasm and pep, it creates an infectious atmosphere. Enthusiasm trumps everything else. It brings them up to your level of excitement.

If you're selling something you believe is terrific, your body language and tone of voice should show it. I can get so enthusiastic about my company and our service that sometimes I have to catch myself and ask, "Am I coming across too strong?" They will say no, or maybe yes, and then I apologize. That's effective, because it is honest. I am coming clean with them.

Speaking the Lingo

Every field has its own lexicon, an insider's vocabulary. Lawyers, doctors, computer people, landlords, military people – they all use a certain terminology. If you become fluent in the lingo of a certain target company, and use it correctly, you will definitely stand out from the competition.

Read up on the unique situations and characteristics of the businesses you deal with. Go see some clients and quiz them about their operations. Learn how they work. Remember the terms and phrases they use. Then, the next time you call on someone in that business, use the same kind of language.

In my case, I focused specifically on how different companies got onto billing difficulties – what caused an account to go delinquent. I'd listen carefully to their language, and then I'd use the same verbiage when it was appropriate.

In selling collection services to an orthodontist one time, I noticed he never mentioned "braces." No, he used "appliances" to straighten teeth.

"When I put appliances on a kid, the parents agree to pay a set fee every month for two years," he said. "They pay for five months, or eight months, then they miss a payment, then two payments, then three. I am trapped. Do I take the appliances off the kid, and leave him with crooked teeth? Or do I leave them on, knowing that when I take them off I might not get paid? That kind of situation is a major problem for orthodontists when it comes to billing."

From then on, whenever I called on an orthodontist, I focused on that issue. I used the word "appliances." Was I in step with those doctors? Absolutely. Were any of my competitors saying the same thing? I'll bet the farm they weren't.

More "Inside Baseball"

You also want to pay attention to specific industries and the issues they face. I remember trying to get through to a certain funeral director. Every time I showed up, he wasn't around.

But in the interim, I stopped to see another funeral director who was already a client. I had inherited him when my territory changed. And he told me a story that I never forgot.

It was a collection that my company had made from the estate of a German man who died in the United States. This particular funeral home performed the usual services and shipped the body back to Europe. As I came to learn, in Germany the funeral director handles the whole estate settlement. Maybe with lawyers, but they handle it.

When I went back to that first funeral home and finally found the director, I used that story. I said, "We had a client who turned over a guy who died in the United States, but he was from Europe. Have you ever had one of those?" Oh yeah. "And then the body has to be shipped, and then you have difficulty getting paid." Yes again.

All of a sudden I'd get into a conversation with him. "Well," I'd say, "we know that in Germany the funeral director pays out the entire estate. We specialize in this area. We understand the unique situations that can develop. On top of that, we understand that you might be doing work for the family for years and years, settling the estate. We can help you with those kinds of collections."

Now he started thinking about different issues he gets into. I got that sale, and I pulled out that "inside baseball" every time I walked into a funeral home. When you show that you know how a business really works, you establish instant credibility. You're going to get appointments, and you're going to make sales.

Is Tuesday Okay, Or Would Wednesday Be Better?

In talking about "getting in" or "once you're in," I'm referring to either the first time to meet the prospect or when you go back on an appointment. You'll have a reasonable shot at getting some business when you go back in for a formal presentation. The trick is getting to that stage, which is why those initial encounters are so critical.

On most sales calls you've got to fight for your time. Prospects will give you 30 seconds to decide if they want to listen to you. Go on that assumption, and pack into that first half-minute the best stuff you've got. When you have a few really terrific one-liners, it's not that hard to battle for a little extra time.

When I began selling for my own company, NCO Financial Systems, I created a line that almost always bought me time. I'd say, "We market a service that our clients use to recover their own delinquent accounts in-house before using an expensive outside agency. I'd like to set up a meeting to come back and explain it to you. Is Tuesday okay, or is Wednesday better?"

The prospect knows you're going to ask for an appointment, so get that of the way as soon as possible. But so many times, a potential client would say, "Tell me more." And I'd answer, "We have this advance service – a flat fee – that our clients use prior to writing off bad debts. The service is designed to increase your cash flow, decrease your in-house billing costs, and find the truly delinquent accounts – the ones that really deserve to be in collections."

This concept intrigued people, because they had never heard of it before. They'd ask for more details. When you get into this sort of situation, you've got to be careful not to provide too much information. It's a delicate balance, because you certainly don't want to seem rude.

But you can't stand there and keep going, toe to toe. If you do, you'll end up giving them a half-presentation, and they're not ready for that. It throws you out of your rhythm. You won't be able to move logically to your conclusion.

So you have to stop yourself. Thirty to 60 seconds and that's it. It's fine if you do a little warming up, but when you get to the main point – why you are there – it's 60 seconds and then go for the appointment. And ask for it in concrete terms – tomorrow morning and the day after. When you suggest two or three options, you improve your odds.

If the prospect persists in asking questions, what do you do? I would always say, "Do you have 20 minutes right now? If you do, I can give you a very good idea about how my program works." You have to ask for that time, because they won't volunteer it, but frequently 20 minutes turn into an hour. During my whole career in sales, it has turned into an hour with no problem.

When that happens, you can give a presentation on the spot. I'd typically take 20 minutes to lay out most of my plan, then glance at my watch and say, "I could keep going here, but I don't want to abuse your time. I really appreciate how much time you've given me already." If they said, "It's okay, keep going," I could move into the close.

Avoiding 'Unqualified' Presentations

As a rookie cold caller, you need to watch for another common pitfall. When you're talking with a prospect about coming back for a meeting, always ask if anyone else should be there to hear it. You want to bring all the players together. Many sales are lost due to what's called an unqualified presentation, meaning that not everyone necessary to make a decision is in the room.

If you make a pitch to one half of a two-person partnership, for example, you'll find yourself playing catch up, calling back and following up. You will be relying on partner number one to transmit information about you, your company, and your product to partner number two. And you know how that goes. "Oh, by the way, Tom, there was a guy in here this morning selling such and such. Do you want to do it?" Tom asks how much is costs, and then says, "Nah, we don't need to spend that money right now," knowing nothing about what you had so carefully explained.

But what if you have already secured an appointment, and discover afterwards that the other decision-makers won't be around that day? This is a ticklish situation. You want to want to jump on that appointment, because you're excited about it, but you know what's going to happen. At best, you'll have to come back and repeat the presentation, and that's a poor use of your time.

So you have to back off and try to reschedule the meeting. It's awkward, because you have only known the prospect for five minutes, and there you are asking to switch an appointment you just made. You might feel a little foolish doing that. Don't let that bother you, because any reasonable person will understand. Explain the situation and arrange a more fitting date, and leave by thanking the prospect for being flexible.

In the Customer's Shoes

The most successful sales people I know have a sixth sense when it comes to working with potential clients. It colors the whole transaction, from start to finish. They create empathy with the customer, an emotional link. It comes through in the way they show respect for the prospect's time and job pressures, or in the tone of voice they use. It's not an easy quality to define, but I think of it as sensitivity.

It's a vital trait for anybody in selling. Whenever I interview candidates for a sales job, I always look for parts of their story that show sensitivity. After they've told me about some big achievement in their life, I usually ask, "Where do you get your drive from?" Invariably, they mention a parent or a relative. Sometimes they become a little sentimental, talking about someone who's meant a lot to them. Their eyes get a little moist. Their voice grows softer. If they are married with children, I'll ask, "How do you like being a father or mother?" Or I'll say, "Tell me about your greatest sale." If they get all excited about it, that is sensitivity.

During the interview, I watch for my own gut reaction to the candidate. Does he or she make me feel comfortable, or inspire confidence, or seem genuine? Would *I* buy from this person? Beyond the "given" ingredients of sales professionalism – honesty, good grooming, friendliness – there's a whole assortment of intangibles that I look for.

I want someone who is optimistic and enthusiastic, a person with good listening skills and the ability to think analytically. But I also want someone who projects a sense of confidence, and who knows when to be assertive and when to soft-pedal it. These "people skills," when you assemble them into a package, give me a good indication if a candidate has the kind of sensitivity to succeed.

Your sensitivity level depends a lot on your upbringing and life experiences. Maybe you studied psychology in school and have extra insight into the way people think and behave. But for the sake of cold calling, you can get the right idea by always putting yourself in the customer's corner. When you can genuinely identify with the customer, you'll automatically keep his best interests in mind, and the customer will know it.

But sensitivity is more than that. It involves tact, consideration, nuance. It's like intuition – it tells you when to say something and how to say it. So I don't mean sensitivity in being mushy, but also in enthusiasm. The person has to feel it. Whether you're meeting a prospect for the first time, or going back later, sensitivity plays a big role in locking up a deal.

Creating Empathy: A Case Study

I remember a presentation I did one time to a mid-size insurance company in the Deep South. I walked into a boardroom to face eight people. They were at the tail end of a marathon session of interviewing companies like mine. It had gone on for two days. I was the fifth and final presenter.

I noticed immediately that they had their suit jackets off, and the first thing I said was, "Do mind if I take my jacket off, too?" I could tell that these were the kind of people who wouldn't object. Of course, they said, go right ahead. It's not that I was hot; I just wanted us to be on the same comfort level. It would take some of the stiffness out of the meeting and help establish a friendlier tone.

These guys had been listening to presentations for hours that day. I understood that they might be a little bored by now, so I tried to commiserate with them. Before I got down to business, I looked at them and said with a laugh, "Aren't you getting sick of this?" They laughed too and said, yes, they were kind of spent.

"Why don't we wrap this up right now," I said, "and go have a beer?" That went over great. They laughed again. "Everybody you have seen is interested in your business. We all want it," I said. "I don't know how far anybody else came to get here, but I came down from Philadelphia, and I have to get back tonight, because I have a graduation to go to." That helped me become real to them. I wasn't just some sales dude. I was a family man just like them, with kids and dogs and a basketball hoop on the driveway.

Then I went on. "I feel a little at a disadvantage here, because I don't know how to tailor my remarks to you. You're all from different parts of the company – finance, credit, info-tech, operations, customer service. I want to make this broad enough so you all can understand how my company works, but not too narrow to one person, because various departments will be making the decision.

"Please bear with me if I'm not addressing what you want to hear," I said, "and interrupt me at any time with questions. If I can answer them I will, and if I can't I will get the answers." That was very effective. They could see that I was in tough spot, and they seemed sympathetic. The closing started right there.

This wasn't even my account. I was pinch-hitting that day for a sales rep named John. "I'm not intimate with your situation," I admitted before I launched into my presentation, " because I haven't been talking to you like John has been. But his wife just had a baby. That's why he can't be here. And by the way, they haven't named the baby yet. But if anyone here is going to sign the contract, John said he'd name the baby after you."

That drew a hearty laugh, and all but put the deal under lock and key. This company became a client a couple of days later. Did we make the sale because I had persuaded them that we could deliver what I promised? Sure. But it didn't hurt that I had first broken the ice with honesty and humor.

Right from the beginning we had a positive rapport. I credit to that sensitivity, because I'd been able to read the mood in the room, and then mesh with it. These were good people, but they were tired. The last thing they needed was another overly sober and serious presentation.

A bit of levity was all it took to wake them up and get them to pay attention. They appreciated my concern for their tedious selection process. It conveyed a sense that I was interested in them personally, not just in making a sale. There was nothing phony about this. I was just being myself, and I did empathize with them. Some sales reps get so slick that they forget to be nice, regular guys, but that's what sells. I knew we could do a fine job for them, and I made that clear. It ended up as a win-win situation, and that's the glue that creates repeat business and good word of mouth.

Getting to "Yes"

Objections, objections – most prospects will voice at least one. If you've done your homework before the call, you should be able to anticipate resistance points.

- If you expect price to be the primary hurdle, for example, you've got to explain why your product or service costs more than brand X. If you don't, the prospect will never know. So hit the price issue head-on. Target your remarks to deal with that, before the prospect has to raise the question.

- Your presentation should be aligned with the prospect's goals, and you should mention them more than once. And as you mention them, talk about how your product can help the customer achieve those goals. Describe your advantages, what makes your product different. How it can solve their problems and make their lives easier. You have to give people a reason to buy. Then make sure your explanation is crystal clear.

- Each time you encounter an objection, try to determine its root cause. Is the person objecting out of sheer habit, out of loyalty to the current supplier, or out of stubbornness? If the prospect mentions an objection once and never again, it might be just a smokescreen. If he mentions it several times, however, your might be running into a genuine blockade. It might be a deal killer. But then again, it might be a negotiable point.

- To handle an objection successfully, you need to know the specific facts about the situation. Ask the prospect, what is it about brand X that's so much better? When comparing products or services, you need to deal in tangible terms. Then you can base your argument on facts.

Market Research

In the days when I was selling advertising on phone book covers, I always did some market research before going in somewhere. I wanted to understand the companies I called on. Then I married up my research – the size and composition of the market, for example – with figures from the government or a trade association. With the right information I could break it down to the consumer level, and bring that home to the owner or president of a company.

Walking into auto parts stores, I already knew that the average family spent $900 a year on tires, seat covers, wax, and the like. If the town had 10,000 families, they represented a total market of $9 million. If the town had ten auto parts places, $9 million broke down to average-store sales of $900,000.

This was good ammunition. And because I often cited "the government" as the source, my information carried a gloss of authority. Armed with that set of figures, I could fight back against various objections, from an initial reluctance to set an appointment to a stumbling block that popped up during a presentation. I pulled out those facts as needed, to reinforce my main argument – namely, that my program could help the prospect beat the average store or increase market share.

Sometimes you have to go that far to get an appointment. You can't get past every objection, of course, but when you have the facts on your side you can rescue plenty of deals.

Tracking Down Industry Intelligence

Industry information is easy to collect. Almost every conceivable slice of the economy has an association or "council" that collects and disseminates data. Many are headquartered in Washington, D.C. or New York. Some are huge, like the American Medical Association and the American Bar Association. Others are rather obscure, like the Weed Science Society of America and the Architectural Spray Coaters Association.

There are at least 7,000 such groups, and they're all listed and described in one place, a massive directory called the National Trade and Professional Associations of the United States. It's publishing annually by Columbia Books (888-265-0600). These trade groups are treasure troves of information you can use in selling. Columbia Books also publishes the National Directory of Corporate Public Affairs, useful when you need facts on a specific company.

By mining these industry groups for effective facts and figures, you'll be able to zero in on prospects with more confidence. You'll be able to sell the way I sold advertising. That approach can work in all kinds of fields, from funeral homes and cleaning services to travel agencies, sporting goods stores, insurance firms, and even pizza places.

Countering objections and getting appointments isn't brain surgery. But you've got to have the facts at your fingertips, and organized for maximum impact. You have to be ready with lines that can turn rejection into success.

Never Take No for an Answer

Imagine that you have a lawn-care business, and you're trying to build up your customer base. If you cold call – just go through a neighborhood knocking on doors some Saturday morning – a prospect might say, "I already have a lawn service."

How do you respond to that? Here's what I'd say: "I have a customer on your street that I do every Thursday, so the lawn is looking good for the weekend. And since I'm here already, I'd like to do your lawn. I'll charge you $5 less than you're paying now, because I'd be saving on travel time." Tell your customer that you have a vision – "I want to do everybody in the neighborhood."

The customer protests, "But I like the other guy." You don't want to offend or confront. I'd come back with this: "I understand, but I'm a nice guy, too. All I want is a chance. Matter of fact, we'll do the first mowing free of charge, and then you can decide. If you'd like, I can give you some references."

Or you could ask, "Does the other guy plow? He might not, but I plow, and I'm looking for customers I can service all year. If it snows more than four inches, I will be here automatically. I want to be your yard guy for all seasons, a one-stop solution for anything. Wouldn't that keep everything simpler?"

You know it will. What busy homeowner has the time to worry about a slew of people coming to handle lawn fertilization, mowing, shrub planting, and snow removal? This is all part of getting in tune with customers – knowing their concerns, anticipating their objections, and developing solutions.

When springtime comes, drop off fliers about mulching. You knock on doors and say, "I've already ordered 25 yards of mulch to do three of your neighbors' yards, and I'd like to add another ten yards to mulch yours, since I'm already here."

You might not get that customer on the first go-round, but maybe on the third or fourth try you will. You've got to get out in front of people and talk, because they don't know who you are.

If you're running a company, you can't wait for the phone to ring. If you're a gutter-repair man, or a roofer, or a guy who does car detailing, you can't afford to sit around waiting for business to walk in. So if you're doing one roof, get your sign up and go canvas the neighborhood. Knock on doors and say, "Since I'm already working for your neighbor's place, I'd like to do any roofing work you need. Do you have any leaks?"

Body Language: Watching for Buying Signals

When you're delivering a dynamite presentation, two sales should be taking place. You're selling the prospect, obviously, but you also should be reselling yourself on your own company. Remember, the customer has to buy you before he will buy your product.

I've already talked about the importance of a professional appearance – your grooming, your attire, and your overall polish. But now other things come under scrutiny – your mannerisms, your eye contact, your attitude. Do you seem sincere? Do you come across as credible? Are you trustworthy? Sometimes I've been able to mentally float outside my body and watch myself in action. Half my brain would be giving the presentation, and the other half would be checking out my performance.

I'd always watch my body language. How was my posture? If you stand tall and sit up straight, you project confidence. Did I seem natural and relaxed? You want people to like you, and if you seem officious, it puts up walls. Was I smiling and nodding and maintaining good eye contact?

In any group of two or more, I've always found it best to look each person in the eye for about five seconds, and then shift to someone else. You can work a room from front to back, and then start over. It removes some of the nervousness if you pretend you're talking to one person at a time, instead of the whole group.

Most of all, was my body language consistent with my verbal language? If there was a disconnect, I would came across as insincere. Was my smile natural and genuine? With a real smile, the eyes crinkle and the eyebrows go up. A smile from the nose down looks phony. The customer wouldn't trust me and wouldn't buy.

Body Language 101

Never lean back in a chair – it looks like you're about to pass judgment. Similarly, if you stand with your hands on your hips, it conveys an air of condescension. If you put your hands on your pockets, you might seem nervous, especially if you jingle keys or coins. Hands crossed in front of you – the "fig leaf" stance – makes you look timid, while hands behind the back – at "parade rest" – makes it seem like you have no energy. Arms crossed? A definite no-no. That's a signal of withdrawal and detachment. Your arms should be relaxed and hanging down at your sides.

Meanwhile, I'd also be assessing the body language on the other side of the table. If you have to ask someone a sticky question – sticky because the answer will make them uncomfortable, or because they don't know the answer – you will see them fold their arms, cross their legs, and sit back from the table. You have to back off yourself from the table and get them to unfold, because you're not going to sell them when a barrier is up.

I would often be quite up-front and say, "Gee, I'm sorry I asked you that question. I'm not here to hurt you, and if I have offended in any way, I apologize. It's just that I have to know certain things about your business, so I can help you." At other times, I'd just write off that whole line of questioning, and begin talking about something else. And little by little, they would begin to relax again.

Asking for the Sale

There are certain "windows" within the sales process when you can close the deal. Watch for signals that the prospect is ready to buy from you.

If they pick up your literature and start to flip through it, if they suggest ways to handle this thing or that, you're getting a buying signal and you can close. Now, closing is uncomfortable for many sales people. By some estimates, in fact, 60 percent of sales folks, at the end of a presentation, never actually ask for the sale. Maybe they're timid, or they don't want to look pushy.

That's the wall they are hitting. They assume their product or service will somehow sell itself, that the customer will simply say, "Okay, I'll buy it." But what's the point of all your preparation, the entire cold calling process, if you fail to ask for someone's business? After all, they expect you to do it. It need not be a big hang-up.

The defining moment in any sale comes with the closing question. Most sales reps have only one of them. That's fine, especially if it's a gem. You probably have a favorite closing question already, but if you're uncertain about how to phrase it, ask your associates, particularly the veterans, what sort of language they find effective. Or maybe your manager can suggest something.

One of the greatest closing questions I've ever heard was taught to me on my very first sales job, when I was selling space ads. At the end of the presentation I'd ask, "Do you have a logo, or would you like to see what our art department can come up with?" That's a terrific line, and I'm sure it was put together by some brilliant sales minds.

If I had done a great job during the presentation, it was the perfect close. First off, it was subtle – it almost sounds as if you're volunteering to do someone a favor. It was non-threatening, it got the prospect thinking, and it was easy to ask. It didn't always work, but it came through often enough for me that I never used anything else during my year in the world of advertising sales.

If you're nervous about moving in directly for the close, try easing in with some non-threatening questions. What is your mailing address? Do you have a direct phone line so my people can always reach you? You might ask about operational issues, logistics, and other hard-core stuff pertaining to their business, things that might eventually involve your company. This is all very solid ground, and very benign.

Then ask how the deal would work. In my business, it involves settlement criteria. In going after a delinquent account, for example, what recovery percentage can we "settle to" without getting clearance from the client? I have to know. I'll write down that sort of information so I can forward it to my operations people, the ones who will actually be doing the work.

There have been times when, before we'd gotten started –before I even had a signed contract – I've called our ops people and had them talk to my prospect. I would say, "Now, you two are going to shake hands over the phone." It was a way of insinuating the sale, winning favor and confidence by small degrees.

Sometimes I do the same thing with the computer people. Past performance being the best indicator of future behavior, I know that when computer people are involved, they are so busy that a week can pass without a response. I try to head off those problems right away. I have the computer person in my office talk to the computer person in their office, because we need to do computer work before we can get started.

Quick Tip 🏃

Sign Here, Please

Easing into a close is basically how a lot of life-insurance sales agents operate. They call it "building out the contract." They start filling out the application as the presentation goes along. When it's completed, they say, "Okay, that's everything. I just need your signature right here." The whole deal has suddenly become more tangible, and that puts a lot of sales over the top.

My approach is essentially the same, although with a few semantic distinctions. I don't always call it a contract, although it is one. And I never say "sign here," because in our legalistic culture business people are understandably cautious about signing anything. I've always tried to make it sound more casual – "I just need your okay on the bottom of the agreement, right by the X." It seems less intimidating.

That's closing, because you are going on the assumptive – not *if* you are going to do business, but how and when.

I know what you're thinking: What about the lawyers? Lawyers are the biggest deal-killers around. When prospects tell you that their lawyers have to review a contract first, how should you fight back?

I suggest you be very understanding. "Fine, I can appreciate that," I'd always say. "The problem is, when these things land on a lawyer's desk, they often sit for two or three months. What can we do to expedite this, so we can get started before your lawyer sees it? This contract has been blessed by hundreds of lawyers already – there's nothing tricky or offensive in it. It's very straightforward."

I try to maintain the momentum. I don't want the sale to get unsold while we're waiting for a lawyer to get around to it. I'll propose any ideas I can think of to move the sale ahead.

Think Positive

Confidence – that's the juice that keeps you going in sales. Confidence not only in your product or service, but confidence in yourself. You have real value – remember that. It will boost your attitude.

In my talks on selling, I sometimes use the example of Joe Montana, who quarterbacked the San Francisco 49ers for many years. He was one of the all-time greats. He led some of the most electrifying two-minute drives I've ever seen. If the 49ers were down five points with two minutes left on the clock, do you think there was any doubt in Montana's mind that he was going prevail? I loved watching him pick apart a defense and march down the field to win in the final seconds. He had great instincts. If anyone could pull it out, it was Joe Montana.

Or look at Joe Namath back in 1969, when he made the bold prediction that his upstart New York Jets were going to win the Super Bowl. Who was this kid with the hair sticking out the back of his helmet? He was going to beat Johnny Unitas and the Baltimore Colts? People laughed. Unitas was a god in football. But when the dust settled that night in the Miami, it was Jets 16, Colts 7.

That's the attitude you've got to have in selling. You've got to believe in yourself. Who do you want to be when you're going for a sale and the odds are long against you? Do you want to be the Joe Montana of who you are? If you have half the self-confidence of a guy like that, believe me, you're going to be wealthy. You're going to have the money to do whatever you want. You'll have freedom.

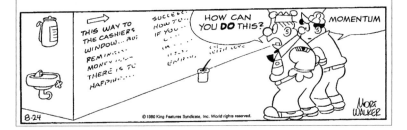

CHAPTER 6

The Power of Persistence

Chapter overview:

- Why following up is crucial to your success.

- How to rescue a lost sale by maintaining contact with the customer.

- Why potential customers won't always see you immediately, but tactful pursuit will win an appointment.

- How to cement the 'sale after the sale' by adding value and going the extra mile.

- How to keep yourself in front of customers with small tokens of appreciation.

- How follow-up took a sales rep from worst to first.

- Why revisiting the site of a sales 'defeat' can lead to unexpected business.

- Why it's vital to treat prospects with respect. Good manners never go out of style.

- How to lock up referrals and keep them coming.

I could not possibly overstate the importance of the follow-up in cold call sales work. Tenacity and staying power are essential to your success. A lot of folks make the sales call, get shot down, and immediately punt. I never give up, even if the sale goes to a competitor. I've landed some of my best clients because I refused to quit.

When you want something, follow up relentlessly. If you don't demonstrate to people that you really want their business, you probably won't get it. You will forfeit a lot of business by caving in early.

True story: Year ago, when I was selling advertising in Connecticut, I had a large number of Greek-American customers who owned pizza restaurants. They all seemed to know each other, and I steadily mined them for contacts and introductions. One time, a pizza man I knew in Hartford referred me to another Greek pizza guy in Waterbury. His name was Gus.

The next time I was in Waterbury, I walked into this good-sized pizzeria around lunchtime and asked for Gus. From behind the counter a man said, "He's not here. What can I do for you?" I replied, "No, that's okay. I have to talk to Gus. It's kind of personal."

He wanted to know what it was all about. "I'll tell Gus," he promised. I stood my ground – "No, thanks. When will he be back?" The guy paused for a second. "Around two o'clock," he said.

Now, there was no way. I knew Gus was there. It was noontime and the place was packed. Maybe he's on a run to the bank, I thought.

At three o'clock, I returned. The same guy told me that Gus wasn't back yet. He kept asking, "What is this about? You can trust me – I'll tell him." Again, I said I could only speak directly to Gus himself. "He might be here at five," the fellow offered. I went back in at six o'clock, and the same guy was still there, bustling around behind the counter, making things happen. "Gus still isn't back," he said.

By now the act was getting old. "I sure wish Gus were here," I told him. "I really have to talk to him. So-and-so in Hartford sent me to see him." That made him stop. He checked me over carefully and finally admitted, "Okay, I'm Gus." I was sort of laughing now. "I know you are," I told him. "You're the only guy here who's really busting his ass. You have to be Gus."

He grinned and gave me a friendly poke – it was like a 10-second warm up. Then I told him what I was selling and used my references – all the Greek restaurants in my customer base. Gus looked interested. He was wearing his apron, wiping off his hands with it as we walked back to the storage room. I gave him a presentation on top of a stack of cases of tomato sauce. When I left that night, I had a new account.

I could have given up on this place after the first or second visit, but it paid off to go back that third time. It was a $400 sale, and with my 45-percent commission, it put $180 in my pocket. That's how I built up my customer base, one by one, never relenting on a potential sale. On the way out, Gus gave me a pizza and the names of a few other people who might like to hear about my program.

Follow Up!

Tell yourself that your follow-up is the best in the business. It doesn't matter if that's not true, as long as you believe it – and act on it. You might have to follow up on a prospect a dozen times before getting either the appointment or the sale. I've been known to pursue a potential customer for several years. Other times, it's just a matter of hammering away over the course of a single day, like with Gus.

Quick Tip 🏃

Proper Etiquette

You don't want to make a pest of yourself – that breeds resentment. There's a fine line between being persistent and being obnoxious. Smart follow-up requires tact, intelligence, and a sense of timing. You can be persistent without being offensive.

I even made it a practice to go back to people who had bought from a competitor. I knew who they were, because I kept a ledger with the names of everyone I'd seen. At NCO Group, as our business became national in scope, I started calling on potential clients all over the country, sometimes in tandem with one of our local sales reps.

I had a database, geographically categorized, listing all the people who had turned us down. The next time I was in Chicago, or Denver, or San Diego, I'd call one or two of them and ask if I could stop by. I just wanted to find out where we had gone wrong. Sometimes we'd have dinner together, and I'd discover that the situation had changed – receivables had suddenly become urgent, or another collection agency was not working out. When that happened, those once-defunct relationships often sprang back to life.

My associate Mark Macrone also thrives on revisiting the site of a defeat. "I've never been ignorant or rude to people who shoot me down. I look at it like, I'm walking into their place of business, when they're in the middle of their business," he says. "If you had sales people standing at your door, being pushy, you might be in a bad mood, too. So I've never been pushy or rude, and that way I could go back. Maybe I got nowhere today, but next week I'm going to stop in there again.

"I don't give up," Mark adds. "There's turnover in business. You walk in a door today, and Mary is the office manager. But six months later, when somebody new has the job, you have a fresh chance to make a sale. That's the stuff we depend on. If you caught somebody in a bad mood on Monday, and they didn't like your tie and threw you out, you might get a totally different reaction on Tuesday."

Follow-up Takes Rep from Worst to First

A salesman named Roger – true story – was the sad sack of the whole sales force. He always finished dead last, and his job was hanging like a loose tooth.

Roger was asked to attend the national sales meeting, the big awards deal. Normally, he wouldn't have been invited, but the company had a particularly nasty motive. After all the prizes and accolades had been handed out, he was called up on stage in front of everyone and introduced as the worst salesman the company ever had – bar none.

It was utter humiliation. After that, I imagine, Roger could have jumped off a bridge. But out of this negative came a positive. The guy dug in. He actually went back and visited all the people he had presented to in the previous year. He asked them, "Why didn't you buy from me? Can you help me out here? I'm trying to get better."

Without the pressure of a sales situation, people were candid. They told him exactly why they hadn't bought. Armed with this new intelligence, Roger was able to turn around and fix the problem areas. People who had rejected him at first became his customers. And the following year, at the awards banquet, he was called back up on stage again, only this time he was honored as the top sales person in the company.

Just because someone doesn't buy from you today does not mean they won't buy from you down the road. That's why follow-up is so critical. You never know what might happen, even after a deal is lost or a customer turns sud-

denly cold. Inactive accounts can be reactivated in a minute. We're talking about elbow grease, and that's why most
sales reps don't do it. If you do, you'll be way ahead of your
competition.

When You Detect a Need, Stay on the Offensive

Some sales trainers advise that you give up on a "prospect" if you haven't gotten anywhere after three attempts
to score an appointment. My own advice: don't give up, if
there is even a glimmer of hope.

Remember, customers and prospects buy when they
are ready to, not when you need to make a sale. If you get
shot down in April, you might have different luck in June
– but you have to be there. So follow up where you have a
fighting chance, where you sense that a need exists.

In the early days of NCO Financial, I set my sights on
a big banking institution based in Pennsylvania, our home
state. They were looking for help in receivables management, and I worked hard to earn us a spot on the final list
of candidates. I got to know all the key players; I understood their demands. At the appointed time, my partner
and I went in and gave a major presentation before a group
of their executives.

Unfortunately, they picked three other companies.
They liked us, they said, but they thought they would bury
us. They thought the business volume would overwhelm
us.

I wasn't about to just walk away. I had invested a lot of
time in this deal. It's true that we were a small company.
Our revenues that year came in at just under $13 million.
But we never considered ourselves small, because if you
think you're small, you are small. We always tried to act
like a large company, because we believed that someday
we'd be one. By thinking big, we had already landed some
Fortune 500 clients.

After losing that sale I could have done the obvious thing – put a tickler in my files to call them again in 18 months. The contract ran for two years. Instead, I decided to stay right on top of it.

A week later I phoned my main contact at the company, "Karen." We were on friendly terms. I asked if she would mind if I kept in touch, and she said, "Of course not – please do." She wasn't just being nice. Karen knew that sometimes contracts go bad, for whatever reason. I said, "Great, I'll call you in a month." Then I stuck a note in my Daytimer to call her in three weeks.

As it turned out, one of the three companies that had beaten us out was already bombing. It had missed an early deadline for some data processing work, and the customer wasn't happy. In fact, they were thinking about bringing in somebody else.

Three weeks to the day after I'd spoken with Karen, I called back at seven-thirty in the morning. I knew she liked to come in early and make the coffee herself. When she picked up, I said, "Hi, Karen. It's Chuck. How are you? I told you I'd call back."

Her tone suddenly was like a tonic. "Chuck!" she said. "It's amazing you should call. One of the vendors we chose is not stepping up to the plate. The computer people didn't do the work we needed, and now we're worried."

I asked hopefully, "Do you think there might be a chance for us?" Karen was encouraging. "Your phone call is timely," she said. "We're having a meeting this afternoon to figure out what to do. Why don't you call me in the morning."

The next day, I called four times before I reached her. When I did, she had great news – "Chuck," she said, "you're in." I couldn't believe it. I ran around the office like a crazy man, spreading the news. It was a tremendous rush. The moral of the story: never quit on a sale, even after you've lost it, because it's not over. It's not over until you think it's over.

That is following up. I didn't wait four weeks to call; I called in three. She was glad that I did. I was showing her the commitment we had, that we really wanted that business, and our conviction that we could handle it. Today, this is one of the largest contracts we have. We've evolved right along with them, together running some leading edge projects in the field of receivables management.

Keeping Yourself in Front of the Customer

In sales the old saying applies: "Out of sight, out of mind." To keep hope alive, you've got to stay visible to potential customers. Make sure they know you're still there.

And do it with some style. Whenever you follow up with someone you've already talked to, create a reason for the call. Give them something free – a newsletter, a postcard, a pertinent report. If you've read an article that is relevant to their business, make a copy and send it over. That shows thoughtfulness and good manners, two things in short supply these days. But people still appreciate being treated well, regardless of the sad state of manners in our culture.

Good manners give you an edge, and sending something is a great way to stay in touch. You do all this either before the sale or afterwards. Attach a business card, and write a little note on it, so they will remember meeting you. Be sure to include a toll-free number, an e-mail address, or a response card with prepaid postage. Make it easy for the person to contact you.

Adding Value: The Sale After the Sale

Whenever there's turnover at the top of a billing department, I go in and meet the new person to resell him or her on our company. They probably don't know who we are, so I give a whole presentation. If they haven't been given the reports on our work, I'll say, "I'm going to run them off right now. Can I use your phone?" I call my office, get someone to run them off, and have them delivered overnight. If I'm still in town, I'll go back the next day and make sure everything is clear. Do I separate myself from the competition? You bet.

Quick Tip 🏃

How Are We Doing?

After a sale takes place, a month or two later, contact the customer. Make sure everything is cool. It's a way of building on the trust you've already established.

I'll call and ask how things are going. Are there any issues I can address for you right now, to make the business relationship more efficient? Are my people responsive? Is customer service getting back to you quickly? If I can get them to say "Yes, your people are doing fine," that's the sale after the sale. They have affirmed that we're doing a good job.

There are more than 6,000 collection agencies out there, and a lot of companies get five or six calls a week from them. You have to defend your turf, and I've always tried to do it by adding value to a sale. After the sale is consummated, I volunteer to run seminars for a client's in-house bill collectors. I teach them what to say on the phone, how to get results. I even hold meetings on attitude and morale. I do all sorts of extra things.

Then it becomes bigger. The relationship goes beyond just collecting money; we get involved in making the business run smoother. And that's the vision for my company – what do we do next? What other products and services can we sell to a client, now that we're already in the family? I've always dedicated a lot of follow-up effort to expanding business within our existing base. It is fertile ground.

The Diplomatic Touch

Even folks who don't like cold callers don't always begrudge a follow-up call, as long as you make it with tact and deference. One of my clients, for example, was the comptroller of a large women's clothing store in center-city Philadelphia. He hated cold calling sales people.

After I got to know him, we talked about this. He thought it was rude to assume you could just walk in and take someone's time. He instructed his secretary to get the salesman's card and set up an appointment, but sometimes he could overhear sales reps outside his office, literally arguing with the secretary for a minute of his time. He never let in people like that.

At the same time, he recognized that sales folks sometimes offered things he needed, and that they had to somehow get in the door. Many times he'd turn them away, but if they came back politely and didn't drone on, he'd make time.

He told me about a large number of personal computers he had purchased. The sale started with a cold call, but it took a while. The computer rep knew he had found a need. If you find that, you've got to peck away at it, but with patience.

The comptroller would tell the computer guy not to call for two weeks, and he would call back two weeks to the day. "He must have called me a hundred times before we bought all these PCs," my client said. "On average, if a person can walk in, put a bug in your ear and leave, he is better off than trying too hard. You got to be smart enough to know what you're supposed to do."

When I interview sales reps for a job, I look for that kind of intelligence, blended with a high desire to succeed. I want someone who can organize his thoughts and give me his or her work history – a person who is selling me in the interview. He's got to be telling me stories about the greatest sales he ever made, and I shouldn't have to ask for them. We're talking about two street guys who wear out their shoes, who go out when it rains and snows, versus somebody who goes in the office and does telemarketing.

And I look for follow-up. He'd better be calling me after the interview, because if he doesn't follow up with me about a job, he won't follow up on a sales call. The people you need should not require follow-up. If they do, you can't afford to have them around.

Case Study: Reaching the Decision Maker

In the early 1990s, I landed a hospital in the Philadelphia area as a client for a test program. I wanted to talk with the comptroller, the top guy on the financial side, because I had some ideas to improve their receivables management, but the lower-level people kept pushing me away from him. The division manager I was working with would never let me meet him.

We ran some great test programs for this hospital. The numbers were strong. But I was never able to jump to the next level and meet the comptroller, who had the authority to implement the whole program. The middle manager ran his little fiefdom like a tin-pot dictator.

Then one day I got word through the grapevine that the comptroller was gone. He had moved on to Wilmington, Delaware, and become chief financial officer for a 1,200-bed hospital. This was my chance. I ran off the status reports on our work for the Philadelphia hospital, his previous place, because I figured he had never seen them. Then I went down and cold called him.

I got there at three o'clock, and an assistant told me he'd be in a meeting for a couple of hours. I stayed right there, had some coffee. I had my guns loaded, and I was ready when I went back in at five o'clock. The secretaries had all gone. As we shook hands, he said, "Yeah, I know who you are."

I showed him the status reports, the results of our tests in Philadelphia. He was blown away. "This is fantastic," he said. "How come I never saw these?" I explained that it wasn't for lack of trying – I had been dealing with a brain-dead middle manager in the patient-accounts division. I said there was a pecking order that made it hard for someone like me to show this to the people responsible for the bottom line. If I had gone over the head of my primary contact, he'd have been angry.

Well, we got into a conversation about what I could do for him at his new hospital. I said, "You are called every day by collection agencies trying to get your business. But the real issue is, which accounts really deserve to go into collections." I told him I had a program that could clean up many receivables before they went bad.

"Let's look at the constants," I said, trying to use deductive reasoning. "One, patients don't even open your statements after 90 days. They already know they owe you, so they just pile them up on the desk. Two, admissions clerks can transpose a number, or fail to get all the information." He nodded his head as I went along. "Three, there are never enough full-time employees in the billing department – never. Four, insurance companies have policies to deliberately slow down payments. If they find some tiny thing wrong, they will reject the claim or pull it off for review. And five, the amount you have to reserve against bad debt rises every year, and you're not realizing that much more money, net, after the collection fees."

I got agreement on all those points. Then I said "Let's see what kind of methods and strategies I can come up with, because we have a tremendous system in our company, a lot of horsepower, to reach people who owe you money. Let's see what I can do for you prior to charging off accounts."

This conversation went on for days. I would call at six at night and he'd answer the phone. Finally, he consented. We started testing a few things, and the tests were done right. We anticipated the problems and factored them into our calculations. We tested and tested and built up trust over two years. Each time he'd give us a little bit more. It got to the stage where I had to bring in my partner, Mike, because it was growing into a major operation. The ops people had to be attuned to the intricacies of the job.

It's very refreshing when I can get a client to sit down with our operations specialists. You want to get these deals straight, in face-to-face meetings, where you can thrash out the problems and solutions. My job as salesman in that situation is to take the egos out of the equation, and keep attention focused on the ultimate objective.

Today we do a lot of work for that hospital. Our involvement with their billing operation is more important than ever in this era of increased outpatient activity and cost pressure on delivery of medical services. And we never would have gotten that business if I hadn't taken the initiative to follow up with that comptroller after he changed jobs.

To me, following up is as normal and essential a part of the sales cycle as breathing. It should be for you, too. As I've said before, we're not messing around here. If you are serious about making good money, never give up on a sale without a fight.

Locking Up Leads and Referrals

At the beginning of this chapter, I described my persistence in getting through to Gus, the pizzeria owner. I scored that as a perfect sale, because not only did I get his business, I also got some excellent referrals. Those in turn led to additional sales, which I then leveraged into still more referrals. When you're able to coax a few referrals out of each one of your customers, you're laying the groundwork for exponential growth.

I've always been fanatical about asking for referrals, because there's no surer way of expanding your business. If you're not aggressively pursuing referrals, you never know how many opportunities you're missing. For a long time I kept a sign on my dashboard – "Referrals." After a while I didn't need that little reminder; asking for referrals became automatic. If you haven't asked for a referral after you've been dealing with a customer, go back in and ask for the names of two or three other people. Just ask, "Who else do you think could benefit from what I have to offer?"

Quick Tip 🏃

Get Letters of Recommendation

When I got into the collections industry, I went so far as to ask my clients to write up letters of recommendation, because credibility is a big issue in that business. Nobody seemed to mind doing it, particularly if I could provide a letter from someone else as an example. So they would write it up, on their letterhead stationery, and give me a few names. Now I not only had some new people to go see, but I had a fresh shot of fuel to carry me for a few days.

Most sales reps wait until they've converted a prospect to a customer before asking for referrals, if they ask for them at all. One of the great advantages of cold calling is that you can follow up even a failed call by trying to get a lead or two. It's a natural outgrowth of the "multiplier effect." When you meet people meet face to face, they get a chance to see what sort of person you are. If they like you, and you seem trustworthy, they're more likely to turn you on to some of their friends, neighbors, and business acquaintances.

Referrals Flow Just from 'Being There

My associate Mark Macrone, one of the savviest sales guys I know, has always taken advantage of "being there" to solicit leads.

Here's how he puts it: "If you're not cold calling, you're using teleselling, or direct mail, or trade shows," he says. "But when you're in someone's office, you have an inherent edge. I can walk into a doctor's office, and if I get in front of Mary, the office manager, chances are she knows the other office managers. I'll say, 'Mary, do you know the person who handles the cardiology group across the corridor?' Sally would be the office manager there. So I'll ask, 'Do you mind if I told her I was just in here?' Mary would have no problem with that. You'd find that she would give you the referral.

"These people have monthly meetings," Mark says, "where the office managers get together to share intelligence. And that to me has always been one of biggest advantages of cold calling – the networking and referrals, which creates a lot of our business. Whenever I get in front of somebody, they're going to give me a lot more information than if I just talk to them on the phone.

"If I don't have personal contact with people," he says, "I'm not going to get good referrals from them. I get talking to people and I might suddenly discover that there's a need for something totally different than what I went in there for. I can end up getting a sale from a cold call like that. If I'd called on the phone, they would have hung up on me as soon as I identified myself."

Another one of our top sales reps, Tim Kleppick, has capitalized on the same advantage. "If you stop in to see someone who's not interested, your odds of getting a referral are much greater, because you've got two personalities who might click," he says. "Even if they're not going to buy, you can establish some common ground in conversation. Then when you ask for a referral, you're not just a sales person to them. You're a regular guy or gal who has to deal with the same traffic in the morning. They're more willing to help. A manager at Doctor White's office is going to say, 'You might want to try Allison in Doctor Smith's practice – I know her.' Referrals just come easier, because you get to know the people."

The Care and Feeding of Good Referrals

A strong referral is like gold buried in shallow ground. You don't need a mineshaft to reach it, just a shovel. It's probably the second most coveted prize in selling after an actual sale.

A third-party endorsement can be more effective than ten presentations if it's handled right, but you still have to sell someone. A referral will work only as hard as you do. And you can't just ask for referrals, you have to earn them. You do that by establishing mutual trust and being proactive in forming your alliances.

Bear in mind that when you get a referral, the source is putting his or her own reputation on the line. They are saying that they trust you enough to involve you with people who could affect their career, their reputation, or their livelihood. You have to treat that with sensitivity and respect.

There are two things you can do with a good referral. You can take it from there, or you can ask the "referrer" for some help. Check out the possibilities for a three-way get-together over lunch or dinner or at someplace like a theater or ballpark. That's probably the best way to meet a new prospect. If the three of you can't physically meet, a phone call from your source to the prospect can break the ice, or you can ask for a letter of introduction.

In any case, you want some background on this person – name, rank, and serial number, along with anything of special interest involving business or personal life. If you are selling insurance or real estate, for instance, it would be useful to know that the prospect is a new father or mother.

Once you've been introduced, how do you handle the approach? Go slow. Don't come across as too anxious. You don't have to sell somebody at the first meeting. In fact, the less selling you do, the more credible you appear. As with any sales call, the key is establishing rapport and trust. At a second meeting, just the two of you, you can get down to business. And no matter how things turn out, follow up with an expression of gratitude – a note of thanks to the prospect, and another one you send the referrer, maybe along with a little gift.

Above all, you have to deliver. In the unlikely event that you fail to follow up as promised, it will reflect badly not only on you, but also on the person who provided the lead. That will knock out any chance for another referral. But worse, it will damage your reputation, and there's nothing more critical to a sales rep than maintaining a good name.

CHAPTER 7

Sustaining a Winning Attitude

Chapter overview:

- Why a positive approach to life is a major asset to success in sales.

- How you can adjust your attitude, knowing it's one thing over which you have total control.

- Why it's important to refuse to be a victim, no matter what kind of hand you have been dealt by fate.

- Aiming high – a personal tale of sheer determination. When you set your goals high enough and resolve to meet the, you have won half the battle.

- Why it's important to maintain balance in your life; the three keys to contentment and personal satisfaction.

- How to keep the peace on the home front when you are working long, unpredictable hours.

- Why it's essential to make time for your children – and have fun with them. This is a dynamite boost to your mental health.

- Why cold calling sales people need a refuge, a place of tranquility where you can recharge your batteries and rejuvenate your outlook on life.

182 Going in Cold

I've always loved those stories about kids who hustle hot dogs at a big league stadium and end up, 15 years later, pitching in the World Series. They had seen those other guys make it to the majors – the "show" – and they told themselves that if those people could do it, so could they.

With hard work and determination – and a winning approach to life – anything is possible. Attitude is your foundation, the underpinning for everything else you do. One way or another, it influences your outlook, your morale, and your ambition. When you have a confident attitude and a drive to succeed, you have what it takes to walk in cold, talk to anybody, and make a positive impact.

Think about it. We gravitate to people who are upbeat and optimistic, and we shy away from those who are gloomy or grim. That's just human nature. That's why the most successful politicians present a sunny face. Who likes a bummer? Who wants to vote for you, or do business with you, if you come across as a brooding or unpleasant?

When you're in sales, customers have to like you. You don't have to be Mary Poppins or some kind of cheerleader, but you do need to come across as a friendly, enthusiastic guy or gal. If you don't, you're pretty much dead in the water. It could even be that you're in the wrong profession.

The good news is that attitude is all in your head. It is one thing over which you have total control. So never despair. No matter what cards life has dealt you, it's possible to bounce back from misfortune, hardship, or even disaster. We see people do it all the time. The human spirit is very resilient.

That's why this book is really about hope – hope that you can develop a new attitude, hope that you can make a new start, or a hundred new starts. You have to let go of the anxieties and fears that are sapping your confidence and blocking your potential. We're all carrying around a lot of baggage, and as a wise man once said, you never know how heavy the bags are until you put them down.

Refuse to Be a Victim

As a kid, I stuttered. Badly. No matter how hard I tried, I could never get the words to come out. It was a constant embarrassment to me, made worse by my classmates. I was the butt of their jokes.

That sort of humiliation can do unbelievable damage to your self-image. On top of that, I had ADD – attention-deficit disorder. That was an undiscovered affliction at the time, but it was clear in retrospect that I had it.

So there I was, a guy with a good head on his shoulders but who couldn't communicate. I knew every answer in class, but the stuttering kept me from speaking up. And with ADD, I couldn't focus on my studies. Every test was a nightmare. It was just incredibly difficult to concentrate. When the pressure of the test was over, I could remember all the answers, but by then it was too late. I always knew the material, but I went through school as a "C" student.

I've done a lot of reading on ADD, and the specialists compare it to having 25 television sets playing in your head at the same time. That was me back then, and it still is. People with ADD can be very creative, but they don't fit well in a traditional academic setting. I sure didn't. And because of the stuttering, I didn't fit socially either. Believe me, it was hell coming up through my teenage years.

But guess what? Out of that negative came a positive. All this adversity gave me the compassion to be a good teacher. It gave me insights into conflicts and difficulties that I had experienced, so I could help students in similar straits. I had a parent approach me one day and say, "You have an uncanny ability to quiet down the big mouths and pick up and encourage the shy kids." That same sensitivity has given me an edge in selling, too, because I've always been able to empathize with customers and read their feelings pretty quickly.

All this happened because I refused to be a victim. Some people who endure the ridicule of classmates never really recover. It leaves a scar on the psyche, a nagging sense of inferiority. But I convinced myself that I had worth as a human being. I was better than that. By the time I started college, the stuttering had stopped, and with that unhappy experience behind me everything bloomed – my self-respect, my self-confidence, and my overall attitude. Without a deep belief in myself, and an outgoing disposition, I never could have made it in teaching or sales.

When I totally broke loose from those adolescent insecurities, it was an awakening. And then, intellectually, emotionally, and spiritually I began the process of saying, "Hold it. I am not going to live my life like this, because it's passing me by."

The point is, you need a healthy attitude to cold call successfully. If nothing else, you need an optimistic outlook to keep going in the face of rejection (more on that later). When prospects shoot you down, remember that you have great value as a person. Look back to the high points of your life, your greatest accomplishments, for reassurance.

Taking Charge of Your Life

The origins of attitude are a little mysterious. Genetics must be involved, because some people are just born with a good nature. But for all of us, I think, life experiences have a shaping effect.

If you were a popular and successful as a kid, the star quarterback in high school and a dean's list student in college, chances are you have a cheerful outlook on life. After all, it's been good to you. The same holds true for a woman who has excelled in sports or been president of the student body. With real accomplishment comes genuine self-esteem.

But what if you're like most of us, right in the middle – Mr. or Ms. Average? What if fate has dealt you a bad hand? Are you destined to go through life with a chip on your shoulder?

Hardly. In fact, there's no reason your attitude can't be terrific.

Years ago, I found some powerful attitude support right in the beginning of the Bible, in the Book of Genesis. It says that we were made in the image of God. So we have a piece of what it is like to be God – just a little piece. But if you have it, you have a foundation for your attitude. It is up to you to water it, nurture it, weed it, and help it grow. On an intellectual level, it helps to believe that, if we are made in the image of God, we have a piece of that perfection.

You can draw a lot of strength from that kind of affirmation. It was enough for our country's Founding Fathers to pledge their lives, their fortunes, and their sacred honor to the cause of independence. They wrote about inalienable rights endowed by the Creator – life, liberty, and the pursuit of happiness. That was the moral basis for the American Revolution.

Quick Tip

Getting Your Head Straight

Many things in life can adversely affect your attitude and personality. Other people usually cause them, like the kids in school who laughed at my stuttering. That's why the country has armies of psychotherapists – too many people have been screwed up. By believing you are made in the image of God, however, you can wipe away all that human stuff and go right to the source. You tell yourself that no longer will you allow those negative human factors to dominate the way you feel about yourself. You're not going to give them that kind of leverage over your life.

What I'm suggesting here is that you take charge of your life and get your attitude positioned for success. If you want to make it big in sales, and decide to add cold calling to your repertoire, you've got to believe in yourself enough to change the way you operate.

It can be a little scary. Once you start making changes in your routine, the people you work with will take notice. They'll be saying, "Hey, you're not the same way you used to be. What's going on?" You might face skepticism and faultfinding.

That is the "human stuff" that can mess you up. You can't let it bother you. I'm writing this for those of you who want to make an additional $20,000 next year, or more. If you're earning $70,000 today and want to reach six figures, you *have* to change your methods and the way you think. If you don't, next year you will make the same $70,000. But you won't even attempt to make that leap without a strong belief in yourself and the determination to punch up your career to higher level.

Aiming High

When I started selling collection services for a company called IC Systems, my territory was southern Connecticut, along the coast, from New Haven on down to Bridgeport and Greenwich. Every sales rep was required to bring in $12,000 of new business each quarter. The typical sale was about $300, so you needed 40 new deals every three months, on average. I had a personal goal to hit my $12,000 quota in two months, however, because once we went over that mark we jumped to a bonus level. That meant an additional $100 in commission per sale, and my family needed the money.

Late in the second month, while closing in on my goal, I caught a cold. Within a week it had turned hideous, like the cold of the century, but I was still out on the road. I stopped to see a customer of mine, a chiropractor, hoping to get some referrals. After listening to me talk for a few minutes, he said, "Chuck, what have you got there? It sounds like pneumonia."

Quick Tip 🏃

'Make No Small Plans. They Have No Magic'

When you are hell-bent on hitting a goal, sometimes it takes sheer determination to push on through the tough times. Without it, it's easy to fumble away your potential. There is simply no substitute for determination. Nothing is more common than people who have squandered their talent and brains and settled for mediocrity. Other people with the same native abilities have risen to the top. The only difference between them is determination to hit their goals.

What I'm saying is, dream big. Or as the great architect Daniel Burnham once said, "Make no small plans. They have no magic." Burnham revamped the city of San Francisco, redesigned Chicago, deeply influenced the modern skyscraper, and designed such phenomenal buildings as the Manila Hotel and Washington's Union Station. He dreamed big and made it happen.

Set your sights high. Tell yourself that you are going to achieve big things. Because if you believe you can, you will. Maybe you'd love to have that ski cabin or beach house. If you set your goals high enough, and resolve to meet them – convince yourself that you are going to meet them – you have won half the battle.

In fact, he was pretty sure it was. This fellow was also into acupuncture, and he asked if he could treat me. He stuck four needles in various places on my body and got me back to where breathing came a little more easily. Then he sent me to a physician, who made the pneumonia diagnosis.

The doc put me on some medication and ordered me to stay in bed for a week. I didn't like being sidelined that long, but I postponed most of my scheduled appointments and stayed in bed for several days. But the fourth day was the last day of the second month, my deadline for hitting bonus level. I was still sick – if you've ever had pneumonia you know how bad it can be – but I needed just one more sale to hit the $12,000 mark. I was determined to make that goal, no matter what. I had an appointment that morning with two dentists, oral surgeons, who worked in Bridgeport, a good 70 miles from my house.

Still perspiring from fever, and feeling horrendous, I managed to make the drive and dragged myself into their office. The good dentists had sympathy for my situation, but it wasn't sympathy that won the sale – a contract to collect for past-due accounts. It was determination. I felt high – lightheaded and groggy – as I watched them sign the papers, but I got home and made a full recovery.

Keeping Your Balance

If you practice what I've been preaching here, you are going to be very busy. If you take up cold calling as a means to build your business and reach financial security, it will require long hours and hard work over a sustained period of time.

It's well worth the trip, or I wouldn't be urging you to take it. As the old saying goes, if you risk nothing, you risk everything. But there is a danger. You can easily become so absorbed with business that you'll take your eye off the things that matter just as much, or more. What good is financial success if the rest of your life is in shambles?

A wise and wealthy man told me years ago that if you want to live happily, you need to maintain balance in three areas of your life – your relationship with your business, your relationship with your family, and your spirituality, whatever that might mean to you. It's as if you're sitting on a three-legged stool. If one of those things is missing, he said, or is insignificant in your life, you are out of balance and probably don't even know it. Just as a plant needs sunshine, water, and soil, you need to have these three things working in harmony to enjoy a healthy, fulfilling existence. It is not an easy balance to achieve, which is why the country has armies of therapists and marriage counselors.

Cold calling sales people, I think, have an unusually tough time maintaining good balance. Their jobs are pressure-packed and time-consuming. Paydays can be inconsistent. Their emotional states can swing wildly from week to week, governed by success on the job or failure. All that can make for a chaotic existence.

The risk is magnified for sales people involved in running growth companies. Entrepreneurs sacrifice mightily to create something out of nothing. It's a noble endeavor – without entrepreneurs we'd still be living in caves. It is futile, however, to look for the meaning of life in the ephemeral institutions that mankind has built, including our own.

You set yourself up for disappointment if you rely on company building for rewards that it cannot deliver. But try telling that to an entrepreneur so lost in work that he or she can hardly see straight. He thinks he's putting together a legacy, but a company is an imperfect hedge against mortality. Things fall apart. Even stone wears away. So it's a mistake to equate your business, or your job, with yourself, because a business does not a life make. A life well lived is a lot more than that.

Out of Kilter

There's a great observation by a successful mutual fund manager – I think it was Peter Lynch of Fidelity Investments. When he retired early, he remarked, "On my deathbed I'm not going to wish I'd spent more time at the office." That is wisdom. That's saying, "Hold it a minute. I've got to reflect on what the heck I'm doing with my life." Men seldom talk that way. It's not macho. Or maybe the rest of their lives are so fouled up that they *prefer* to spend more time at the office.

It's easy to throw your balance out of whack. A sales rep determined to make it big tends to put business first, letting everything else slide. If you are gung-ho about your work, putting in 55 or 60 hours a week, you need to step back and reexamine your priorities. I'm not saying that's wrong – maybe you need to log that much time right now to reach a specific goal. But be aware of the price you're paying.

I remember talking to a couple of guys who were laughing at this issue of balance. They were trying to make the point that only one thing counts, and that's business. Well, that only lasts so long, and then people burn out.

Still, you need to address your primary job responsibility – making sales and bringing in new business. Long hours are inevitable, and you're bound to run into unpredictable situations, because the best-laid plans go haywire once you plunge into the day. Let's say you're driving home at six o'clock, and decide on impulse to hit one last prospect. You're only doing your job. But the call takes longer than you expected, because the customer likes what you're saying. In the end though, he says, "Let me think about it," the classic rejection. And by this time, you've missed dinner.

On the Home Front

In speaking to sales groups about balance, I say that at work you're doing a hundred miles an hour – you're redlining it. That mental speed is the accumulation of all your anger and frustration. You've got money pressures like crazy, and you've gone an entire week without a sale. You had three deals you expected to close, and none of them wrapped. You're down on your company, your job, and where you are in life. There's no one to blame, so you blame yourself, and that gets you angry, too, because you're a good guy.

Even though you're doing everything right, nothing is breaking your way. It's all going higher and higher, and you're revving up to 80, 90, a hundred miles an hour. All of a sudden you hit your house at seven o'clock, and your house is doing five miles an hour. Guys nod their heads at that and say, "Yeah? How about if it's doing *two*?" You barge in, take all the pressures that built up during the day, and dump them on your family.

Your kids don't care what happened to you that day. They don't even know what you do. They're glad to see you, but you're in a grouchy mood. Dinner was an hour ago, there are toys all over the floor, and the place is a mess. The kids are running around, and it's noisy. You want to establish some order, the way you do at work, but your house doesn't operate like that.

So what happens? You might explode, pushed over the brink by the household pandemonium. You don't want it to happen, but it might happen. It's a common thing. And then not only is your work life out of kilter, so is your home life. Similarly, if you're having a great day on the job, but your relationship with your family is on the skids, when you come home at night that good day will evaporate, because you're walking into a hellhole. Unless you have an unusually understanding spouse, who sympathizes with the stress you are under, your marriage could start to buckle.

Remedial Steps

For the good of everybody concerned, you have got to stop this. How? By talking about it with your spouse and your children, if they are old enough to understand. Don't get angry; just try to explain the strain you are under, the rejection you face every day, the constant fight to get ahead. It can be a very healthy process, a catharsis, a clearing of the slate.

Then tell yourself you are going to turn over a new leaf. You are not going to let a bad day at work poison the atmosphere around the house. Set some boundaries. Try to compartmentalize, so you keep your work life separate from your private life. While driving home, play some music that makes you feel good. Plan a night out , so you've got something to look forward to. I always took my wife out on Friday night, no matter how tired I was. Friday night was party night for me, especially if I'd had a great week. Focus on positive thoughts.

Dissolving these home-front tensions requires working smarter, scheduling your day more tightly whenever possible. Make your time on the job count. If you have an active clientele, you'll have to deal with a lot of extraneous day to-day issues, but balance those against the fact that your principle duty is making new sales. Get to work at seven or eight in the morning, put in a solid ten hours, then leave for home at six – and arrange for dinner to be at six-thirty or seven at night. Invest in a cellular phone, so if you are going to be late, at least you can let your family know.

Make Time for Your Kids

There are few things more vital to a sense of fulfillment than spending time with your children. If you are a typical parent, your kids mean the world to you. That's really your life's work – raising your kids to be successful individuals. When you get involved in their lives, it also helps you unwind from those job pressures.

There are countless ways to enhance that time together. When my kids were younger and into scouting, I became a scoutmaster. You can coach Little League, take the kids camping or hiking, or just help with their homework every night. The closer you are to their lives, the more they will know they can always talk to you. Whatever you do with your children, you will get it back in spades and it will be a source of rejuvenation and satisfaction.

Incidentally, I think golf is a terrible sport for a family man. I know we live in the age of golf – everyone seems to play it – and I like the game as much as the next guy. But when you have young kids, you have no business spending your weekends on the course – unless you take them with you.

I know two men who play 18 holes every Saturday and Sunday, and one of them is already divorced. He's a golf fanatic. He might become a low-handicapper, but big deal. His family life has come apart at the seams. If you love golf, marry someone who likes golf as much as you, and get your kids a starter set when they turn three or four and teach them to play.

Of course, if you do your golfing during the week, while entertaining clients, that's a different story. Some of my sales reps cut a lot of deals out on the course, because the atmosphere during a round of golf tends to engender sociability and comradeship. It can be a terrific way to build a friendship, at least on a business level.

Of Heart and Soul

When work life and family life are clicking smoothly – or especially when they are not – your spiritual nature, your soul, still needs nourishing. If you have a relationship with God, however you define God, at least you have an outlet. It might be a priest, a rabbi, or a minister, somebody you can turn to for a spiritual lift. You might say, "My life is in such turmoil right now. I can't handle this. I don't know what the heck to do about it." Talk it out and ask for advice.

If you're having a horrendous time at work, when nothing is going right, a spiritual dimension gives you another place to go. Many, many times, in the lonely depths of a sales slump, I stopped in a church somewhere and sat quietly for 15 minutes. That helped me to put things into perspective, so I could deal with them with a cool head. You can draw strength from the "higher power" that says, "Take it easy. It's not that bad. Things will get better."

If you can achieve a balance in those three areas – your work life, your family life and your spiritual life – you'll feel good about yourself and you won't spend any time on a psychiatrist's couch. Without turmoil and confusion to throw you out of whack, you will be able to focus on selling.

Selling is about making money, not for money's own sake, but for what it can bring you. If you follow the principles expressed in this book, you will make a lot of it. After that, it is up to you to invest it wisely, in ways that bring you serenity and happiness. Create your refuge against the storms of human existence.

Finding Tranquility

Everyone needs a place to go where it's calm and peaceful. Remember the old Drifters tune *Up on the Roof* – "...I've found a paradise that's trouble-proof." We could all use something like that to recharge our batteries and remind us why we work so hard.

In my own case, I bought a horse farm in Chester County, Pennsylvania. Driving in here at night is just the ticket after a tough day. Leaving a quiet country road, I proceed up a long gravel driveway, cruise past the barn, and park under a huge, ancient oak.

The house is a great, rambling place, built in 1740, with half a dozen bedrooms upstairs, each with a fireplace.

This is the Pennsylvania horse country of foxhunts and landed gentry. The farm looks out on an idyllic view of pastures and forested hillsides. Lush in the summer and majestic in the fall, with the trees blazing with color, the countryside in winter is a world straight out of Currier & Ives. The local folks sometimes ride through the snow on horse-drawn sleighs. My whole family knows we have something very special here, and we all love it.

This is what money can bring you. I didn't have to buy a horse farm. I had a perfectly nice house and a log cabin in the mountains. But because I did buy it, neat things have happened in my life. My children are revitalized in nature. They're into the horses. They swim in the creek. They pitch in on chores to help keep the farm running smoothly. It has become a gathering spot for even my oldest kids and their friends, who are already out of college. My wife, June, and I get to see more of our children.

My eldest son says he can't wait to bring his own kids to Grandma and Grandpa's farm – and he doesn't even have a girlfriend yet! I couldn't have made a better investment. And in retrospect, I couldn't have made a better move than when I left teaching for the great game of selling.

CHAPTER 8

Coming to Grips with Fear and Rejection

Chapter overview:

- Fear of cold call selling stems from intimidation. It's a powerful force that can stop a sales rep from even getting started. But fear can be controlled and conquered.

- How to work cold calling into your sales repertoire gradually, to reduce the pressure and fear.

- Taming the "gray ghost" of rejection, a creature who rides in the trunk of your car but wants to take over the controls.

- The best defense in cold call selling is your sense of personal value. Positive self-esteem can build an inner bunker, a coat of armor against the slings and arrows of rejection. Tips to enhance your self-image.

- How to take inspiration from the giants of history, people who faced truly petrifying ordeals. Your fear of cold calling will seem puny compared to their feats.

- The best approach to defeat the dragon of fear is to confront the dragon head on. Recognize that fear is hard-wired into us, but don't let it rule your life.

- When you're hitting the wall, it's critical to stay on the attack. Techniques to help maintain your momentum.

- A Little League pitcher faces down the fear factor.

- When frequent rejection clearly can be blamed on your product or service, you need to make a switch.

Fear. It's one of our most primitive instincts. When a saber-toothed tiger was chasing a cave man through a forest, you think that guy wasn't terrified? Down through the eons that sense of fear and angst got hard-wired into our brains. And it comes up big whenever I suggest that a sales rep give cold calling a try.

Why shouldn't it? Walking in cold on total strangers doesn't come naturally. It's normal to be nervous about it – at least at first. But when nervousness builds into uncontrollable fear, the problems begin.

I've seen lots of sales guy and gals knocked out of the box in the first inning, as we'll see below. Going into a cold call, they thought they had their nerves in check, but the slightest pressure brought on a near-paralysis. Some of those folks swore off cold calling on the spot. Others managed to deal with it somehow, and then watched as that sense of fear faded bit by bit until it was it gone.

I was part of that second group. Believe me, on my early outings I felt lots of anxiety. But I couldn't afford to be ruled it – the effects were too debilitating. Somehow I had to get a handle on it, so I could concentrate on business.

My coping strategy was simple. As a former history teacher, I knew the heroic exploits and the great figures from the American past. I had often used them to inspire my students. Now I began using them to inspire myself. These were tales of people who had confronted extraordinary peril – off the charts compared to my level of fear.

Think for a minute about Lewis and Clark setting off to explore the wild American West, knowing they were entering a menacing world in terms of weather, dangerous beasts, and potential hostilities with the likes of the Sioux nation.

Or how about the troops who stormed Normandy Beach during the D-Day invasion of France? They knew as they crossed the English Channel that night that, come morning, wading ashore, they would face withering machinegun fire? You think they weren't scared?

And don't forget the early astronauts, who strapped into their space capsules never knowing if the booster rockets would explode on the launch pad. Talk about the right stuff!

For sheer guts and daring, though, few people can top George Washington – at least in my book. His role in leading the American Revolution was truly heroic. For an extra shot of courage I would picture Washington at Valley Forge during that brutal winter of 1777-78. His troops were freezing. They had no shoes. The fate of the Revolution lay in doubt. And remember, Washington didn't have to fight this war. As a gentleman farmer with a nice life at Mount Vernon, he could have stuck with the status quo. Instead, he put it all on the line.

When you read that line in the Declaration of Independence – "We pledge our lives, our fortunes, and our sacred honor" – you know this was dead-serious business. Failure meant the gallows. When those patriots sent off that document, they had spit in the face of King George III. Turning back was impossible.

And there was Washington, taking on the world's most powerful army with this ragtag bunch of volunteers, who were bleeding in the snow at Valley Forge. You think he wasn't afraid? You think he didn't have sleepless night wondering, "What the hell have I done?"

Try that on for size when you're working up the nerve to make a cold call. Is your fear worse than Washington's fear? All you're doing is making a sales call. What's the worst thing that can happen? You won't make a sale. So what? Nobody is going to hang you.

Once I made that comparison, my fear diminished. It was still there, but it no longer had the power to hold me back.

Confronting the Dragon

No matter what I say about fear, nothing can quite prepare you for the anxiety of that first cold call. You're walking in cold on an unqualified lead, knocking on the door of a total stranger. Your stress level is going to be up at the red line.

That's normal. But be warned: as you walk through that door, you're mind will be reeling with multiple fears – fear of rejection, fear of being chased out, fear of looking bad. If you are naturally shy, it's that much tougher. Some people don't even like going to parties where they don't know anyone.

But whether you're a wallflower or the life of the party, cold calling will bring on some big-time uneasiness for any rookie. I consider myself to be a friendly, outgoing guy, and reasonably self-assured, but as a neophyte in this business I could sweat through a shirt just walking ice-cold into someone's office. I felt actual fear or something very close to it. The worst part was the apprehension, never knowing what awaited me on the other side of the door.

I came to realize that the best way to slay the dragon was to confront the dragon. The only way to win was by continually putting myself in stressful situations, where I had to perform. It was contra-phobic – you go for the thing that scares you the most. That was the only way to beat it.

Even today, after 15,000 cold calls, I still feel a little pang of anxiety when I'm walking into a charged atmosphere – the executive suite of a *Fortune* 500 company, say, or a major law firm. But now I know why I feel that pang, and how to handle it.

Think You're Too Tough to Feel Fear?

Maybe you think you are impervious to this fear factor. That's great. I hope you're right. But before you get too cocky, consider that I have seen grown men – people I was training – fall apart in cold call situations.

I'm talking about macho guys; people you'd believe could do anything. They acted the part. They had the right jokes, wore the right clothes, the whole nine yards. We even did some role-playing, before hitting the streets, to get the feel. They knew what to expect on that first cold shot – or thought they did.

But walking in together on an actual call, I have watched them crumble at the front desk. Someone is saying, "C'mon, c'mon, hurry up." They get nervous and start mumbling. Under pressure they forget what they want to say or how to say it. Their thought process comes unhinged. Suddenly, they realize that they are looking really bad; they are blowing the opportunity. They start to panic and begin searching for the fastest way out, so they give a business card to somebody and beat a hasty retreat.

After a few days like that, your confidence is in shreds. You feel beat up and bloodied. You start to think your product stinks, your job stinks, and your company stinks. Right there, your effectiveness is crippled, but in cold calling you can't afford that. Your next call had better be as good as your first one. If it's not, your lack of intensity will show – and customers will see it. That's a sure path to rejection.

At War With Yourself

Fear is perhaps the deadliest of killers in the world of sales. It stops some people right in their tracks, with demoralizing impact. When you let fear dominate you, it will slow you down every time, weaken your presentation, and undermine your resolve. It pits you at war with yourself.

And there's no easy out. You simply have to deal with it. If it helps at all, keep in mind your motivation for doing this: You want to make good money.

As part of our psychological makeup, fear is bred into us from an early age. It grabs us right from the playground. The first time we deviate from the other kids, they make fun of us. At home, if we do something without permission, we're subject to punishment. Then comes school, where we are outranked by teachers, principals, coaches, and professors. All these authority figures teach us that making a mistake, taking a risk, or even skipping a practice subjects us to criticism or punishment.

When your self-esteem takes a hard blow, you don't forget it. Fear of failure, fear of ridicule, fear of risk-taking – they become second nature. That instinct is reinforced on a lifelong basis, as the media pounds fear into us. We are blasted every day with bad news, an incessant bombardment of all the horrific things that happen to people, all the grief that can befall us. Instinctively, we hunker down and learn to play it safe.

Now imagine you are a sales rep just getting started in cold calling. You are carrying all this psychological baggage and you are only dimly aware of it. It lurks deep in the subconscious, a dark and nebulous force. And there you are, standing in the hallway of an office building, looking at a door and wondering if you should knock. You know that behind that door is a potential customer – the managing partner of a law firm, a company president, a purchasing agent.

Suddenly they loom as authority figures, with the power to intimidate. In some nameless way, all those entrenched fears start sapping your confidence. Your mind fills up with apprehension, and questions come flooding in. What if I really blow it? What if I make a spectacle of myself? What if they put me down?

This is the primary reason why that question is asked by every candidate for a sales job – "Is there much cold calling involved?" They fear being shoved back into the position of a being a little kid again, up against authority.

It makes no difference if you are approaching an office assistant or the owner of a company. It doesn't matter if you told yourself in advance to be cool, calm, and collected. Walking in there, you feel vulnerable and exposed. And you are at risk – at least that's the way it feels. You don't know if you'll meet with a frosty reception or even a hostile one.

And what happens? Your anxiety shoots up. You get rattled. Then you freeze. Someone confronts you and demands, "Who are you?" You say, "I'm Joe Blow with Ace Paper Company, and I'd like to see the person in charge of office supplies." The other person says quickly, "We don't need any of that. We're in good shape for paper."

You have to fire back with another line to try to get through. You can't let someone making $20,000 a year shoot you down. Right on the spot, you need to come up with the right words to *make* them want to see you. You have to find somebody around there with a little savvy.

You don't have the time or energy to fool around. You want to make the call, get the appointment, and be out. But if you can't come up with the right language, if your self-esteem isn't strong, if you don't value yourself, your product, and your company – if you are immobilized by fear – well, then you are in trouble.

The Self Doubts Begin

As you gnaw on fear and rejection, negatives thoughts some creeping in. You question your judgment: Did I make a bad decision about what to sell? Sure, that's the problem. "I'd be great if I were selling the right thing" – a lot of sales people say that. They see guys and gals making $300,000 selling medical equipment and feel like they're selling weed-whackers – in Alaska.

Friends and family members pile right on. "Why are you doing this?" they'll want to know. "Why are you selling this crap?" The problem isn't you – you are now convinced about that. Therefore, the problem must be the product itself, or the service.

Ever hear the expression that when you point at some-body, three fingers are pointing back at you? When you blame your product for dismal results, three fingers are pointing back. Why can other people sell it? What are you doing wrong?

Or what are you doing right that you need to do more? In our culture we obsess on what we're doing wrong. Stop for a minute and ask yourself, what am I doing right? And what is stopping me from making sales?

Asking the question is the beginning of wisdom. If you answer yourself honestly, then you've got something more concrete to work with, and you can build on that.

The Best Defense – Your Sense of Value

When talking to my own sales people about fear, I use a "seesaw" analogy. On one side of the plank you have conflict and competition – heavy forces. Balanced against them on the other side is nothing but your self-esteem. Which side, I ask them, will prevail?

When you make a cold call you enter an uncertain environment. Just for starters, you are disturbing someone. The "prospect" has never heard of you before and maybe has never even heard of your company. He goes on alert, sensing trouble. Your sudden presence creates tension.

As you gather the gumption to proceed, you need confidence, poise or courage. Call it what you will, it stems from your self-esteem or self-value. This is bedrock, your foundation, your essence. It is the one thing that can carry you through when the chips are down. But no matter how strong your self-esteem might be, it's vulnerable to attack.

In a competitive arena, customers are judging you all the time. So are your managers and peers. They're watching to see if you'll make your numbers. They're telling you that you're doing a good job, maybe, or a bad one. When people begin criticizing your performance, your self-confidence drops. Your anxiety level in turn begins to rise. You get a little paranoid. And out in a sales setting, that's going to show.

If you are just starting to cold call and feel plagued by fear and doubt, remember that you have value. That is what I tell my sales people. Remember that we thought enough of you to hire you. We believed you'd be an excellent representative of our company.

I build them up as people of honesty and integrity. I say that we trust you and support you – that this whole organization, from the top all the way down, is standing behind you. We will do anything to help you get business.

Quick Tip 🏃

The Four-point Checklist
I've always remembered a little list of affirmation points somebody had pinned on a company bulletin board. We were supposed to tell ourselves four things before every cold call: I believe my company is the best. I believe my products or services are the best. I believe I am the best. I believe that when my customers buy, they will always be better off.

That's not a bad way to talk yourself into knocking on another door. The point is, you are it! Tell yourself that – "I am it! I'm the best." And believe yourself when you hear it.

Nobody ever told me things like that, but that's what I tell them – constantly. I believe in them when they don't even believe in themselves. The finest teachers in this country try to convince kids that they can achieve impossible dreams. Simply because someone believed in them, suddenly those kids *do* accomplish amazing things.

In giving my reps lots of praise and encouragement, I'm really trying to convince them of their personal value. I know what they are up against – a culture that looks down on sales people. Out in the field, facing hostile fire, positive self-esteem is their best friend. It's like an inner bunker. When the bombs of rejection and adversity start falling, there's no better protection than an invincible self-image.

As a company we give our reps every tool we can – a good mix of products and services, the flexibility to structure sales in different ways. We treat them well and back them to the hilt. But we can't give them a sense of value. It can't be manufactured. It's got to come from within.

Earlier I mentioned that phrase from the Bible – we are made "in the image of God." Whenever I remembered that, it made me feel pretty good about myself, no matter how sales were going. It was an affirmation that I was okay. That's the sort of self-talk you need to motivate yourself.

It's very important that you have self-affirmation. It might be nothing more than looking at yourself in the mirror, standing there shaving, and saying "I'm smart enough, I'm likeable enough, and I've got a great product. I can do this because, doggone it, I'm good enough."

The Character Issue

I was doing a seminar one time when a sales manager asked what characteristics I like to see in a sales rep. I told him, "I want a person who is trustworthy, loyal, helpful, friendly, and courteous."

Some guy in the back row made a crack – "What are you looking for, a Boy Scout?" I shot back, "Why would you settle for anything less to represent you? Why not shoot for that, and see what you get?"

I saw a glimmer of recognition when I explained that I really wanted someone with guts. A person who has integrity has the guts to do the right thing. It's a character issue. Some people will ridicule that, but what are they really ridiculing? Probably their own inadequacy to do it, their own lack of courage.

Phase into Cold Calling to Diminish Fear

When brand new sales recruits join our company, I often spend a few days with them in the field. There's no better indoctrination than hitting the streets together. That's where cold call selling happens, so I take them straight into the arena.

No matter who they are – shiny new college graduates or experienced sales people – there's always anxiety about starting to cold call. They want to know why it's really necessary. What's wrong with direct mail or telephone work? Haven't we heard from all the "experts" that cold calls are futile? Isn't there an easier way to get business?

I try to explain to them that cold calling is useful in many different situations. It's not an all or nothing proposition. Use it to supplement what already works for you – there's no need to junk the rest of your arsenal.

When you have written or called someone and received no answer back, you just show up. Or when you have turnover in an account – go see the new contact. You go to see a client, and there are four other businesses in the same building, and it's early afternoon. Go see a couple of them. The whole point is to increase your number of transactions because you never know where they might lead. Remember the "multiplier effect," the way you can thread a sale from one person to another.

Quick Tip

Never Forget – You Have Nothing to Lose

The new sales reps at my company are just like me when I got into cold calling. They have that ingrained sense of fear and it grabs them as our "basic training" comes to a close. After two or three days, I'll pull up in front of an office building and say the words they're dreading: "Well, what do you think? Are you ready to handle this one alone?"

That question freezes them, but I try to be reassuring. "I know you're nervous," I'll say. "Don't worry about looking bad in front of me. Don't worry about nerves. I'll be right there with you. Nobody can hurt you. You have nothing to lose. Focus on that – you have nothing to lose."

This is probably the best question you can ask yourself in that situation – "What do I have to lose?" The answer, of course, is absolutely nothing. You've got nothing now. If you get an appointment to come back, that's great. If not, well, at least you tried, and if you have found a need you can always go back.

During those training days in the field, the new reps see me strike out routinely. Once you see your teacher, your mentor, get shot down, it's easier for you to get shot down. You learn that it's nothing personal. It's just part of the game.

Cold calling doesn't mean you never use direct mail or phone work. You can do all that. But there will be times when cold calling is what you have to do. Don't be afraid to get your hands dirty. It will give you one more arrow in your quiver. If you want to make another $25,000 next year, adding a cold calling dimension to your repertoire will help you get there.

When you venture into cold calling in stages – mixing it with your usual routine – the fear is broken up and diluted. There's less pressure on you to do it all at once. As time passes and you get your footing, the fear begins to lift.

A Little Leaguer Confronts the Fear Factor

A friend of mine had a son on a Little League baseball team. The boy was one of the younger kids on the squad, but he had a great arm. In the backyard he constantly practiced his pitching. The coach always stuck him in the outfield, however, because he didn't think the kid could pitch in an actual game.

Finally, a day came when his team was getting shelled in a big game. The coach had gone through all the usual pitchers, but the other team kept scoring. In desperation, assuming the game was lost anyway, he called in my friend's son from the outfield and handed him the ball. This was his chance – he was going in to pitch.

The bases were loaded and there were no outs as he went to the mound and threw a few warm-up pitches. The boy was nervous as he eyed the first batter, a tall 12-year-old lad – the "clean-up" hitter. This was different from throwing in the backyard. There were people in the bleachers and an umpire was behind the plate. The kids on the other team were jumping around, anxious to start cracking some big hits off this untested new guy.

He struck out the first batter – three straight called strikes. The next hitter grounded out. The third batter popped up back to the mound. Three up, three down. He went on to finish the game, pitching three scoreless innings. His team began to hit and clawed their way back to win the game.

That night he told my friend – his dad – that he was terrified when the coach sent him in the pitch. What if he walked in a bunch of runs? What if he couldn't throw strikes, what with all that pressure? What if his team-mates made him the "goat" for losing the game? All those thoughts rushed through his mind as he got ready to throw his first Little League pitch.

"I was really nervous and scared, Dad," he said. "But after I struck out that first kid, I told myself I could do this. I could really pitch. And by the next inning I couldn't wait to get back out there. I wasn't afraid anymore."

That same kid went on to become one of the best pitchers in the league and was the starter in the all-star game.

It just goes to show that fear is only in our heads. If you're afraid of something, take it on. You'll be surprised at how quickly fear will vanish after a little success. Our 10-year-old pitcher had just learned a big lesson.

Coping With Rejection

Rejection is an inescapable fact of life in sales work of all types. It permeates a sales rep's existence the way calories permeate cheesecake. In the case of face-to-face cold call selling, however, I think rejection is particularly painful. It's more personal. You're not just a voice on the phone. You are standing there, in person, giving it your best shot, and you're being rebuffed.

Quick Tip

Cardinal Rule
Nothing is more lethal to a sales career than the belief that you're not up to the job.

You try to be rational about rejection. You tell yourself that it's not *you* that's being rejected. But no matter how you rationalize it, rejection can undermine your self-confidence. Like some insidious force, it eats away at you. You feel yourself sinking. It rekindles those old feelings of failure, and that can be disastrous.

I've had days when I walked in 20 or 30 doors and nobody would see me. There have been weeks when I'd given five or six presentations and struck out every time. You try to figure out why they're not buying, and they won't tell you. You try to close a few more times, but you don't get anywhere. They say they want to "think about it." It would be Thursday afternoon and the whole week would be going miserably. You had just poured out your guts for an hour, and you're tired, and they don't bite. I've been rejected thousands of times. I know it's tough.

You leave a little piece of yourself in there when you get rejected. After you've been put down time after time, you feel raw, like a slab of meat in a butcher shop, with the bones sticking out. The worst thing is, maybe you gave away that piece to somebody who doesn't even have the capacity to make a decision. It might have been a receptionist, a secretary, or some minion who made the decision that they don't need what you have. You know you should only be talking to the people who count, but you allowed someone below that level to bounce you out. All you have to show for your trouble is a couple of business cards.

Now, what happens? You feel like a whipped animal. In your demoralized state, you won't be thinking clearly. Your composure falls apart, and your anxiety level shoots up. Your eyes will drop lower, you posture will get a little droopy.

You don't know who to blame, so you start blaming yourself, or your job, or your company. You might even blame your overall station in life, and kick yourself because you didn't become an airline pilot or a banker – something with a steady paycheck. In our country today, in the current culture, it's not okay to fail. Nobody remembers who was number two in anything. Nobody remembers who lost the Super Bowl five years ago. With that kind of pressure, when you fail, you can get depressed. But the plain truth is, if you're out there selling, you're going to be failing sometimes.

Taming the 'Gray Ghost' of Rejection

Back when I was selling collection services for a company called IC Systems, I hit a major slump one month. Sales just weren't happening, and my attitude was in the dumper. I felt like a failure. Looking for someone to talk to, I called my manager. "I'm sorry," I said, "but I've got to unload on you. I'm sick of these people. I'm sick of getting shot down. I'm tired of all this."

He was a decent guy who had weathered his own horrendous days in the field. And he said, "I agree with you, Chuck. They're a pain in the neck. This business would be a lot easier without customers."

I gave a sad kind of laugh, but I felt better knowing that he understood what I was going through.

Then the manager said something about rejection that really stuck in my mind. He told me that I had this thing living in my car. He called it "the gray ghost." The ghost starts out in the trunk, he said. If you let him, he slips into the back seat. By the third day, he is in the front seat next to you, and by the fourth day he's sitting in your lap. Before you know it, he's driving the car.

You've got to get the gray ghost back in the trunk, he said, and then lock it. His point was that you can't afford to gnaw on rejection, because it will poison your outlook and drain your energy. If you drag around the baggage of the previous day – the anger of rejection – you are dead. It will only get heavier.

Whenever your own gray ghost gets into the driver's seat, you've got to wrestle your way back into control. You've got to stop a downward spiral before it gets serious. It's okay to feel lousy for a while – it's perfectly normal. But you can't wallow in self-pity, and you definitely can't carry that feeling over to the next day. If you do, customers will sense your lack of enthusiasm. You have to stop telling yourself that your job stinks. Just say it five times – stop, stop, stop, stop, stop. Negative thoughts aren't going to get you anywhere or do you any good.

Hitting the Wall

You can expect to hit a lot of stone walls once you start to cold call. It's okay to hit the wall. If you're not hitting it, you're not going anywhere. You're complacent. When you hit the wall, oddly enough, you know you're advancing. I tell my sales reps that when they hit the wall, come talk to me. I won't look at it as a negative. I'm glad they're hitting the wall; it tells me they're charging hard out there.

Giving a sales talk one time, I told the group about the wall. I said you can try to go over it, under it, around it, or you can start knocking down the wall. Bring the sales manager out with a cannon, I advised. I explained all this with a chart. Well, the sales manager took it and had me sign it. He hung it in his office and used it as a cornerstone all year – how to knock down those walls.

Vince Lombardi used to say the best defense is a good offense. That worked well for his Green Bay Packers and it can work for you. Stop feeling sorry for yourself, and go on the attack. Get back out into the field. See somebody new. Or visit an existing client and ask for a few referrals. Keep slugging.

The day I landed one of my best clients, a large marketing company, I had made 25 cold calls and gotten nowhere. I was feeling so sick and tired that I almost packed it in and went home. But I forced myself to stop for one more call, the 26th, and that's when I struck gold.

Quick Tip 🏃

When you make a lot of calls and plant a lot of seeds, the outcome of any one call isn't that critical to your overall success. It's like buying a mutual fund. While one stock in the portfolio is declining, another might be making a big upward move. That's diversification, and it pays off in selling as well as in investing.

You've got to be like the tortoise, in the story about the tortoise and the hare. The most successful sales people I know are the ones who just keep on going – the "steady Eddies." Sure, rejection bothers them, but only a little. Remember what the pundits always said about President Reagan – that he had a Teflon coat; nothing bad stuck to him. That's how a good sales person handles rejection. They let it bounce right off. They don't let the bastards get them down. They know that selling is a numbers game, so they keep posting big numbers, hoping for some hits.

Rejection Lands on the Headshrinker's Couch

Rejection becomes such a problem for some sales folks that they seek therapy. Surfing the net one day, I discovered a short article called "Handling Rejection – The Secret to Sales Success." The author, a practicing psychologist named Norm Ephraim, had seen a lot of sales people. They had come in for professional help to cope with rejection. They'd tried motivational books and tapes, but nothing seemed to work.

Ephraim recommends that they confront the beast head on. "What really helps you handle rejection is to recognize that there is a part of our minds which *always* takes disappointment seriously," he writes. "This part connects us to childhood emotional feelings of insecurity. Any disappointment, frustration or loss will make us feel anxious and small, what I call a child state.

"The key to handling rejection," he advises, "is to have compassion for such young feelings. All too often, people are self-critical when they feel vulnerable. This only makes us feel bad. What really works is when you can say, 'Look, this *was* a disappointment and it hooked childhood feelings in me. Okay, so how can I best take care of myself and get back on that horse and get going again?' Such self-compassion and active coping can have amazingly positive results," Ephraim declares.

Even Nice Guys Get Rejected

No matter how nice a person you are, you're bound to hit rejection in any cold calling program. That's a fact of life. Potential customers don't always need what you're selling. They might not even give you an appointment. You remind yourself that it's nothing personal. Even so, rejection can be hard to handle, especially if you think of yourself as a good person.

A little story: I once went on a Caribbean cruise, and I was the only guy who bought drinks for the band at the pool. There were four guys in the band, wearing Hawaiian shirts and playing Jamaican music. It was hot, and they were good, and I was there to have fun. So I said to a waitress, "Go ask the boys what they'd like to drink, and ask them please to play *Buffalo Soldier.*" All of a sudden I hear, "Hey, Chuck, thanks mon. We're gonna do a little Bob Marley."

What did it cost me? Twelve bucks to buy a round of drinks. I did it again the next day. They came over to where I was lying by the pool, and said, "Thank you, mon. Very nice of you. We get thirsty up there."

It was a little thing, but it mattered to those guys. If I were up there jamming in the hot sun, I'd sure like it if someone bought me a cold beer. A gesture like that comes from sensitivity. I put myself in the customer's place, in terms of the band. If you keep the customer front and center, with genuine concern, you will always do the right thing.

Quick Tip

'Nobody Can Make You Feel Inferior Without Your Permission'

We deal with fear, rejection and self-esteem as we choose, because we live within our minds. We live with fear as we choose to, rejection as we choose to, and self-esteem as we choose to. The behavioral consequences of those emotional human states are not predetermined.

Making the best of the situation is up to you, and you have plenty of choices. You have the choice about your attitude, your determination, and your self-image. There's a little gem of wisdom I used to tell myself; I think it came from Eleanor Roosevelt: "Nobody can make you feel inferior without your permission." There is lots of truth in that.

I've always regarded myself as decent fellow, which made rejection a little tougher to take. If you know down deep that you're a good-hearted soul, that you are well meaning and square dealing, getting a rude reaction from some "prospect" is like an insult. You can't understand how it can be happening. You know it's just business; it's no reflection on you. But while you are learning the truth of that, it is hell.

Rejection subconsciously takes us back to the playground, when we were eight years old. When kids get rejected – when they're not picked to be on the team, or when they flunk something in school – they cry, kick, and scream. They sulk. But now you're an adult, and that sort of reaction won't fly.

When you run into heavy rejection, you have to step back, examine the situation, and grab hold of yourself. On an intellectual level, you have to face the facts. Then you move on.

When Your Product Really *Is* the Problem

If rejection becomes more than you can handle, take a hard look at your business. Is the problem intrinsic to your company or your product?

The trouble might be a poorly structured sales program. If you have enough clout in your company – heck, even if you don't – see if you can't convince management that there's a better way to operate. I always knew what the problem was at IC Systems, for example, when I started selling collection services – it was price. Customers had to pay up front. They had to pay a percentage after that, but some up-front money was required. That was an ironclad requirement, and it killed a lot of deals.

When I finally got my own company, NCO Financial Services, I designed our sales program for flexibility. Customers could pay up front, they could pay a straight percentage, or we could tailor a deal to any given situation. I did not want to walk out without a deal – ever. After all that work to get an appointment, I didn't want to lose the sale because of a couple of hundred dollars.

By building flexibility into our system, we had the agility to finesse almost any circumstance. That kicked us into high gear, and that's when I began to close on more than half of my presentations.

Take a look at your own sales program. Can you suggest improvements? Are there ways to make it more nimble, more adaptable? If you have good ideas, run them up the flagpole and see if anybody salutes. You need to give yourself the best possible shot to land new customers.

Surviving Rejection Day by Day

Whenever rejection drags me down, I use a variety of techniques to put my gears back into drive. They're not

especially profound, but they supply a degree of comfort.
Think of them as safety valves.

- To refocus, stop for coffee at ten in the morning.
While figuring out your next move, write notes on
your business cards.

- During the day go through a car wash. It breaks up
the routine.

- Pull off the road and read a chapter from a positive-
attitude book, or stick in a tape on positive thinking.

- Working your way through an office complex,
duck into a men's room (or ladies' room) before
approaching the next door. Throw some cold water
on your face, comb your hair, and make sure your
fingernails are clean. It's a way to regroup.

- After a bad week, never leave the field on Friday
until you have an appointment for Monday. All
weekend you'll be pumping yourself up.

- If I was having a terrible day, sometimes I'd walk in
a door and start a conversation by saying, "I'm having a really bad day. How's your day going?" It was
human, and it let me take control of the situation.
Most people would respond, "Yeah, my day is going
pretty bad, too." Then we'd get into the reason for
my visit.

- Do what an army does when it's in disarray? It gets
back to basics. The troops polish their boots and
clean their rifles. To a sales person, this means you
get back in your car, get back in the field, go see
some good customers and ask for referrals. Start generating contacts again. Walk in a bunch of doors and
find some folks who will talk to you. Get the whole
process churning. Do whatever it takes to break out
of your funk. Don't let rejection pull you under.

Quick Tip 🏃

A Sound Track for Selling

Your car is your sanctuary. Treat it like one. Slide some good music into your tape deck. I always did that when I wanted to feel good about life and get myself psyched up for another call an hour later. I did that religiously. Sometimes I'd get myself on such a high that I'd practically rip the door off the next place I was going to see.

"Nobody Does It Better," by Carly Simon – that became my song. I told myself, nobody does it better than you, Chuck. Nobody walks in doors better than you do. Nobody breaks the ice better than you. Nobody closes a deal better than you.

That's what I'd tell myself, and that's what helped me handle rejection. Maybe you have your own song that fires you up. Give it a try. It works.

Little things like that recharged my engines. I wouldn't let my bummer of a day hold me back. Instead, I'd make it work for me. That kind of thing relieves the pressure. In any negative there's a positive, but while you're going through the negative you don't always know what the positive is. You're too intimate with the pessimistic side of the issue. Stop for a minute and think – how can you turn rejection around and put it to work?

Keep Fear in Perspective

History has been my passion for years. I taught it in school, and I continue to devour biographies. All this knowledge comes in handy in sales. Early in this chapter I mentioned how I draw strength from the titans of American history. But in fact there is endless inspiration in the stories about the giants of the past. Compared to the adversity they endured, your problems will seem like pip-squeaks.

What were my troubles with rejection compared to the dangers faced by Magellan or Christopher Columbus? Talk about courage. Magellan believed he could circumnavigate the globe, sailing west from Europe and ending up back where he started. He dealt with mutiny, the defection of part of his fleet, freezing weather as they rounded the tip of South America, and the unknown vastness of the Pacific Ocean. Magellan himself was hacked to death in the Philippines, fighting a warring tribe in waist-deep water. His crew finally limped home to tell the tale. He was a towering figure, and when I reflected on his voyage my own trifling worries about fear and rejection seemed ludicrous.

Some other examples:

- I'm always fascinated by life stories of people who went against the odds, who put everything on the line and never gave up. One of my favorites – and this ties directly into cold calling – concerns Thomas Edison and the invention of the electric light bulb. Edison didn't know that it was impossible to make a light bulb. Every other scientist and inventor knew it was impossible, so they didn't even try. Edison tried about 10,000 times before he got it right. His story reminds me of all the critics of cold calling who claim it doesn't work. A lot of sales reps believe that and never even give it a try. Personally I ignored the critics – cold calling had always worked for me. Because I didn't know what could not be done, I succeeded.

- There's a story about the time Edison's New Jersey factory burned down. As flames engulfed the place, nobody could find Edison. His son spotted him running across someone's yard. "The factory's on fire," he said, " and we were afraid you were inside." Edison replied, "Yes, I know. I'm looking for your mother. I want to make sure she doesn't miss the biggest fire we've ever seen." Most people would have been devastated. Not Edison; he got right back to work the next day, bringing in materials to rebuild. Attitude is the key. He wasn't about to give up. He wasn't going to sit around feeling sorry for himself. The next time you're feeling down because nobody is buying, remember Edison. What are your problems compared to his?

- General George Patton – there's another inspiring guy. In late December 1944, as allied armies drove across France, the Germans staged a massive counterattack near Bastogne. They broke through American lines and surrounded the 101st Airborne Division, cutting it off completely from relief. Patton's Third Army was a hundred miles to the south when he got word that the division was trapped. He told General Eisenhower he'd get to Bastogne in 48 hours. His troops rolled north through deep snow night and day over Christmas, reaching Bastogne on December 26th. In some of the fiercest fighting of World War II, Patton's forces smashed into the Germans in the Ardennes. The Battle of the Bulge was the last gasp for Hitler; he had gambled everything on stopping the allies in France, but he hadn't reckoned on dealing with Patton. The Third Army threw back the panzer divisions and saved the 101st. The outcome of the war was no longer in doubt.

- Throughout history we find remarkable people who held a true course in the face of terrible trouble. Consider Abraham Lincoln. As a lawyer, he knew that the South had the right to secede from the Union. Put yourself in his shoes. He had to decide whether to launch the nation into the Civil War. You just have to decide whether to knock on another door.

To keep myself bucked up on the cold calling trail, I also thought about my grandfather, who left Italy in 1910 to come to America. He had no money, only a trade as a stonecutter. He didn't speak the language. He left behind his parents, his brothers and sisters, his friends. He got on a boat, crossed the Atlantic, and made his way to Vermont to work in granite and marble. Imagine leaving behind everything that is familiar and venturing into the unknown.

When I thought about him, and what he had risked, I asked myself, Why am I afraid to make a cold call? What's the big deal here? I have the support of my family and my company. I'm in my native land. I speak the language. Nothing can hurt me. So what if this call doesn't pan out? There are a thousand other places to go.

...And Finally

You don't need to look to the giants of history to draw vicarious courage. Perhaps there's something in your own past where you came face to face with real danger. Maybe you were in the military and survived a narrow scrape. Maybe you lived through an earthquake or a fire or a killer hurricane.

It could be practically anything. As you gather the courage to walk into someone's office, think back to those situations when the stakes were very high. Your fear of going in cold will seem trivial by comparison.

All these tactics – safety valves, heroic tales, taming the "gray ghost" – kept my fear manageable. They got me through the early days and put me on the road to success as a cold calling sales guy. After that, it was a matter of time and effort. The more calls I made, the further the fear receded in importance. As fear and anxiety fade, your effectiveness shoots way up. You'll eventually feel comfortable and confident in almost any face-to-face sales situation.

But you have to do it to get these great results. It doesn't come free. You have to keep knocking on doors, keep pounding away.

MY LIST OF GREAT MUSIC TO MOTIVATE
AND RESTART YOUR ENGINE
—Make a CD for the car—

1. Theme from Rocky- *Bill Conti*
2. Welcome to the Jungle- *Gun's N Roses*
3. Knocking on Heaven's Door- *Gun's N Roses*
4. Born to Run- *Bruce Springsteen*
5. We Will Rock You – *QUEEN*
6. We Are the Champions- *QUEEN*
7. Panama- *Van Halen*
8. China Grove- *Doobie Brothers*
9. Brother Loves Traveling Salutation Show - *Neil Diamond*
10. So-Laimen Live performance- *Neil Diamond*
11. I Am I Said- *Neil Diamond*
12. Nobody Does it Better- *Carly Simon*
13. Here Comes the Sun- *Beatles*
14. Summer Wind- *Frank Sinatra*
15. Won't Get Fooled Again- *Who*
16. Nessun Dorma- *The 3 Tenors*
17. Rock n' Roll- *Led Zeplin*
18. Indiana Jones Theme- *Led Zeplin*
19. I Need a Hero- *Bonnie Tyler*
20. Jump- *Van Halen*
21. We're An American Band- *Grand Funk Railroad*
22. Does Anybody Really Know What Time It Is? - *Chicago*

CHAPTER 9

Getting Your Manager on Board

Chapter overview:

- Honest, open dialogue with your manager breeds a partnership of trust, friendship, and mutual support. Engaging your manager in your success provides an invaluable asset.

- Working with your manager, not just for him or her, enables you to talk more freely about rejection, sales slumps, and the travails of your job. You will have a comrade in arms.

- When you show your manager that you understand his or her job pressures, you earn gratitude and enhance trust.

- Hitting "the wall" – when you need help, ask for it. Your manager should know that the problem will work itself out, once you get past the wall. A few safety values to help you cope.

- How to curb the anxiety when your manager is riding with you on a sales call. And how to get the most out of your time together.

- What to do when your manager is incompetent or gets into trouble: practical steps for self-preservation and continued success.

- For managers: Are you a friend and guide to your sales reps, or a tough, demanding boss? Motivating people isn't hard. Some practical steps to keep your people fired up and make you more successful, too.

- Money is not always what sales people value most. Everyone wants recognition for a job well done. For managers, a few ideas you can use to show appreciation, and they don't cost much.

- As a manager, it's your job to "soften up" potential customers. Here's how to do it without stepping on the sales rep's toes.

Cold call selling is lonely work. Out there in the field, flying solo, sales reps have to deal on their own with everything from emotional highs to feelings of failure and rejection. It's no wonder so many of them finish up the day on a barstool.

But a bartender's distracted sympathy doesn't count for much. You really need somebody who understands what you're going through in good times and bad. You need a real friend. Maybe you're fortunate enough to have a spouse or a golfing buddy who always lifts your spirits. Or maybe you don't.

What you do have, however, is a sales manager. And forging a strong alliance with your manager is one of the wisest moves you can make.

The Payoff from Frequent Contact

Early in my career I landed a job selling collection services in southern Connecticut, along the coast. My manager was based in Boston, some 90 miles to the north. Once every quarter we'd get together for a sales meeting, but that wasn't enough contact for me. I made it a habit to call him once or twice a week.

On account of my initiative, we formed a real partnership. As a result, he became very familiar with my style of selling, my goals, and my personality. In fact, we became friends. I never had any qualms about calling him on a Sunday and saying, "John, I could really use you on Wednesday. I'm giving a presentation to a committee of six people and I'd like you there to help with the sense of parity." Whenever possible, he would drive down and we'd make the call together.

John was a terrific manager, brimming with ideas and always eager to help, but the other sales guys didn't use him the way I did. They were probably afraid of appearing weak. They thought a request for help might be misconstrued as a sign that they were not up to par.

This ties into fear. To overcome anxiety, John and I laid our cards on the table from day one. "John," I told him at our first meeting, "there are going to be situations where I'm going to want your help. I don't want you to ever think that I'm hiding from you, or that I'm afraid of you, or that I'm not good enough for this job."

He appreciated my directness. All good sales managers have spent time in the field. They know what it's like out there, and the best of them can identify with your plight. If you're in over your head on some deal, ask your manager for help. Tell him or her that you're outnumbered going into a presentation, and you really want to close this sale. Could he be there to field questions you might not be able to handle? Could she come in to lend moral authority and create the appearance that you're operating as a team?

If your manager is any good, it should not even be an issue.

Work With Your Manager, Not Just For Him

You mission is to bring in business, and your manager's reason for existence is to make you more successful than you already are. It's a critical relationship for anyone in sales, and the value it produces depends on your approach.

My career has encompassed all sides of this issue, from salesman to sales manager to building and training a sales force in my own company, where sales managers report to me. I've seen what works and what doesn't.

If you think and act like a typical employee, you will be treated like one. But if you aspire to be a manager yourself some day, take on extra responsibilities. Be a leader. Make yourself a real player. My own attitude has never been that I worked *for* someone. I worked *with* them. It was always a partnership, and consequently the dynamics worked in my favor.

This goes all the way back to my days as a schoolteacher. I once had a principal, for example, who liked to listen in as we taught lessons. Under union rules, she had to give two weeks' notice before coming into the classroom. It was really a sham, because she was never going to see a typical lesson that way – she was going to see a show. So I gave her permission to drop in whenever she wanted to – unannounced – or to eavesdrop on my class anytime, over the speaker system. In my view, we were in this together. The point was to give these children a solid education. It required a team effort.

Now bring that kind of thinking into the sales world. Many reps tend to hide from their managers. They see them only when it can't be avoided. It ends up becoming an almost adversarial situation. That's understandable if you're worried about hitting some sort of quota or goal, but it's almost always a mistake.

When you take a proactive stance, you can establish much friendlier terms with the one person who can be your coach, your counselor, and your confidant. When your manager is less your boss than your partner, your anxiety level eases. You can lay everything is out in the open, with no hidden agenda and no secrets. When you create an atmosphere of mutual trust, you'll be able to talk more freely about problems you are encountering on the job, or any other issues bothering you regarding the product line, maybe, or the company in general.

Think how refreshing it would be if you could call your manager and say, without any fear, something along these lines: "I'm in a slump. I'm a good sales person and I've shown quality – I think we both know that. But I'm hitting a wall and I don't know why. It's been two weeks without a sale. I need you to come ride with me and tell me what I'm doing wrong."

In saying that, you are breaking the unwritten rules of the system. You are admitting a problem and singling yourself out. But the manager isn't your enemy. He's in your corner, or should be. His role is to be like a tow truck – to help pull you out of your slump, not to blame you for sliding into a ditch.

Quick Tip 🏃

Need Leads? Check With the Boss

Managers always have leads going through them. Walk in once in a while and ask for them. You never know what might have just come in the mail. Your manager might have a stack of business cards or a database of potential customers. She might have heard about a client that suddenly wants to ramp up your business relationship.

I used to collect cards by the dozen, and they were free for the asking. I'd give a sales rep a card and a little briefing about a potential prospect, whatever I knew about the situation. A lot of sales came from those little exchanges, but they didn't happen unless the sales person called me or walked into my office and asked.

Sales Managers Are People Too

Don't forget that managers labor under their own pressures. They have to make their numbers and report to the next higher person on the corporate food chain. All managers battle with that issue, and they're always applying pressure on their reps to step up production. It's a pain for all concerned, but it's necessary.

In my experience, the best way to handle that is to be up-front with your manager. Tell him or her, "I understand the stress you're under, and I'm doing my damndest to make sure we hit our goals. I am on the team. I'm with you."

Comments like that go a long way towards building a mutual comfort level – as long as those comments are true. If you're showing up for work at 10 o'clock and knocking off at three, however, then you are lying to the manager. It will eventually catch up with you. But if you are honestly giving it your best effort, you have nothing to hide. When your manager has confidence in your work ethic, it's so much easier to talk to him or her when you're in the doldrums.

Hitting the Wall Together

As a manager, I always urged my sales reps to "use" me. Any time it was possible, I'd kick into action to lend a helping hand, by riding along on a call, getting together for more training, or by providing anything else the sales person required to make the job easier.

I also warned them about hitting "the wall" – before anyone hit it. It doesn't matter how much money you're making or how well you're doing, you are going to hit the wall – and not once but several times. It's inevitable.

Suppose you've just had ten months when you were selling phenomenally well. You're on track to break a record. All of a sudden you hit a wall and you go dry. When you have bad months in February and March and realize you're already behind schedule for the year, you are hitting the wall. You are hitting it financially, emotionally, and mentally. And you're attitude is suffering.

Talk with you manager ahead of time about the wall, so you'll know how to handle it. Get him or her on board with you, so it's safe to bring it up. I've had sales guys come up to me and say, "Chuck, I'm hitting the wall, and I know exactly in what area." Because we had established a level of trust, they felt free to say that. They knew I wouldn't take it as a personal failing.

If a sales rep was coming off a strong year, when he made $40,000 more than the year before, he'd be dealing with a whole new set of concerns. You don't just make an extra $40,000 without encountering more customer problems, more administrative issues. He had never had to handle all those things before, and suddenly he was hitting a wall. So we'd talk about it. We'd brainstorm some solutions, ways to mitigate those new problems, so he could get refocused on selling. That was my job – not to do his work for him, but to guide him out of the swamp.

Taking Your Manager for a Ride

Here's the situation: You have an important sale on the line and you need help to lock the deal. You call in the cavalry and now your manager is going to be there when you go in for the close. You're nervous. You've never done this before. What if he thinks that you don't handle yourself well in front of the customer?

The best way to suppress anxiety is to control the situation.

In a few companies where I worked, sales managers would do a so-called "ride with." They would ride around with the sales reps, one at a time, and say practically nothing for most of the day. It was as if they were invisible. During a presentation, they'd silently observe and take notes. At the end of the day they'd write up a little critique – an analysis of your performance during that particular out-ing, your strengths and weaknesses.

If you've ever experienced something like that, you know it can lead to paranoia. So what do you do? Diffuse the tension by tackling the situation head-on.

Before starting out on a "ride with," I'd say: "Listen, Eric, I don't know everything, but I know where I stand and I know where my sales skills need work. I want to increase my income by $25,000 a year, and I want to use you as a resource to help me get there. Show me the way to do it. Give me the vision to get to that next level. What do I have to do to get there?"

When you are upfront about your needs – and get them across in a respectful way – you create a positive buzz in the car and start off the day on a hopeful note. If your manager is any good, if he has been in your shoes, he will respond to the challenge. He's going to like your intensity and desire, and he'll want to help you. When you develop a trusting, open relationship, a good manager will return the favor in spades. So by all means, when you need reinforcements to close a deal or just lend an ear, don't be afraid to call in your coach.

When Your Manager Is the Problem

Okay, here's a twist. What if your manager is hitting the wall and you are not? Suppose your manager is unhap-py with the company's direction, or territories and commis-sions are being cut, or there's a power struggle under way. The manager might be leaving, but you can't be sure.

What do you do? If you get enmeshed in internal politics and are forced to take sides, you might choose the losing side. Keep your head down, stay out of the line of fire, and go right on selling – just do your job. Who knows – if the manager leaves, you might be promoted into that position.

It's a great opportunity. But if you let yourself get bogged down in company squabbling, you might end up as damaged goods. There will always be office politics and arguing and low-intensity warfare. Every company goes through ups and downs. Let somebody else deal with that stuff. Just get out the door, go meet some new people, and tell your story. You'll be fine.

What if your manager is incompetent? If you've been in the sales business long enough, you've probably had managers you have admired for their professional skills and others who can't help you out, or won't, because they're operating out of their depth.

How do you handle working for a boss who's unfit for the job? It's not easy. You can try looking elsewhere for guidance, to other managers or to someone in the home office. It's a negative situation, but look at the upside.

In your career, you'll have sales managers of varying abilities – the good, the bad, and the furniture. The thing to remember is that you can learn from every one of them. You learn how to be a manager by taking the good traits and qualities from the best of them and incorporating them into your style. Conversely, you learn how *not* to be from the bad ones. You learn how to avoid, as a manager, those things that bugged you as a sales rep.

For Managers Only: Spending a Day with Your Sales Rep

Managers can work wonders to energize a sales force when they use the right techniques. In corporate America today, there aren't many sales managers who spend time riding with their troops. They've forgotten what it's like to chomp in first – to break the ice with potential customers. It's really a shame, because this is a terrific way to get to know your reps and what makes them tick.

You, as a manager, would be well served by carving out some time to give this a try. When it comes to building morale, there's nothing like dedicating a day to making the rounds with one of your people. If you want to encourage self-confidence in your troops, don't just tell them that they have value, *show* them.

How should you handle this situation, once you're in the car together? With sensitivity, good humor, and a little understanding of psychology. Try to eliminate anxiety, any notion that your presence is a threat. Whenever I do this, we first meet for coffee and start with a conversation, opening on a positive note. I explain that I want this day to be as productive as possible.

For starters, I'll ask the sales person to list three or four areas where he or she feels completely qualified, where he doesn't need any help at all. Suppose those areas are breaking the ice, making appointments, and giving presentations. We discuss those aspects of the job, and I congratulate him about this, that, or the other thing. In talking about those things, the rep feels pretty good. His self-esteem is up. He now feels that he has a friend – me – and that friend has said he's doing a good job.

Consequently, he's more apt to admit that there is this one area – countering objections, for example – where he feels a little weak. That's when I'll say, "Okay, today we are going to focus on that. For eight hours, that's all we're going to work on. Just that one thing." We play question and answer. He throws the most common objections at me, and I counter them.

If we drive 50 miles for an appointment, and the prospect is a no-show, I understand. "I know how you feel," I'll say, "because it's happened to me a lot of times." The idea is to have a little fun while making the rounds, and to work on that one deficiency, because I want my reps to grow in their jobs and make more money.

Job One: Building Up Your Reps

During a day together with one of my sales folks, we'll talk about different techniques, different customers, why clients buy from us versus from our competition. It's a golden opportunity to find out how my sales reps are doing – how many deals they have going, how big the wave is, how wisely they are using their time.

If they have spare time, are they walking in five or six new doors? Are they concentrating on only the big sales and not the small ones – do they have a case of "bigitis?" Eight-five percent of the business marketplace is comprised of companies with fewer than 20 employees. If the sales person is only going after large clients, in hopes of big commission checks, he's forfeiting a lot of business. No matter how small the deal is, it's still a win, and a small company you call on today could be a big company in four or five years. You can grow right along with it.

I've had sales guys we inherited from companies we acquired, and they were freaked out when I started riding with them. After we bought the collections division of a company in Cleveland, for example, I spent a week there with the two sales people who "conveyed" with the deal.

I went back to Cleveland a month later and we had dinner together. I asked how they felt when we were together on the road. One of the guys said, "Chuck, you scared the hell out of me. I didn't want to look stupid in front of you. Nobody ever rode out on calls with me before – certainly no managers or executives."

I said to him, "That's kind of sad. It tells me that they've forgotten what it's like to be on the front lines. You *are* the front line, the best I've got out there. To hell with the computer unit, the postage unit, the long-distance company, and everything else – nothing starts without the deal. You are the guy who's got to make it happen. And my obligation is to help you and make you successful."

I explained that the lifeblood of their business was in the field. That's where the customers were. Go see them, I said – often. Those customers are fighting their own battles every day in the marketplace, and if you aren't there with them, why do they need you? If you're out of sight, you're out of mind, and your competition might slide into that opening. Besides, every time you visit an existing customer you've got an opportunity to ask for referrals.

The key to spending a successful day with a sales rep is to build him up. Don't point out all the things he's doing wrong. We live in a culture where things are always right or wrong. As soon as you start talking that way, the walls go up and people take a defensive attitude.

If the rep's objective is to make $20,000 more next year, you don't attack his method. But you might need to remind him that using the same old method won't be enough to get there. If he works the same way this year as last, he's going to get last year's results. He's got to make some adjustments. That's where you come in, with fresh thinking and practical suggestions.

Your Duty As a Manager: Soften Up the Targets

One of the most valuable things you can do as a sales manager is plow the ground for your people. When you do this effectively, they can come in and reap the benefits, and everybody wins.

Let me cite an example. I went out to St. Louis one time to ride with one of my newer reps when he visited some large clients. One client was a hospital, and we discovered that it was part of a 25-hospital consortium that swapped information about financial-management software programs. It was like a user group, and we happened to meet the gentleman in charge of the operation. I volunteered to talk to the members about dealing with problem accounts, and he accepted.

The group was getting together the next day, and I went in and spoke for an hour on the whole issue of managing accounts-receivable, using case studies of other hospitals in our client base and how they were handling the problem. We discussed early-out billing systems and ways our company customized programs to meet the needs of each situation. The whole thing went over very well.

As a result, my St. Louis sales rep was able to close sales with seven of those hospitals. He was overjoyed. He called and told me the "war stories" about landing these new clients. Why did he get them? In his view, it was because I had given that presentation. It built a sense of trust that we were serious players. That gave him additional credibility when he went in for the sale.

This is what you can do as a sales manager – soften up the ground so your reps gain an advantage. You can't do this on a constant basis, because you don't have that sort of time. Tell your people to use you for those tough situations that have large potential, not the onesies or twosies but for those deals that need an extra kick from a senior person in the company.

Quick Tip 🏃

Motivating Your Reps – On the Cheap

When I was building my own territory, I'd always get letters of reference from customers and tape them on a wall. Later, as a manager, I'd instruct my reps to get letters, make copies, and send them to all the other sales people. They could see, on a customer's letterhead, what a terrific job we were doing. At NCO I even framed letters like that and filled up a whole wall with them, for all the employees to see. It was evidence that their work was making a difference. And my sales guys sometimes read these testimonials before going out for major presentation, as a pick-me-up. Little things like that give a sales force more self-confidence, and they don't cost much.

Manager's Notebook: Little Things That Matter

It's critical to let your reps know where they stand, before anyone gets into trouble. Nobody likes to be kept in the dark.

One of a manager's most unpleasant tasks, for example, is firing someone. You don't really terminate an employee; they terminate themselves – that's a good way to look at it. The sales person might be trying, but he's not making any money. The company is investing in this individual, and it's losing money on the deal. The numbers aren't adding up. You are just the bad news bearer.

Tell your people that you won't terminate them; they will do it to themselves. Tell them that a termination might be inevitable sometime in the future, but it's up to them to avoid it. Make it clear that it's not something you'd ever enjoy – in fact, you would dread doing it. But say that you'll do it for your own preservation as well as for the financial success of the company.

Once you explain that, you will feel stronger as a manager and your sales reps will feel more confident, knowing that they control their own fate. It makes for a healthier climate, because it demystifies the whole process. You won't fire someone, they will fire themselves.

On a cheerier note, find out what motivates each one of your sales reps. Ask them, and write it in their files. What gives them gratification, besides money? Ask them how they'd like to be rewarded. They'll be honest with you. According to employee surveys, money isn't always the number-one issue. Sometimes it ranks lower than "recognition." Everybody likes praise, acknowledgement of a job well done, but in today's fast-paced business world, many people never hear it.

If you want success as a manager, be the exception. Make it clear that you value your people. It doesn't have to be an anything lavish. Send flowers to a sales rep's wife with a note saying, "Your husband had a great week. Congratulations!" Give your best people tickets to a concert or a ball game. Tell them to go out to dinner – on you.

Maybe invite them both – sales rep and spouse – to a nice restaurant. When the drinks arrive, offer up a toast. You raise your glass and say, "I know what it's like to married to a salesman. You have a tough job. I just want to let you know that we really appreciate the support you provide on the home front."

Something like that goes a long way. There are hundreds of small but telling gestures you can make, little tokens of your gratitude. Use your imagination and come up with some good ones, because, believe me, they can be dynamite as motivators.

We all want to feel appreciated – it's in our nature. And if your sales people don't feel appreciated, and if the money is comparable somewhere else, they will leave. Then you do have a problem.

CHAPTER 10

Making Good Money

Chapter overview:

- When your income is sufficient to meet your expenses, you risk sliding into a "comfort zone." Escaping from that zone is critical to your success. It begins by recognizing that you have hit a plateau below your potential, then taking steps to build up your income. Examples.

- Why escaping your comfort zone is not a one-time event. You need to devise strategies to break out every time you reach a new level.

- Thinking outside the box to increase your leads and customer contacts.

- How to avoid the trap of spending too much time in the office. Serving existing clients and cleaning up paperwork is important, but the ticket to new business and financial success is not in the office – it's in the field.

- For managers: how to encourage your reps to reach beyond their comfort zone and strive for higher sales objectives.

- How to "stretch" when setting annual goals, without fear of penalty if you fall short.

- Why it's vital to set personal goals. When you have something tangible to shoot for – a new house, a boat, another child – your motivation to work harder will intensify.

- Crunching the numbers as you plot an assault on the next income level.

- For managers: running the perfect sales meeting.

Early in my career, when I was selling insulation, I used to walk into stunning houses on the Connecticut River. They were spectacular places, worth millions of dollars. I'd say, "Wow, I'd love to live in a house like this. Why can't I?"

I was living in a three-bedroom condo at the time, with a growing family. A million-dollar house seemed as remote as the moon. But thank God I had that job, because it showed me the kind of houses that were out there. That began the process of expanding my mind. I decided that somehow I had to get from where I was to where I wanted to be.

If you have a dream – a really nice house, a vacation home, a carefree retirement – you can't just pay it lip service. Financial security won't happen by itself. Forget about winning the lottery. Attitude, ambition, and discipline are the keys. You've got to believe in yourself, and you have to be willing to put in hard work.

We've already seen that cold call selling is a numbers game. When you put up big numbers of calls and presentations on the front end, you will reap corresponding rewards on the back end, in sales and commissions. I've watched this come true throughout my career.

But it's not enough to simply tell yourself that "Yes, okay, it's a numbers game." When you say that, it's got to go into the ground. It has to go all the way down. And then you have to act.

Escaping From Your Comfort Zone

Too many of us fall into a trap that stops us well before we reach true financial success. I call it the comfort zone. Think of it as a siren song that seduces us when we're already making enough money to live decently. You're doing better than the guy next door. You can pay all your bills. You're not feeling any real financial stress. When you are comfortably situated like that, it's human nature to say, "I'm doing fine."

And you might be – for now. The trouble is that you might be stagnating at a level that will never give you a realistic shot at your dreams. If you've always wanted a second home – a beach house, maybe, or a place in the mountains – you might never put together the resources to buy it. You won't be able to travel to places you've always wanted to see. Whatever your dream is – another child, a boat, an African safari – it can silently slip away as you hunker into a comfort zone.

That trap has snared me several times. Fortunately, I've always managed to escape, and you can too. The first step is to recognize that you're already sheltered inside a comfort zone. Next, you've got to draw up a battle plan to fight your way out. Then you need the will power to pull it off.

When I was teaching school at the junior high level, I always taught my students that they could be anything they wanted to be – it was all a matter of attitude. After I'd been saying that for five years, I began to question my own situation. I had a positive attitude. I wanted to be able to afford some nice things – like a house, for starters. But I knew I couldn't support a family and live the life I wanted on a teacher's salary a year. So I left the classroom in hopes of making more money in sales.

Quitting teaching was a huge departure from my comfort zone, because I had no job waiting for me. It was a risk, but one I felt compelled to take.

Five years later, after selling everything from stocks and bonds to insulation, I was selling collection services in Connecticut and pulling down about $35,000, the most money I had ever made. My wife, June, was working part-time as a nurse. With our combined incomes we were in good shape, and my work ethic, unfortunately, reflected it. My sense of urgency had begun to dull. I was no longer pushing to make last minute calls at six o'clock, the way I had before. I just wasn't as "hungry."

Once again I was in a comfort zone, and I had to find a way out. We had three children at that point, and we decided that we didn't want someone else raising them in a day care center. That was our immediate goal – we wanted to see if we could survive on my income alone.

But the thought of merely scraping by didn't excite me. I wanted to double my earnings. I had gone into sales, after all, because it's a field where you can determine your own destiny. You're not beholden to some corporation for a small raise each year. You can make big leaps. And I had some dreams of my own. I love to travel, and I wanted to see the world – Rome, the Pyramids, the great museums. And I didn't want to see them just once. I wanted to be able to go any time I wished.

Running the Numbers

My manager existed to help make me more successful, so I called and asked him to hold a meeting on the comfort zone. "What are you talking about?" he said. I explained that I was comfortable with the money I was making, but when I looked ten years down the road, or 15 years, I wasn't doing okay.

My kids would be in college by then. Where was that money going to come from? I didn't want to have to scramble around and borrow. I wanted the tuition money banked in advance. So I asked him to raise my consciousness and help launch me to a new level.

We sat down and crunched the numbers, calculating what it would take for me to jump from $35,000 a year to $60,000 – good money at the time. Let's say my method to make $35,000 required me to walk in 40 new doors every week. Out of those, I'd average about 15 appointments, and I'd close sales on five of them. My call-to-sale ratio was

8:1. If I quickened my pace to 60 calls a week, I could set up 22 or 23 appointments and sell seven or eight of them.

Those two or three additional sales every week, each one worth about $140 to me, on average, would translate to $20,000 more in annual income. That would put me at $55,000, or maybe $60,000 if some big-client decisions broke my way.

The very act of talking about this gave me a different mindset. I knew I was better than $35,000. I had met the $100,000 sales people, and they didn't particularly impress me. If they could do it, so could I.

To pump myself up, I thought back to a movie I played every year when I was teaching. The film was called *They Said It Couldn't Be Done*, and it was phenomenal. It featured clips of the actual construction of some of the world's most awesome engineering feats – the Panama Canal, the Golden Gate Bridge, the Eiffel Tower. It talked about the building of Hoover Dam on the Colorado River, near Las Vegas. It was the heaviest structure ever put in one place by man. They poured concrete nonstop for two years, working in conditions of tremendous adversity and sickening heat.

If they could do *that*, I told myself, then surely I can do *this* – double my income. All I needed was a strategy to make it happen.

A Comfort Zone Escape Plan

I set up a "war room" in my office – that is to say, the dining room of my condo. On one wall, I taped a map that included my territory, all the towns on and near the Connecticut coast. I marked where I lived and stuck in pins to signify client locations. Then I went to work, attacking my market with a renewed intensity.

Some of my clients were in buildings that also housed a number of other companies and medical practices. I zeroed in on those locations like a smart bomb, determined to work them until I'd sold everyone in the building. The people in these places all knew each other, and steadily, by leveraging one deal on top of another, I was able to make major inroads. There was one building alone where I ended up with 12 clients.

Vertical markets, where you sell to a particular specialty, represented another ripe opportunity. Again, there were some natural starting points. I already had many of the anesthesiology groups in New Haven and Bridgeport. Now I resolved to lock up that whole sector of the medical community.

I went after it with such gusto that I was generating leads and referrals that spilled out of my territory. In any medical specialty, from anesthesiology to orthopedics, the top people all know each other. Physicians in New Haven were providing referrals to their friends in different parts of New England. My clients would call the other docs and say, "You've got to see these guys."

No financial credit came my way when those referrals led to business for one of my colleagues, but that didn't matter. I wanted to grow the whole company, and strengthen its identity in the marketplace. I thought we should own Connecticut. There were 13 of us selling in New England, and I thought we were good enough to lock up the whole region. If we raised our profile high enough, we'd all benefit.

How to Keep Generating Leads—Even When You're Swamped

As my cold calling tempo picked up speed and new clients came aboard, I ran up against a wall. It was getting tougher and tougher to sustain my call rate and still do all the necessary follow-up work.

On top of that, as my client base expanded it required more maintenance, leaving me with less time in the field. I needed to find a more efficient way to get myself in front of potential clients. So I went back to see my manager, and we brainstormed some ideas.

He came up with a winner: Why not place an ad in the newspaper, he said, and hire someone to make appointments for me? What was there to lose by experimenting with something like that? It seemed like a reasonable idea, so we drafted a little plan.

By paying an assistant a certain hourly rate, we figured, with a small bonus for an appointment that led to a sale, it could be affordable. Nobody else in the entire IC Systems sales force, more than a hundred people around the country, had ever tried that. But I needed something to stimulate my production, so I was game. I placed this ad in the paper – "Independent sales rep looking for professional person to work from home two or three days a week, to help make qualified appointments."

Thirty people responded. I ended up hiring a legal secretary who was home with a new baby. The job was perfect for her. She was poised and smart, and she lived in the middle of my territory, so a lot of her calls were local. (I was paying her phone bill.) I typed out a script – essentially the same one I used for walking in doors – and gave her a quick course on salesmanship and the fundamentals of my business – selling collection services.

She caught on fast and began hitting the phones, targeting categories where I'd had good success – medical and dental practices, plumbing and heating contractors, fuel oil suppliers, and a few others. After that, we met every couple of weeks to regroup.

It turned out to be a fabulous move. My sales went crazy – I was picking up an extra two or three deals a week because of her. A lot of sales people reserve Monday to make calls and schedule the week, but with this system I had a two-pronged approach. I was out there working the streets, as usual, canvassing for business, while she was generating action by phone, setting up appointments.

She always knew where to reach me. Sometimes she'd call while I was at one appointment with the news that she had just booked another one for me, an hour later, with someone around the corner or even in the same building. It was great for efficiency – it economized my travel and let me squeeze more production out of my time in the field. Before long I was on track to make my goal – $60,000.

That's what it took to break out of my financial comfort zone – big changes in my operating mode. First I stepped up my cold calling pace, and when that wasn't enough, I took a risk on something I'd never done before. I had to trust someone else to make appointments for me. There was no assurance that the strategy would work, but it paid greater dividends than I had dared hope. Without it, I couldn't have jumped to that next higher level.

My association with the legal secretary lasted seven months, and ended only when IC Systems promoted me to regional manager and transferred me to Pennsylvania.

Danger Signals

Let's assume that you feel comfortable with your financial situation. You tell yourself that you are doing just fine. You're not killing yourself out at work – you have time for both family and golf – and your income is enough to make your monthly "nut" and have something left over.

You have two cars in the garage, and you're squirreling away the money to take the kids to Disney World. You're not hunting for new prospects with quite the same zeal as before, because the old fire to get ahead isn't burning so brightly anymore. You're living mostly off your existing accounts.

This trap is very seductive, and a lot of sales people end up staying there, victims of their own contentment. But look at the price you pay when you don't try to fight your way out. You won't ever be able to buy that ski condo you'd like, or the car you really want. Paying for your kids' college education will loom as a major headache. You'd like to build up a big retirement fund but you can't save as much as you will need. You figure that somehow things will work out.

If that sounds familiar, you've got to shake yourself. You're better than that, and you know it. Don't be lulled into thinking that you're doing the best job you possibly can.

Quick Tip 🏃

Quick, Get Out of the Office!

Take a close look at how you manage your time. You might be spending too many hours in staff meetings, or busying yourself with paperwork. It's easy to get bogged down with internal operational issues. Good sales people, who have loads of clients and contacts, have to spend some time on customer maintenance – there's no getting around that fact.

You can fool yourself into thinking that you're working, because you are dealing with these things. And you are working, but not on the primary mission. Your money isn't in the office. It's out on the street.

You have to strike the right balance in there, a balance of your time within the job. You do what's necessary to satisfy your base, but tilt the scales in favor of selling. Jettison some of that fringe stuff, and get back in front of customers. You've got to be bringing in fresh sales, because new business is your lifeblood. That's what makes you grow.

No Guts, No Glory

If you are serious about making real money, prepare yourself for some changes. This takes backbone, because we all resist change. Remember what I said earlier, that you are at war with yourself? This is a classic battleground. But just by talking about breaking out of your comfort zone, concretely and with sincerity, you will begin the process.

As you gear up for an assault on the next income level – from $60,000 to $100,000, say – convince yourself that you're capable of getting there. Tell yourself that you're a sales professional. And what does a true professional do? He gets better at his work. He grows in wisdom and competence. He gets smarter. You gain an inner strength when you believe that you've got the right stuff to make it to the top.

That's part of what I've tried to get across in this book – you need the courage to change. If you don't change the way you work, you'll just tread water. You won't make another $40,000 next year. Taking up cold calling for the first time – that's a huge change. Upping your call rate from 30 a week to 50 – that's big.

Shifting into cold calling or accelerating your call rate doesn't necessarily demand a radical departure from your current routine. You can start with some smaller steps. Make a resolution that every week, no later than Wednesday, you will talk to somebody new about your company. If you do that religiously, it will become automatic. When Wednesday comes around, and you haven't approached a new prospect yet, a bell should ring in your head.

Or this: Before giving an important presentation, call some of your good customers in the same kind of business that you will be dealing with. Ask if they know anybody over at company X, your target. And if they do, see if they'd mind placing a call on your behalf. That way, when you walk in there, you're on an up-tick.

Once you see the positive outcome of small changes like these, you'll be less afraid of taking a larger risk. You'll be able to step into the unknown with more confidence. In our desire to be so perfect, a lot of people become immobilized. They don't want to look bad or be embarrassed, so they do nothing that could bring on embarrassment.

You have to get past that. So what if your nose gets bloodied up a little bit? Change carries risk, but you can't shrink from it. To break loose from your comfort zone, you need to embrace change, with intelligence, diligence, and the determination to succeed. If you can do that, you're going to be a highly effective sales person, and a wealthier one to boot.

Without Change, Your Income Will Stagnate

Think of the comfort zone as a wall that's blocking your path to a six-figure income. Stand at the wall and identify the problem. Then use all the resources at your command to reach the other side.

Talk to your manager; get some ideas. Keep an open mind to new approaches, the way I did when I decided to hire an assistant. Somehow you've got to increase your number of customer contacts.

It might require starting your days earlier and finishing them later. There might be mornings when you have to get out of bed at five-thirty and chip ice and snow off your windshield, then drive an hour to your first appointment. You'll be thinking, "This is nuts. It's ten degrees outside. It's still dark, and I'm already on the go."

That's okay – escaping from your comfort zone, by definition, can be uncomfortable. On your way home, at six o'clock, you decide to swing by one last place. You know there's a better chance to get some "face time" with a decision-maker after the staff people have gone home.

That happened frequently enough in my case that we pushed our family dinnertime back to eight o'clock, so we could still eat together. Even then, there were nights when I'd roll in two hours late. My wife would be disappointed, but at least we both knew we were working towards something worthwhile. We were in this thing together.

Unfortunately, a lot of sales folks never confront that wall. After reaching $60,000 or $70,000 a year, for example, they stop growing. They settle into a pattern, and they're not willing to change a proven strategy. They're afraid of taking a risk, afraid that they'll screw up and lose what they already have.

Or perhaps they're just lazy. They'll never admit that, but everything they do – the way they sell, the hours they put in, their lackluster follow up – will ensure that they'll never become really successful. They plod on next year the way they did last year, with identical results. They become prisoners of their comfort zone, not only because they fear failure, but also because they fear success. That's why they don't reach very high.

Aim For the Stars When Setting Your Goals

In my own company, NCO Financial Systems, discussion about the comfort zone usually surfaces at annual goal-setting time. If I sense that someone's not really stretching, I'll try to act as a mentor. I'll talk about the dangers of standing still. I want my people to succeed, not only for the company's sake, but also on a personal level.

There was one young salesman, for example, whose objectives for the coming year seemed beneath his ability, so we had a little chat. "John," I asked, "how come you set them so low?" He said, reasonably enough, "Well, I want to make sure I attain them." I responded, "Yeah, but why not go for another $30,000 instead of $15,000? You know you can do it."

John was very direct with me. "Chuck," he said, "do you realize what I'd have to do to make $30,000 more?" Sure I knew, I told him. I had done it myself. And I explained some techniques we could use to bring his numbers to a new high.

"Go for $30,000," I suggested, "and we'll work on it together. So what if you come up $5,000 short. I don't care how bad it might look." There is a psychology to setting goals. People are afraid that at the end of the year they won't make them, afraid they'll look foolish, so they low-ball it.

But now I'm the boss, telling John to go to the stars with me, and that I'll help him get there. I said, "Why not write down two goals? Do one that you share with the company, and another one that you share only with your manager. That way the company isn't relying on a forecast that is too high. But the one with your manager is a personal thing."

Quick Tip

Cement Your Goals – Make Them Public

Tell your sales manager that you're the greatest prospector in the world. Who cares if that's true? What's important is that you believe it. Tell the manager that you're going to make $25,000 more next year, and ask for his or her help – not to do it for you, but to provide guidance and support.

Then write down your goal for the year, and tell everyone. Tell your family and friends. This ties into fear, because the last thing you want to do it subject yourself to ridicule by not hitting your goal. When I was in my thirties, I told everyone that I wanted to retire when I turned forty – not that I wanted to retire, but I wanted the financial independence to make it an option. With financial freedom, I knew, everything else would come.

And guess what? When I hit forty, they reminded me. They remembered. When you tell people your goal, you cement it. It's no longer just a piece of paper sitting in a drawer.

The Manager's Job – Getting You Psyched

You need realistic hope that you can reach your goals, naturally, and it is your manager's job to provide that hope. How many people get hope given to them today? How many times have you received accolades for a job well done, or had someone in authority sit down to raise your consciousness above a certain level?

I go out of my way to do things like that. I constantly encourage my people to fulfill their aspirations. I'm sensitive to that, because so few people did that for me on the way up.

In discussing goals with a married salesman, I'll sometimes ask if his wife works outside the house. If she does, how much does she make? He'll usually say $35,000 or so. Then I'll ask what would happen if she stopped working tomorrow? What would you do? How much do you rely on her salary to keep your household running? Are you sliding into a comfort zone because of that second income?

For saleswomen, I might pose the same questions about her husband. Wouldn't it be great, I'll say, if you could support the whole shebang yourself, so you could bank that second income and build up a nice nest egg? Or one of you could stay home with your young children. When you dangle a clear incentive, the goal becomes more real.

Then we'll talk about strategy. What makes sense as an action plan? Never mind the clichés about working smart – how hard will you work? How many hours will you put in? Are you willing to be out in your market from seven-thirty in the morning until seven at night?

And we'll talk techniques. It's a numbers game, and referrals are vital. Are you willing to ask clients for letters of recommendation, signed and on their letterhead? That's an uncomfortable thing to do, especially if you have to follow up a few times before getting those letters. It's a small thing, but it pushes you out of your comfort zone. You're trying something new.

I've had dozens of these little "chats," and invariably they inspired my sales folks to crank up their effort a few notches. In many cases they'd whip through that year at a record pace. All they needed was the confidence of someone high up in the company that they could do it. Because I believed in them, they believed more deeply in themselves.

Try to apply that to your own situation. Do you need that extra shot of fuel to kick yourself into higher gear? If you do, go see your manager and ask for it. Tell him you need a pep talk. Explain that you feel ready to take your production to a new level, but you don't want to be all alone. Get him to build you up. It really helps.

Quick Tip

Picture Your Dreams

Some Sunday afternoon take your family and go through a few open houses. Look at places that cost $50,000 more than the house you're living in, or $100,000. Have the real estate agent run the numbers, and translate that into the income required to make the payments, compared to what you're paying now.

Then you have a meeting with your spouse, and say, "I think I can do this. It would cost us $500 more every month, but I know I can do it. Do you want to go for it?" Get everybody on board, make it clear that sacrifice will be required, and then develop your strategy.

Now, what happens if you knuckle down, follow your plan, and suddenly, instead of making $50,000 a year, you're on course to make $75,000? You might enter a new comfort zone at that level. It's natural to pause for a time and consolidate the situation, but don't lose your momentum. You've come this far; why not go higher? Keep raising the bar.

Escaping from your financial comfort zone isn't a one-time deal. New traps always lie in wait. The key is to remain alert to the danger, and keep knocking down the walls. Visualize how your life would improve – all the neat things you'd be able to do – if you could double your income. Then find a way to do it, and plunge in. If you believe in your heart that you can, you will.

A Perfect Sales Meeting – With Yourself

In most sales meetings I attended as a rep, the managers preached at us. It wasn't much of a two-way street. They just dumped numbers and goals on us for a few hours, or they paraded up somebody to talk to us. Maybe you, as a manager, tend to run your own meetings along those same lines.

Let me suggest an experiment. Try running a meeting where you open with a question – "Hey everybody, how much more money would you like to make next year?" Suppose there are 20 sales people. Everyone writes down a figure and then you do the math. As a group, the sales department wants to make, say, $1 million more next year.

That number is your new working base. You say, "Okay, guys and gals, we want to increase commissions by $1 million. Now, if that's what we want to make, how to we get there? What is our most profitable line; how can we leverage existing business; how many more calls do we have to make?" You boil down that $1 million to specifics.

Next you talk about the 80/20 rule – 80 percent of the revenue is produced by 20 percent of the people. So out of these 20 people, four of them are going to produce the 80 percent. Then you throw down the gauntlet. "How do feel about that, you 16 other people? According to the way the numbers work, you are only going to bring in 20 percent of our total. Are you happy with that?"

They're not happy, of course – they better not be. "We don't like that," they'll say. "What can we do to change it? How can we make it more equal?" At that point you can begin zeroing in on individual goals. You're asking your sales people to grow up and be responsible.

That turns into a hell of a sales meeting when you work it right. But most sales reps aren't that lucky; they might never experience a perfect sales meeting. So what do you do? You hold that meeting with yourself.

Figure out how much more you want to make next year. Let's say it's $20,000. Attack that number scientifically. If every sale brings you $400, for example, you need to make an additional 50 sales. Ask yourself some tough questions. Which accounts are you more likely to grow? Is that new business going to come from old or new customers? How many more sales calls do you need to make, if it takes ten calls to arrange three appointments and three appointments to land a sale?

Are you willing to make that kind of sacrifice, to make an additional 500 calls next year? That means knocking on two more doors a day. When you start focusing on expanding your sales efforts, you have to step up your intensity.

Take some time to contemplate all this. Be honest with yourself. Assimilate all the facts and extrapolate the extra work required to build up your income by $20,000. You can't just say that you want to increase your sales next year, because if your volume is $1 higher than this year's, you have succeeded. One of the best reasons to set goals is that it gives you a professional challenge. If you don't reach for the stars, you can't get there.

You're thinking like a manager when you establish some hard but achievable goals. And you're managing the most important career of all – your own.

NOTE:

I was trying to get an article printed in Inc. Magazine about our company. We had made the Inc. 500 list of fastest growing companies four years in a row with pure gut-in-your-face sales...<u>not acquisitions</u>. You never know where relentless pursuit will lead you...and I never believed my last ditch effort would result in this article on cold calling. I met Jay at 6:30 a.m. Monday and told him to pick where he wanted to go. Talk about pushing the envelope!!!

48 Hours with the King of Cold Calls

By Jay Finegan

(Editor's note: This article originally appeared in <u>Inc.</u> magazine.)

The marketing sophisticates say cold calling is dead --
that it's too expensive, too untargeted, and too ineffective
to pay off. Chuck Piola, 15,000 cold calls and one fast-grow-
ing company later, disagrees

Center City Philadelphia on a raw winter morning.
Chuck Piola bursts out of his black Mercedes singing in full
throat (this time it's the Drifters tune "Under the Board-
walk," handled off-key but with feeling) and scans a cluster
of skyscrapers. He points to a building with particularly
striking architecture.

"Let's try that one," he says. It's the Bell Atlantic Tower,
52 stories tall. He strides quickly through the lobby, carefully avoiding eye contact with the security guards. In the
elevator he glances at the buttons and pushes 40, a shot in
the dark. The elevator rises, and Piola pops out. Straight
ahead is a law firm he's never heard of before.

"I wonder if you could help me out?" he asks the receptionist, opening with his favorite line. "I represent NCO
Financial Systems. We specialize in discreet recovery work
for companies having trouble collecting receivables. Our
clients include Bell Atlantic, a lot of doctors and hospitals,
and even the Philadelphia 76ers. I happened to be in your
building, and I wondered if I might see whichever partner
handles your finances." His tone is upbeat and cordial.

The receptionist, polite but skeptical of unannounced
visitors, gives him the once-over. He seems to pass. "That
would be Mr. L.," she says. She points to an inside line. "You

can use the phone back there." Alas, Mr. L. is not available. Piola thanks the receptionist and leaves a business card.

By the elevator, a tall gentleman is meticulously fitting wraparound glasses behind his ears. A detail man, notes Piola as he strikes up a conversation.

"Beautiful offices," he remarks. "Are you with the firm?" The man is. "Arthur Newbold," he says, extending his hand.

At a glance, Piola notices that Newbold's shoes are unshined and his slacks pressed carelessly if at all. Either a nobody, Piola thinks, or someone so high up that he's past the $900 suits, all the show. Piola decides it's the latter and again makes his familiar pitch. At the end he mentions Mr. L.

"No, no," says Newbold. "The person you want is Rich Rizzo. He'd handle that."

Piola thanks him and returns to the front desk with the new information. Newbold, it turns out, is a partner, and the receptionist sits up a little straighter at the mention of his name. She cheerfully provides Rizzo's number and again offers the inside phone. Rizzo picks up, and, yes, he is interested in learning about NCO Financial. But today is impossible, he tells Piola. They agree to an appointment two days hence.

"Bingo!" says Piola. The first cold call of the day, and already things are looking good. The 400-lawyer firm has millions of dollars' worth of outstanding fees, and Rizzo is the partner who handles finance.

*   *   *

True cold calling -- the face-to-face pursuit of unqualified prospects -- has long carried a whiff of the unseemly. But today it is in complete disrepute. By some estimates, a single industrial sales call now costs $400 or more, what with travel expenses, support costs, pay, and benefits. Few companies want to risk that outlay on a crapshoot, so they equip their reps with leads generated by telemarketing, direct mail, and trade shows.

"The days of sending a foot soldier out in the field to randomly call to qualify are over," says Gary Hultgren, director of sales training at Moore Business Forms, a $2.5-billion company in Lake Forest, Ill. "Cold calling has almost become a dirty word because of the economics. I don't see how anybody does it anymore."

Gary Hultgren, meet Chuck Piola. In a 15-year sales career dating back to when he sold phone-directory advertising door-to-door, the former high school history teacher estimates he's made some 15,000 cold calls. He thrives on "going in raw," as he puts it, taking the business to the street.

In 1986 he teamed up with Michael Barrist to revive NCO Financial Systems Inc., a collection agency started by Barrist's grandfather in 1926. Today, with 63 employees, they operate from a sprawling suite of offices in Blue Bell, Pa., near Philadelphia. Their client base -- 64 when Piola started -- has reached 1,700. Their computer-directed machines generate some 120,000 collection letters each month. And NCO's billings have reached $3.5 million a year, growing so fast that the company has made the *Inc.* 500 three years running.

Piola, the executive vice-president, heads a sales staff of six. And he credits the company's rapid rise not to some highfalutin marketing system but to old-fashioned shoe leather -- walking in doors and telling his story.

Sure, he's heard that cold calls aren't cost-effective; he just doesn't believe it. "Some accounting operation crunched those numbers," he says, dismissing the point as though waving away the merest gnat. What the bean counters ignore, he contends, is the multiplier effect. "When you cold call, you maximize your opportunities. You meet people. You can thread a sale from one person to another, and you never know where it's going to lead."

On this day -- the first of two he's set aside to work Philadelphia's high-rent district -- it has already led to Rich Rizzo. Piola says he never would have reached him through direct mail or telemarketing. Rizzo took the call, Piola says, because he mentioned Arthur Newbold.

"You've got to put yourself in a position to meet somebody who'll be receptive, and that won't happen unless you see people," he explains. "The goal of the cold call is to get the appointment. You have to at least get up to bat."

Back on the street now, he darts into Two Logan Square, another tower.

In an hour he works his way down the building, hitting 10 companies -- law firms, insurance outfits, ad agencies, investment banks. At each stop, of course, receptionists protect the entrance. Getting past them on the phone can be tough -- that's their power base. But face-to-face cold calls are rare enough now that this defensive perimeter is easily penetrated. "Nobody knows how to handle cold calls anymore," Piola says. "I get through because there's no system to stop me."

A little charm goes a long way, too. Piola spends a few minutes with each one he meets, tossing a compliment or two, cracking a few jokes. He smiles a lot, which comes naturally. "You've gotta love people to do this job," he says. "And I sincerely do." In the windowless world of the high-rise receptionist, Piola's presence is like sunshine. That makes an impression.

He's much the same each time he meets a potential client. He looks for something to talk about, some common ground. It can be a picture on the office wall, the view, or failing that, something general -- the traffic, sports, the economy. Rarely is he stumped for a topic. "The salesman's job is to find the hot button," he says. "You have to become real to them, because up to that point you are just a business dude. The ice hasn't melted at all. You can get so fancy on sales techniques that you forget to be a nice, regular guy. But that's what sells."

At Two Logan Square, however, he finds no takers. Not one to gnaw on rejection, Piola cuts into another office building. He wanders into more law offices and securities firms. Then, peeking out of the elevator on the 21st floor, he spots some big game -- Sun Refining and Marketing Co., part of giant Sun Co.

Here he finds no human face out front, only locked doors and a card-key entry system. But there's a phone on the wall, and he manages to lure out Larry DeAngelis, the general credit manager. DeAngelis doesn't have much time to chat, but he and Piola exchange cards. When Piola telephones, the next day, DeAngelis agrees to a meeting two weeks later.

Out on the street at noon, Piola blends in easily with the lunchtime business crowd. He's wearing a cashmere topcoat over a double-breasted, blue pinstriped suit. A quiet paisley tie is knotted crisply on a starched white shirt. He always shines his shoes the night before he cold calls, so his wingtips glisten. He has an expensive leather briefcase, cuff links, and an Omega watch.

His outfit is no accident. Collection agencies suffer from a shabby, Columbo-like reputation. Piola knows that and counters it. Cold calling is both an art and a science, he says. It requires a fluent understanding of body language, the ability to talk to people on all levels of workplace society, and above all, a carefully cultivated image.

Today, working Philly's business elite -- "the suits" -- Piola wants to project a conservative, understated look. "People have to buy *you* before they'll buy your product," he preaches. "They are buying your polish, your conviction, even your grooming. It helps a lot if you look successful. People have to know immediately that you're not some bimbo."

Over lunch at the Corned Beef Academy, Piola recounts a war story -- his recent cold-calling conquest of Pittsburgh National Bank (PNB). He'd flown to Pittsburgh to service an account at Mellon Bank. NCO collects its delinquent credit-card debts. The appointment ended early, leaving a few hours to kill. So Piola walked into PNB and scanned the directory. He found the name of the VP for credit policy. Let's call him Ted.

"I go up -- I'm now on the top floor of the bank," Piola says. "I ask the receptionist where I can find Ted. I've just missed him, but she buzzes me into the executive area to see his secretary. The glass door opens, and I walk down this hallway with Persian rugs and mahogany paneling, to Ted's office."

It turns out that he's not the person to see. Neither are the next two people Piola is referred to. "Meanwhile," he says, "I'm walking around this place like I own the bank -- you need to feel that way when you cold call. You can't be intimidated."

Finally, he finds the vice-president in charge of the whole recovery department. She won't see him without an appointment, or so he's been told. But after hearing what NCO does, she ushers him into her office. "I was there for an hour," Piola marvels. "We talked about everything, even philosophy. She slaps me on the back when I leave and writes down the name of the guy I needed to call."

The upshot: PNB gives him some $350,000 of sour consumer loans to collect, on a one-third contingency basis. That works out to about $115,000 for NCO.

"It blows my mind," Piola says. "At 11 o'clock I was outside on the street. Five minutes later I'm in the sanctum sanctorum of one of the country's 20 biggest banks. It shows you that this interference thing is just a head trip."

This day in Philadelphia yields no such luck. On the last of 25 calls, he takes a wild stab at the regional headquarters of the Internal Revenue Service. "People owe it money, right?" he says. The commissioner, however, declines to be seen.

*   *   *

Early the next morning Piola guns his Mercedes back into the city. First stop, a car wash. Part of the "aura" of cold calling, he explains, is feeling good about yourself. And that goes for your car, your socks, and your tie. "You don't want any irritations," he says. "Maybe I'm being picayune, but all these little glitches that bother you during the day can crimp your performance when you get that 30-second shot in front of the right person. If my socks keep falling down or I don't like the tie I'm wearing, I'll go buy new ones."

Maybe clothes are on his mind, for his first call is on Nan Duskin, an upscale women's clothing store on Rittenhouse Square. He already has the account; he just wants to touch base with Larry Gustison, the vice-president and chief financial officer. Gustison is busy, but he waves Piola in.

"Chuck can always see me," Gustison says. "But as a rule I hate cold calls. It's rude to think you can just come in and take time, especially if you don't know the person."

Piola chews on those words as he drives across town to Wills Eye Hospital. "Larry's right," he says. "You don't want to fight people, you want to sell them. And he's very busy, which is unusual. I think most people go to work wondering what they're going to do for lunch. So I don't buy this business that nobody can see you without an appointment."

On a good day, Piola can make 30 cold calls, do three or four presentations, and schedule an appointment or two. He operates on "the assumptive." His attitude is that people want to see him -- or *would* if only they knew his business. "We're talking about management of accounts receivable, which can be a nightmare."

Cold calling his way through the hospital now, leaving cards everywhere, he encounters, by chance, Ruth Humm. She's been in the medical management field for 15 years, and Piola has worked with her before. She's glad to see him. "Chuck always has some good jokes," she says.

Humm is new to her job managing an ocular-oncology practice, and assumed Piola had a contract with it already -- 70% of NCO's client base is medical. Since he's here, however, she does have one thing: a New Jersey man, already reimbursed by his insurer, has stubbornly refused to pay the eye surgeon.

Piola warms to the challenge. "After four or five months in our system he's going to get 45 or 50 attempts," he says. "We'll send letters; we'll do skip-tracing; we'll get a neighbor to tell us where he works and go after him there." Humm seems pleased. "Our secretary here is the first bulldog," she says, "but Chuck is the Great Dane with the louder bark." She hands him the file and signs a contingency contract. It's a $2,800 account.

That's small beer compared with his final quarry of the day -- Independence Blue Cross, a monster insurance company. Like most, it has unpaid premiums, overpaid claims, and the like. A few months earlier Piola had left an NCO brochure for John Foos, the chief financial officer. Now, driving over, he gets on the car phone to a secretary he met that day. It's not Foos he wants, she says. It's someone named Tom Ford, the manager of corporate cash. "Manager of corporate cash," Piola muses over the phone. "Nice title." The secretary chuckles.

Minutes later, he's on the 40th floor, executive real estate at the Blue Cross headquarters. Tom is not the guy to see, either, Piola learns, and he gets another name. He hits one blind alley and then another. Eventually, he's directed to Rosemary Park, senior VP of the risk-management division, down on 41. Yes, indeed, Park says, she is very interested in a presentation. They set a date.

What probably influenced her, Piola reflects later over a Dewar's and water, is that he had started at the top, with John Foos. "His name counts everywhere in that building. The fact that I had never even talked to him didn't matter. I'd paid my dues because I had tried to see him, and then using his name was like hard currency around there."

*   *   *

In the end, however, Rosemary Park canceled the meeting, saying something had come up. Rich Rizzo at the law firm kept his appointment, but nothing came of it. Oddly enough, it was Larry DeAngelis at Sun Refining and Marketing who provided the most promising breakthrough of those two days.

"Chuck is the only person who has ever made a personal call on me for that kind of service," DeAngelis says. "I was impressed."

The business he gave NCO wasn't large -- two corporate collection accounts totaling less than $10,000. But as Piola sees it, it could be the start of something big. "What turns me on is that a small company like mine was actually able to go in and do a deal with a *Fortune* 50 company like Sun," he says. "And it happened on a cold call."

Tips From a Master

After 20 years of 'going in raw,' Chuck Piola shares his thoughts:

The **best time to reach a decision maker** is early in the morning or late in the day. "Try to catch people on their way into the office, before the secretary arrives. That minimizes interference."

Piola's **favorite opening line:** "I wonder if you can help me out?" "*Everybody* likes to help," says Piola. "Put people in that posture right away."

Almost any business could successfully use cold calls. "If I had a cleaning business, I'd cold call apartment houses, industrial complexes. You don't know what won't work if you don't try it."

The multiplier effect: "Cold calling maximizes your contacts. You meet people -- in the elevator, the hallway, the reception area. **Everybody you see is a resource.**"

Multiplier-effect corollary: **"Never assume the person you're talking to isn't the decision maker."**

How do you get people to see you? "If you walk in the door and are a breath of fresh air for them, you're not an infringement on their time. They'll make room for you."

Even **in slow times, stay consistent.** "You might cold call for three weeks with no results, but you'd better make your calls that fourth week as good as when you started. If you don't, prospects will feel it."

"You can't take rejection personally. **Nothing should bother you.**"

"You have to come up with a reason for someone to see you, and you usually have 20 or 30 seconds to do it, so **be ready to think fast.** If you're getting shot down, find something that will go 'click' and get a 'yeah, maybe' response. Then ask for the appointment right away: 'Would Tuesday be OK, or would Wednesday be better?' Go on the assumptive."